CRIME, VICTIMS AND JUSTICE

Crime, Victims and Justice

Essays on Principles and Practice

Edited by

HENDRIK KAPTEIN
University of Amsterdam

MARIJKE MALSCH
NISCALE, Leiden University

ASHGATE

Published by
Ashgate Publishing Limited
Gower House
Croft Road
Aldershot
Hampshire GU11 3HR
England

Ashgate Publishing Company
Suite 420
101 Cherry Street
Burlington, VT 05401-4405
USA

Ashgate website: http://www.ashgate.com

British Library Cataloguing in Publication Data
Crime, victims and justice : essays on principles and practice
1. Restorative justice
I. Kaptein, H. J. R. II. Malsch, M.
345'.001

Library of Congress Cataloging-in-Publication Data
Crime, victims and justice : essays on principles and practice / edited by H.J.R. Kaptein and M. Malsch.
p. cm.
Includes bibliographical references and index.
ISBN 0-7546-2354-8
1. Restorative justice. 2. Victims of crimes. 3. Criminal justice, Administration of. I. Kaptein, Hendrik. II. Malsch, M. (Marijke)

HV8688.C72 2003
364.6'8--dc22 2003058370

ISBN 0 7546 2354 8

Printed and bound in Great Britain by
Athenaeum Press Ltd, Gateshead, Tyne & Wear.

Contents

Preface

Plans for this collection of essays began with a conference held in Amsterdam on 1 December 2000: *Restorative Justice: Criminal Justice for Victims?* organised by the Paul Scholten Institute (the research department of the Law Faculty of the University of Amsterdam), and NSCR (The Netherlands Institute for Research on Crime and Law Enforcement, Leiden). Speakers were prominent scholars from Canada, the United Kingdom and The Netherlands. They represented various fields of law, psychiatry, philosophy and the social sciences. This book contains updated editions of key papers presented, together with additional essays originally written for this volume.

The central topic of both the conference and the book is restorative justice, its relationships to current criminal justice systems, and its possible benefits for victims and offenders. As might be expected, not all contributors were equally in favour of newly introduced aspects of restorative justice. Also, even explicit proponents of restorative justice regarded the introduction of restorative justice in the criminal justice processes problematical in more than a few respects. Thanks to these diverging opinions, ensuing discussion and its condensation in the essays presented here, this book may well present a highly interesting collection of views on the potentialities of restorative justice. A brief overview of contents, in authors' alphabetical order, may serve to introduce main subjects.

Ybo Buruma airs substantial doubts about restorative justice as a strong overall model. In contrast to Ezzat Fattah, he maintains that restorative justice may do well in less serious cases, but does not offer any acceptable answers to serious crime. Different victims suffer from different consequences of crime, he contends. Presumably they cannot be put on one line in all respects, when restorative justice models are to be considered. Moreover, offenders' and victims' positions are regarded to be unequal in most cases. Thus it is argued that 'returning conflicts to serious crime victims and offenders' is not a good idea. According to Buruma, criminal procedure and punishment have to do with inflicting pain on offenders in the first place. Thus criminal law is interpreted as not primarily concerned with redistribution of costs or with restoration, as is civil law.

Ezzat Fattah is of a rather different persuasion. He describes the introduction and the progress of victim-centered or victim-oriented policies and objectives in Canada and abroad. Still, his conclusions are not highly optimistic: although some progress has been made and some results have been achieved, to him it seems that the situation of the vast majority of victims has hardly improved. In his view, redress for victims has, until now, been only secondary to having offenders severely punished. Fattah contends, then, that nothing less than a paradigm shift, a shift from retributive to restorative justice, can truly satisfy victim needs, achieve victim empowerment, and ensure that victims are actively and fully involved in the justice process. Also, Fattah discusses a number of important but overlooked benefits of restorative justice. Moreover, he notes some dangers to, and of, the restorative justice paradigm.

Ian Freckelton extensively discusses the Australian experience of criminal injuries compensation, also in – again extensive – comparison with a number of other countries. Developments are argued by him to be strongly related to changing governmental attitudes toward the needs of victims. Freckelton notes that eras of victim blaming were followed by increased awareness of the effects of crime upon victims, leading to the introduction of new schemes and legislation. He states that state funds were reduced again later, in times when costs of the schemes appeared to increase. Compensation of non-material damages is shown to have been possible under some schemes only.

Marc Groenhuijsen discusses restorative justice problems and projects from the perspective of The Netherlands criminal justice system and comparable systems. He seems to agree with Fattah and Wright, among others, in stressing the importance of restorative justice. At the same time, he extensively discusses pressing problems of epistemology: is restorative justice a new paradigm or not? Is a paradigm chance needed in order to do criminal justice to victims? It is contended that the question of effective implementation cannot be fruitfully tackled without developing a well-reasoned notion of the precise theoretical status of reform efforts in this area. In the end, piecemeal reform is argued for, among other reasons because of officials' resistance against prospects of complete abandonment of current criminal procedure and punishment.

Hendrik Kaptein aims at developing outlines of 'civilised criminal law', in which full compensation for victims is to be realised by offenders' efforts. Penal servitude is taken to be the constructive core idea of retribution as integration of forfeit, punishment and restitution. Also, an attempt is made to base criminal procedure and punishment through penal servitude on principles of moral psychology transcending criminal law, concerning relationships between actorship, wrongful harm, resentment, apologies, reparation and reconciliation. Punishment as infliction of pain must be done away with completely, it is contended, to be replaced by penal servitude. Offenders' pain is taken to be no more than a probably not unwelcome by-product, then, in restoration of original positions of respect and self-respect for all concerned. Apart from completely different kinds of sanctions, civilised criminal law is thought to be not completely different from current criminal law, thus offering possibilities for piecemeal reform.

Marijke Malsch discusses the consequences of having to appear in open court for victims who are summoned to act as witnesses. Her research shows most witnesses to be reluctant to appear in open court and to make statements in front of defendants, the other professional process participants and the public in the gallery. Some other victims, however, seem to be helped by such a public appearance: dealing with the consequences of crime is said to be enhanced by public recognition of the crime and the victim's suffering. Certain characteristics of The Netherlands criminal justice system turn out to protect victims' interests: they are often not required to testify in open court. A newly proposed law will, when introduced, make victim impact statements possible in the Dutch criminal law system. One of the goals of the new law is a therapeutic one. Malsch discusses the question as to whether this goal will be reached by new legislation.

Åsa Rydberg looks at aspects of restorative justice from the specific viewpoint of The International Criminal Tribunal for the former Yugoslavia. This tribunal hopefully will contribute to processes of reconciliation in the region of the former Yugoslavia. However, until now there is no special role or position in the proceedings for victims other than as witnesses. Rydberg explains the various protective measures for witnesses which have been developed for the international court, such as the use of video-conference links in exceptional cases, various measures to protect victims' privacy, and arrangements with local police authorities for post-trial protection in the countries of residence of witnesses. The Tribunal does not deal with the issue of victim compensation: such claims may be brought before national courts or other competent bodies. Surprisingly, there seems to be a certain lack of restorative elements in the court's procedures.

Martin Wright focuses on the question as to what should be done when one person harms another. The criminal justice process, focusing on offenders, does not treat victims very well, according to Wright. Restorative justice claims to do it differently: the basic principle is to offer help to persons who have been harmed. Dealing with offenders comes later. How is this principle to be realised in practice? Early restorative justice programs generally focused on offenders, taking reparation mainly to come down to payment of amounts of money or so many hours' work. More comprehensive programs and schemes should govern processes, it is argued, in order to make them more 'victim-friendly'. Highly relevant questions remain, such as: will restorative justice deter crime? May it deal with 'victimless' crime? And so on. Wright is of the opinion that restorative methods, unlike those based on punishment, contribute to the ideal of a stable society. Its principles are thought to be applicable in other parts of society as well, above all in schools.

So much for the contents of this book and the impressive amount of scholarly and practical work on restorative justice involved in it. If only these concepts and theories, or any human endeavour, could make an end to crime. No crime, no victims. And no books or whatever on restorative justice.

Still it is to be hoped that this book may contribute not only to the advancement of restorative justice scholarship and wisdom, but to justice for crime victims all over the world in the first place. Whatever is to be thought of criminal law in relation to justice for victims, it remains a depressing fact that the great majority of these victims are still left alone.

What kinds of reform of criminal procedure and punishment (and of society) are to alleviate this sad situation may well remain in doubt for some time. In the meantime, all practical possibilities within current criminal realities are to be exploited in order to do at least some justice to victims, however imperfect. And let it not be forgotten that no justice for victims and offenders may do away with the basic need for care and compassion, for victims and for offenders.

H.J.R.K.
M.M.

1. Doubts on the Upsurge of the Victim's Role in Criminal Law

Ybo Buruma*

Even a sceptic has to acknowledge the remarkable changes in the last 25 years regarding the way in which the police, judicial authorities and scientists think about victims of crime. I remember my 1973 class when criminology professor Willem Nagel said: 'If you read about a murder – suppose it was your child, your brother'. Then he waited a moment and continued: 'Suppose your child was the defendant in the dock'. Of course at the time we, the students, were also thinking of the victims before the moment of silence, but we had to be taught that criminal procedure was about defendants: the interests of the victims were supposed to be subsumed under the general public interest. Nevertheless the same Willem Nagel was the man who introduced the term 'victimology' in the late 1950s in The Netherlands.

Not only in The Netherlands but also in many Western countries legal or organisational changes have in recent years taken place in favour of the victim. It is tempting to speculate about the causes. Maybe the horrors of the 20th century have to do with this: who would dare to silence the victims of the holocaust, the gulag, the killing fields or turn away from the testimonies for instance before the South African Truth and Reconciliation Commission? Maybe, to venture a second possibility on an altogether different level, it has to do with secularisation: we are not compassionate anymore because God asks us to be and because we are all sinners, but because we position ourselves in the place of the victim.[1] A third possibility is that the cultural feeling that the victim speaks on behalf of us all, is related to the rising crime figures since the 1970s. Crime has become a social fact, not an aberration, not an exception to the rule but something we have to deal with, knowing that the government is not able to prevent it completely. The suffering of the victim is nowadays the measure of moral evaluation, while in the 19th century (and before) the victim was looked at with distrust.[2] This is related to a new way of dealing with tragedy – in the past the victim was being blamed, in mid-20th century welfare states the community or 'politics', but more and more we are tempted to blame

* Nijmegen University, The Netherlands.

1. My cousin I. Buruma has spoken of a pseudo-religion of kitsch and death, in 'The Joys and Perils of Victimhood' *New York Review of Books* (8-4-1999).

2. G. Vigarello, *Histoire du viol, XVIe-XXe siècle* (Seuil, Paris, 1998).

and to punish individuals because they are responsible for suffering (even in almost no-fault cases).[3]

Against this general background the appeal of restorative justice and victim's rights may have been formed because of the relatively disappointing outcome of traditional theories on punishment. 'Just deserts' (as well as older ideas on retaliation) is in the end a very negative idea that can bring you almost everywhere – it may start as a liberal program of thinking to protect offenders against the uncontrolled discretion of judges and prison administrations and it may end (sometimes accompanied by ideas of protecting the public) with rationalising robot-like sentencing and increasing levels of punishment. General deterrence is a concept in which the offender is used as an instrument to teach others, who – as criminological studies teach us – are not being deterred from most (and especially not from the most important) crimes. In addition, rehabilitation programs have the image that they almost never work; that is not a really fair image, because there are successful interventions – in and outside institutions – especially if they are addressing multiple risk factors with a focus on interpersonal skills.[4] So, although there are reasons to defend the position that it is a pity that the correctionalist rationale is fading, it is a fact that it is – in The Netherlands and I suppose also in the Anglo Saxon world.[5]

There may therefore actually be 'a long standing state of crisis regarding the meaning and justification of criminal law and punishment'. In this chapter I want to discuss whether restorative justice and/or strengthening of victim's rights are indeed an answer to it. In order to do so, I will stipulate a difference between restorative justice and victim-oriented criminal law and I will use this difference by comparing severe, ordinary and minor criminal cases.

Victim-oriented criminal law and restorative justice

Although the concept of restorative justice could be used in a lot of different ways, I will restrain myself and just state that I am using the concept in a very broad sense – for all kinds of ways of reacting to crimes that are not primarily motivated by retribution or prevention. I am thinking about individualised ways of mediation as well as community-oriented forms of reintegrative shaming. However I would like to stipulate a difference between (fundamentally non-punitive) restorative justice and a victim oriented criminal law approach.

3. See for instance M. Douglas, *Risk and Blame* (Routledge, London, 1992) and Paul Ricoeur ed., *Le Juste* (Esprit, Paris, 1995) with reference to M. Delmas-Marty, *Pour un droit commun* (Seuil, Paris, 1994).
4. See for instance the studies of the Loeber/Farrington group as published in the Office of Justice Programs, *Juvenile Justice Bulletin*, on Serious and violent Juvenile Offenders (May 1998).
5. D. Garland, *The Culture of Control* (Oxford University Press, Oxford, 2001).

First a few words on the victim-oriented criminal law approach. In several countries in the Western world a legal recognition of victim's rights in the context of criminal law came about in the mid 1970s. Many Criminal Injuries Compensation Boards were founded in those years: in The Netherlands in 1976. Later, since the mid-1980s a series of legal developments took place. In 1985 the National Victim Support Organisation was founded. That same year an important Commission on legal provisions for victims in criminal procedure was founded: the Commission Terwee.[6] The so-called Terwee Law came into force in 1995, making it easier for the victim to ask for civil damages in a criminal procedure.[7] If the judge decides to grant the claim of the victim he ordinarily also imposes the measure of compensation, which means that the public prosecutor has to help the victim in getting the money: if the convict does not pay, the prosecutor can confiscate his earnings and the convict can even be put behind bars. From a dogmatic point of view this combination may be remarkable: something that must be considered as a civil verdict (be it in the context of a criminal trial) is enforced by substitute imprisonment on the initiative of government.

The new law also secures the right for the victim to read documents from the criminal dossier (art. 51d CCP), the right to legal council (art. 51e CCP), the right of the victim who has joined the case in the first instance and whose claim has been denied, to appeal on his own (art. 421.4 CCP) and the right to be informed properly and quickly about important steps of the police or the prosecutor concerning the case (art. 51f CCP), including – according to the instructions – the right to be heard personally by the prosecutor in severe cases. Recently an *Instruction second opinion investigative enquiries* enabled the victims of severe crimes, or their relatives, to ask for a second opinion, when the chief public prosecutor thinks he has to stop the investigations because of too little advancements. Another recent development is the possibility to provide victims with information about the offender's release, but this is actually only happening in sex cases and seemingly without a proper legal basis, which seems to be necessary because of convict's right to privacy (art. 8 European Convention of Human Rights).

Although I am not altogether happy with all these changes and the focussing on the victim, I cannot deny their existence. Presumably victim's rights will be one of the most important issues in criminal law and procedure in this century to come.

This victim-oriented criminal law has to be differentiated from restorative justice. It is basically punitive and not primarily 'damage-centered' or 'conflict-centered' as I suppose restorative justice is: the perpetrator is still in the middle of the procedure, although the victim can have his say as well. Some

6. Report of 3 March 1988; see also Instructions of the Prosecutors-General (central office of the prosecutors) 'De Beaufort-richtlijnen' from 1986 and 'Vaillant-richtlijnen' from 1987; and Parliamentary pressure as published in the documents of Parliament *TK* 1989-90, 21345, 3, p. 1.

7. Law of 23 December 1992, *Official Journal (Staatsblad)* (29, 1993).

adherents of restorative justice may be right in thinking that damages settlement, one of the different goals of restorative procedures may be brought about more easily outside the repressive context of police officers and prosecutors. In the Dutch 'Instructions for the police and the public prosecutor's office regarding the victim' provision is made for quick and efficient settlement of damages. The idea was that especially in minor cases the victim and the offender could work out a compensation which would result in the prosecutor not pressing charges. Still it does not seem to work very well.

In the late 1990s the Dutch government recognised the importance of restorative strategies, such as ADR and especially mediation.[8] This interest underscores the wish to return the responsibility for dispute settlement to the parties and/or communities involved and to alleviate the pressure on the courts. Being a bit of a sceptic I am inclined to see the interest of neo-liberal government in alleviating the pressure on the courts: it is cheaper to let people pay for law than to give law to them.[9] However this may be unjust, too cynical and undervaluing the good intentions of some of the government officials involved.

In order to evaluate the difference between the two ways of thinking it may be illuminating to make a difference between types of offenders. There are enormous differences between the greengrocer of whom some apples were stolen, the man who has been burgled and the girl who has been raped. These differences should be recognised if one is to discuss the position of victims and/or the possibilities of restorative justice. I will discuss the examples mentioned above in order to differentiate between cases in which in my opinion a basically punitive attitude is fitting and cases in which restorative ways of thinking may be appropriate. Finally I will discuss the largest and most difficult category, that is the category of cases that may demand a victim-oriented criminal law.

A basically punitive approach: severe cases

If we consider the most problematic victims – for example (the relatives of) victims of murder or rape – I cannot help but start from a traditional legal perspective. Severe crimes should not be looked at as 'problematic situations' – problems between people that should be given back to the people – but as crimes, infringements of collective morality. There is a fundamental reason as well as a sociological prediction to support this supposition.

By the act of punishing a norm that has been violated is recognised. Although one could say the same in cases of shoplifting and burglary, it is especially regarding high profile cases that the 'act of not-punishing' – the clumsy expression is intended to emphasise that we are not talking about an omission,

8. *TK* 1999-2000, 26352, 19 & 22.

9. See also on restorative justice in terms of privatisation S. Gutwirth & P. de Hert, 'Grondslagentheoretische variaties op de grens tussen het strafrecht en het burgerlijk recht' in K. Boonen *& al.* ed., *De weging van 't Hart* (Kluwer, Deventer, 2002).

but about deliberate not punishing in restorative justice – is questionable because of this fundamental thought. A substantive norm (such as the right to life or the right not to be tortured – that is deliberate inhuman treatment causing very serious and cruel suffering) may be imperative for certain government action, according to the European Court of Human Rights. That Court has decided in many cases that the right to life (as well as the right not to be tortured) implicate the duty of national governments to investigate alleged killings by officials. I do realise that the Court has never said that for instance a killer-cop should be punished (see for example the McCann-case).[10] Here I am just interested in the line of reasoning: certain governmental reactions are requested because of substantive rights of the citizens. The duty to act is in this perspective a result of the legal system itself. No policy can change that – neither an unsympathetic one like an authoritarian pro-torture policy, nor a sympathetic restorative justice policy. There are certain norms the violation of which requires punishment. Of course this line of reasoning does not count for – for example – government regulations that cannot be held dear to the value system of a community of citizens and therefore this fundamental idea will usually not stand in the way of the decision not to punish infringements on these regulations. However, there is an outer limit – one can only argue where the line has to be drawn.

Less fundamental but nevertheless not unimportant (and for many a pragmatist presumably even more important) is the sociological prediction that non-punitive reactions to high profile cases would diminish the legitimacy of government and/or of law. The issue here is not human rights and legal governmental obligations, but popular acceptance. In some cases a non-punitive reaction would not be accepted. In Holland there has been the case of personal reconciliation between a policeman who had been shot at by a RAF-terrorist. The colleagues of the policemen – one of them badly injured himself – found that to be unacceptable, although the reconciliation took place when and partly after the terrorist had been serving a long time in a German prison.[11]

I do not believe restorative justice is a good idea from the point of view of the victim and the offender in these cases. In many high profile cases there is an unequal relationship between the offender and the victim. Take a relatively debatable example (maybe it is not the best example for 'high profile cases') such as date rape: one would think that the girl would be in a bad position to bargain, be it only as a consequence of the psychological difficulty and danger of secondary victimisation. From the point of view of the offender there is also a problem: how can he defend himself against false reports? If he does not accept mediation the girl will bring her allegations to the attention of the

10. European Court of Human Rights, 27 September 1995 (McCann and Others v. the United Kingdom), Series A no. 324; see also ECHR 19 February 1998 (Kaya v. Turkey), *Reports of Judgements and Decisions* 1998-I, p. 324; ECHR 4 May 2001 (Hugh Jordan v. The United Kingdom).

11. F. Denkers, H. van Hoogen, C. Wackernagel *& al.*, *Begrepen onbehagen: Politie en Rote Armee Fraktion verzoend* (Vermande, Lelystad, 1999).

media. If he accepts his responsibility he could worsen his position if the prosecutor would prosecute.

That is why the outcomes of the Restorative conciliation project in The Hague (The Netherlands) are not surprising. Here the idea was that conciliation could have an emotional, but supplementary relevance apart from, but not instead of, criminal law: offenders and victims are said to be completely at liberty to participate – there is no criminal law threat in the background. There were 118 requests – especially from parole offices (*reclassering*) and victim support (*slachtofferhulp*) – in two and a half years, which led to 19 cases of direct conciliation. The private research enterprise that evaluated this project has done its utmost to stress the qualitative importance of the project – that is the possibility for the victim to accept and show his vindictiveness and for the offender to show his regrets. Notwithstanding these positive intentions the results are not convincing: in most of these 19 cases either the offender or the victim did not want to continue.[12]

In this perspective it is interesting to note that the Economic and Social Council of the UN stated on restorative justice programs that:

1. the offender should take responsibility *vis-à-vis* the victim and affected communities – otherwise restoration and reintegration will have no chance at all.

2. the cases referred to the restorative justice system can only be those of which it is acceptable not to prosecute – because judicial discharges based on agreements out of restorative justice programs should preclude prosecution in respect of the same facts (*ne bis in idem*).

3. the cases referred to the restorative justice system can only be those which it is possible to prosecute, because in cases where no agreement can be made, the cases should be referred back to the criminal justice authorities.[13]

So in my view very severe cases such as murder and rape ought to be kept outside the scope of restorative justice. I know that some can cite examples of restorative dealing with serious crimes, especially in terms of victim benefits – alongside criminal justice rather than being a replacement of it – but this does not seem to be a good idea.[14] The bottom line of my argument regarding these severe cases may be described as follows: because it is not acceptable not to prosecute, restorative justice is out of the question. Of course one could think about giving a more important role to the victim in these criminal procedures, to be discussed next.

12. M. van Barlingen, G.J. Slump & H. Tulner, *Tussenevaluatie Herstelbemiddeling* (Van Dijk, Van Soomeren en Partners, Amsterdam, 2000).

13. Economic and Social Council, *Basic principles on the use of restorative justice programmes in criminal matters* (20-4-2000).

14. T.F. Marshall, *Restorative Justice: An Overview* (Center for Restorative Justice and Mediation, University of Minnesota, Minnesota, 1998).

Victim-oriented criminal law: ordinary cases

Bearing in mind the starting position of the Economic and Social Council I would say a punitive approach is necessary in severe cases and a purely restorative justice approach – maybe even outside the realm of criminal justice – may be possible in mild cases, but I will come back to that later. However, fundamental problems arise if we look at the important category of intermediary cases, such as burglary. Could we leave it to a priest to decide about restorative justice or prosecution? How do we decide if (and when) these crimes can be dealt with in a restorative justice-like way? Before answering these questions, even more important is the question of why we would enter this new venue at all.

It may be argued that solidarity with the victim is the reason for a restorative justice approach instead of a penal approach. However this solidarity does not compel us to embrace restorative justice, because it could also be argued that this solidarity can give us a new basis for criminal law in general, such as the traditional legitimising theories. Victims seem to offer a wonderful basis for re-embedding social relations and re-embedding trust in the law and its upholders. May we say that in the past we punished because a sin has been committed (*quia peccatum,* retaliation to restore order), that later on we punished in order to prevent people from sinning (*ne peccetur*, presupposing trust in experts) and that from now on we punish because there was suffering or because suffering ought to be prevented or in order to let it stop. This line of reasoning might be defended, but I will not go for it and I will explain why.

Discussing the possibilities of a victim-oriented criminal law, one should bear in mind that historically the basic idea of criminal law is that it has to do with deliberately inflicting pain by government or the judiciary to an offender. It is not like civil law about redistribution of costs or a restoration. Why? Because criminal law has been from the outset a way to deal with people who want to punish others – who want to inflict that pain for their own sake. From Solon's days inflicting a punishment was a question of power – power of the landlord, the commander, the father of the household – and (because of the interests of the community as a whole) the judges had the task to stop too Draconian use of these powers by limiting them and weighing the interests of both sides. This has nothing to do with the question as to whether you like it that criminal law has to do with inflicting pain – or with retributive or consequentionalist thinking in the ordinary sense – but with the political wish to stop people from starting vendettas and to stop others from dealing with less powerful people as if they were their slaves. One might want to make criminal procedure more fruitful by incorporating possibilities of repair, but criminal law is no successor to Roman civil law.[15]

15. See for instance D.M. MacDowell, *The Law in Classical Athens* (Thames and Hudson, London, 1978); P.W.A. Immink, *La liberté et la peine: étude sur la transformation de la liberté et sur le dévelopment du droit pénal public en Occident avant le 12e siècle* (Van

I believe that criminal law is still important to prevent people from taking the law into their own hands. On this assumption it is understandable why in the end the suffering of the victim is not a relevant basis for punishment. Criminal law demands that the suspect is proven to have committed the alleged act with a sufficient level of guilt and not enough justification to be exonerated. If that is the case a punishment will be meted out. If we do not find it necessary any more to prevent people from taking the law into their own hands, a case can be made for abolishing criminal law, but if we do find it necessary, we have to accept that criminal law is about making people suffer. This can only be done properly by looking into all circumstances of the case and into the personality of the perpetrator. If the level of guilt of the offender is low – it was not an intentionally committed crime or one could almost speak of a justification or an excuse – there could be some reason to be merciful: everyone can imagine himself to be in the same place as the offender. In that case he should not be punished severely, whatever the impact on the victim.

That is why solidarity with victims should not fundamentally affect criminal law. However, one can try to find possibilities for the victim to have compensation for his bad luck. One line of reasoning may be, that the objective damage that has been caused is an indication for the severity of the punishment. Because of the increasing appreciation of the feelings of the victim, it could be asked whether the suffering of the victim could be the basis for punishment. If so, the judge should estimate the subjective damage done, namely the suffering. Of course the prosecutor will tell the judges about the damage, even about the psychological impact. Victim impact statements, written down by a police officer shortly after the traumatic event, can be useful in our Dutch system where we quite easily accept written statements.[16] However judges are fully aware that 'myths of innocence and victimisation are a powerful obstacle in the way of confronting unwelcome facts'.[17] For instance, facts that lessen the impact for the victim. That is why for the assessment of the damage written statements at one specific moment are not sufficient, and that is why the actual assessment should be based on standards which enable us to decide as objectively as possible – as we try to prove the intention of the suspect as objectively as possible.

I will not deny that this idea is a result of my inclination to doubt the general trustworthiness of the statements of victims. I would like to venture two reasons for this inclination. First, some victims are unreliable themselves. Every insurance company knows the phenomenon of excessive claiming: in 3 out of 10 burglaries the insurance companies do not pay.[18] And one-quarter of all hooligans and one-quarter of all suspects of fencing stolen goods, carrying a

---

Gorcum, Assen, 1973). See also M. Hildebrandt, *Straf(begrip) en procesbeginsel* (dissertation, Erasmus Universiteit Rotterdam, Rotterdam, 2002).

16. See about this writing down by police officers *TK* 1999-2000, 27213, 1, p. 9-10.

17. A. Krog, *Country of my Skull* (Cape, London, 1999).

18. H. Huys, 'Schade door criminaliteit' *Index* (vol. 7, 4, April 2000).

gun or stealing bicycles have themselves been a victim of violence.[19] These victims know that in modern culture being a victim is a reason for pious inquiries about their suffering, but almost never for questioning their own actions. Nevertheless it cannot be denied that most victims are reliable.

This brings me to a second reason to doubt the trustworthiness, or should I say usefulness, of the statements of victims. There is a huge difference between the way victims appreciate their ordeal. Even if the victim as a person is highly reliable and if he would be completely 'transparent' regarding the impact of the crime, this could still give rise to enormous problems. It is hard to accept that the guy who broke another guy's nose in a café brawl would be sent to jail if the victim was mentally traumatised by the blow, but would be given the opportunity to give the victim some money if the victim was not mentally traumatised. From the perspective of equality that is hardly fair. Moreover, one could also say that it would be hard to accept that a very dangerous participant in the brawl would not be sent to jail if the impact on the victim was small, while he would if the victim had been a weaker person.

So I do not think the suffering of the victim should serve as a basis to assess a certain level of punishment. The harm done should be looked at as objectively as possible. Nevertheless it could be held, that it would be preferable to give more voice to the victim in the criminal procedure. That is why recently a Parliamentary initiative was taken in The Netherlands to introduce the right to speak for victims and for surviving relatives.[20] The discussion on the Victim Impact Statements was timely in view of the European Council Framework Decision of 15 March 2001 on the Standing of victims in criminal proceedings.[21] According to art. 3, 'Each member State shall safeguard the possibility for victims to be heard during proceedings and to supply evidence'. If this means that all victims have the right to be heard at trial, the Dutch definitively have to change their system. In my opinion this would be bad for the system and bad for the victims.

Let me be clear on one point: my doubts are only pertaining to the position during trial. I would welcome improvement of treatment of victims immediately after the crime and in the period until the court session. There are examples of horrific shortcomings of the law in action, such as the case of an 18-year old girl who had been murdered in The Netherlands, and where the police and public prosecutors completely failed to properly inform her father, Mr De Ruijter de Wildt and other relatives.

My doubts concern a stronger victim orientation in court. That could easily lead to a competition of interests between fair justice for the victim and a fair trial for the defendant. One should realise that it is hard for the judges when they have to weigh not just two interests – those of the defendant and of the public – but three.

19. C. Jol, 'Daders als slachtoffers' *Index* (vol.7, 4, April 2000).
20. *TK* 2000-2001, 27632, 1-3.
21. *OJ* (2001) L 82.

More specifically I fear that in many cases victim impact statements will in the end be counter-productive for most victims, although I will not deny that for some, like Mr Kloppenburg, the father of a courageous boy killed, it is important to be able to express themselves as victimised relatives in court. My opinion is based on current Dutch practice as well as the comparative findings of De Keyser and Malsch. In my own experience the position of the victim in court is ordinarily a simulacrum of influence: he can say something, but in the end the victim is helpless again, because the judge interrupts him, does not seem to understand, looks friendly to the defendant, gives a lower punishment than expected. Comparative research seems to indicate the same: victim impact statements have (almost) no influence on the level of punishment, while Erez found only marginal effects on the satisfaction of these victims.[22]

These latter findings were to be expected if one considers some facts regarding post-traumatic stress disorder. Rates of PTSD of 80 per cent were observed when rape, life threat and injury were present in an individual's history.[23] Most crime victims with PTSD have to live with depression – so who could blame them for their vindictiveness? These people need to be recognised, but especially they need social support in order to stop their feelings of isolation and helplessness: trauma clouds self-esteem – the biggest trap after victimisation is the trap of learned helplessness. They have to find a place in the world again, a place where they have some control over their own lives. As Gulag survivor and poet Joseph Brodsky said: try to avoid seeing yourself as a victim.[24] In the first days after a traumatic event it is important that the police (and victim support groups) give the victim his (psychological) due. If the victim has to wait until the court session before he can give a victim impact statement, he stays in the trap of learned helplessness. The various procedural steps are out of his control. When the big day of the trial arrives the whole thing is out of his control again and he may well feel humbled once more. Support for victims? Sure. But giving them more important roles in court is deceiving them. What they get is prolonged helplessness. Then one can really say that the murderer made more victims by tarnishing the memory of the deceased with the bitterness he invoked in the relatives.[25]

22. J.W. de Keyser & M. Malsch, 'Is spreken zilver en zwijgen goud?' *Delikt en Delinkwent* (vol. 32, 1, 2002), pp. 5-20; E. Erez & P. Tontodonato, 'Victim participation in sentencing and satisfaction with justice' *Justice Quarterly* (1992), pp. 393-427; E. Erez, L. Roeger & F. Morgan, 'Victim harm, impact statements and victim satisfaction with justice' *International Review of Victimology* (5, 1997), pp. 37-60.
23. D.G. Kilpatrich *& al.*, 'Victim and crime factors associated with the development of crime-related posttraumatic stress disorder' *Behavior Therapy* (20, 1989), pp. 199-214; H.S. Resnick & D.G. Kilpatrick, 'Crime-related PTSD: emphasis on adult general population samples' *PTSD Research Quarterly* (Vol. 5, number 3, 1994).
24. J. Brodsky, *On grief and reason: essays* (Farrar Straus Giroux, New York, 1995); one could also think of the people in the photographs of Sebastiao Salgado: strong people in desperate situations – human beings, not victims – who did not surrender.
25. D. Tutu, *No Future Without Forgiveness* (Rider, London, 1999), p. 113.

It is hard to draw any definitive conclusions. Nevertheless I would say it should not be up to the victim to decide whether a punitive or a restorative action should be chosen. In severe cases that would be wrong because of the normative importance of punishment; in 'ordinary' cases it would be wrong because of the overwhelming influence of subjective factors. It could only be different with minor offences.

Possibilities of restorative justice: minor cases

The cited words of the Economic and Social Council implicate the necessity to keep one's mind open to the possibilities of restorative justice. It can even be said that there are substantial reasons for this as well. Since the 1980s there has been a drastic increase in punitiveness in The Netherlands: more prosecutions, higher penalties – an increase not only to be explained directly by increasing crime rates. Youth crime is illustrative: 80 per cent of young offenders will not do it again; 5-10 per cent are hard core. These figures are relatively stable.[26] However, nowadays even the 14-year old boy who commits mischief like stealing an apple is placed in the so called HALT-program for youth punishment by the police and has to work for four or eight hours. HALT is an alternative, based on the criminal code, to deal with young delinquents who have committed minor offences: if the youngster works properly his case will not be sent to the public prosecutor's office. One of the HALT-coordinators told me he is astonished about absolutely petty cases leading to these official punishments.[27] He literally had to execute the HALT-program in a case of two stolen apples. Nevertheless no one is complaining. It is a new industry.

In these cases one could imagine that the greengrocer whose apples were nicked would be willing to accept some initiative for Alternative Dispute Resolution – be it in a criminal law context (organised by the police) or organised by social workers or a church. He may be a decent guy, willing to take his responsibility for educating youth. Obviously this has little to do with the new role for victims: it will probably cost the greengrocer more to give the offender the opportunity to confess and to restore the original loss than to simply take his loss. Restorative justice programs may be very good in cases like these, in order to circumvent an exaggerated criminal law system. But it is fair to say that they are even more important from the welfare point of view, as far as they provide opportunities for the offender, the families of victims and offenders as well as the community. The importance of pedagogy or community work seems to come first and there is nothing wrong with that. I do have sympathetic feel-

26. P. van der Laan, 'Jeugdcriminaliteit neemt toe...of niet...of wel?' *Sec* (12, nr 6, 1998), pp. 5-8; there probably is a rise in violence but this is to be attributed to a small group.
27. F.M.J.A. Imkamp, 'Vijftien jaren alternatieve sancties in het jeugdstrafrecht' *Sancties* (1999), pp. 316-324: in 1991 almost 9000 kids were sent to a HALT-project; in 1996 more than 20.000 although there are no valid indications that the amount of relevant crimes has risen.

ings about the *'Echt recht*-conferences' in The Hague schools, modelled after New Zealand Family Group Conferences.[28] Schoolchildren who threatened their mates with a knife were not expelled from school and not punished according to the Dutch HALT system, but were reintegrated by shaming activities. Would it not have been a shame if these juveniles had been officially punished?

The 'independent coping' project (*sociale zelfredzaamheid*) in Zwolle seems to provide another illustration. There, people in one of the poorer communities of a Dutch provincial town are proud to be able to cope with their problems as a result of the project. One of the noteworthy findings is that these people were not bothered most by feelings of insecurity, but by feelings of being slighted and neglected by the authorities. The police considered the neighbourhood to be a no go area. The project stopped this and teams of local police officers, welfare workers and housing project personnel with a large degree of discretionary power were responding to the wishes of the community.[29] The importance of strengthening social efficacy could indeed be thought to be greater than the importance of criminal punishment in certain cases.

We have, however, to acknowledge the tension between this welfare point of view and the public function of law.[30] For example: I am willing to accept that away from the eyes of the public the decision could be made that a person who used to earn his income by means of robberies or drug dealing and is now working in addition to receiving a social security benefit, without paying taxes and without notifying the social security agency, will not be prosecuted for fraud. I would even be glad if this inequality would remain invisible to the public eye, thanks to restorative justice. But the transparency of the decision not to prosecute might easily be lost, possibly leading to a loss in trust in the fairness of the procedure in the eyes of others that are prosecuted for fraud.

A second problem arises if we imagine the man who has beaten up his wife and who will not be prosecuted, because of a victim-oriented restorative way of acting if his wife does not make a case. It is probably better – not only for him but also for the wife and kids who probably have to live on with him – to try to teach him communicative skills. However, one cannot deny that in this way an evil person might escape his just deserts and that a dangerous person is not being forced to abstain from committing serious crime, because the victim said he committed a minor offence, while in truth it was not minor at all. Of course a true believer in the cause of restorative justice may accept this disregard for

28. R. van Pagee, 'Echt recht op Haagse scholen' *Sec* (10-2000).

29. J. Hes, *Recht doen aan de buurt* (Stichting Maatschappij, Veiligheid en Politie, Dordrecht, 2000); these same feelings were noted in J. Meyers, 'Notes on the Murder of my Neighbours' *Atlantic Monthly* (March 2000). See also R.J. Samspon, S.W. Raudenbusch & F. Earls, 'Neighbourhoods and Violent Crime' *Science* (Vol 277, 15-8-1997).

30. C.P.M. Cleiren, *Geding buiten geding* (Quint, Gouda, 2001). See also J. Kocken, 'De strijd tussen verzoeners: rechter versus mediator' in *Recht der werkelijkheid, thema Onverzoenlijkheid* (Elsevier, The Hague, 1999), pp. 77-93.

traditional motives for punishment, but for many this disregard will be more difficult than in the aforementioned social security case.

A third problem arises if one considers possibilities of non-punitive approaches regarding instrumental regulations, for instance in the realm of the 'food and drug administration', tax law, economic law and the like. Ordinarily these are victimless crimes, apart from general interests. Moreover it is often hard not to consider these regulations as primarily prescriptions from a governmental authority. They have little to do with the morality that governs the interactions between people. Of course, in some of these regulations there seem to be moral undertones (for example in environmental law), but often these undertones are hardly noticeable. In many western European countries there is a tendency to impose governmental fines for transgression of these instrumental regulations outside the realm of criminal law (for example the German *Bussgeld* for *Ordnungswidrigkeiten*). These administrative sanctions are to be distinguished from the more civil law-like solutions from the realm of restorative justice. The latter seem to be better suited to crimes and misdemeanours with moral undertones and with victims (like shoplifting by schoolboys). However, I have to admit that one could also state that other forms of restorative justice ought to be elaborated for administrative and other types of victimless offences.

Nevertheless I do see some opportunities for restorative justice projects. Because restorative instruments will have to be backed up by the judicial system according to the ideas of the Economic and Social Council, in my opinion participation of police or law officers would be required. This holds good even in cases of minor importance where considerations of pedagogy regarding the offender or welfare of the community do indicate a restorative approach. The Dutch system, which does not require a policeman or a public prosecutor to prosecute every known crime, makes it possible to look for alternative solutions. It is up to the prosecutor's office to decide whether prosecution should follow or not, and if not, under which conditions. One of these conditions could be successful participation in a restorative program. So, if the prosecutor decides in these cases to choose in favour of criminal procedure, he has to accept that the role of the victim could be relatively minimal. If he opts for restorative justice he ought to bear in mind problems of equality and dangers posed by offenders.

Justice, mercy and compassion

To recapitulate: criminal law is about deliberately making criminals suffer because of their crimes. Solidarity with the victim cannot be a basis for criminal law. Maybe current retributivist and utilitarian ideas do not offer plausible grounds for punishment, but restorative justice cannot end the so-called 'state of crisis of criminal law thinking' either. One could try to assess the suffering of the victim – no easy thing to do – but whatever the possibilities, one cannot use that assessment as a yardstick for punishment. This does not mean that restorative justice is not an important idea, but it cannot be claimed to be a strong overall model.[31]

Perhaps the restorative idea should be given some scope in ordinary cases, but then it seems that the police and the public prosecution have to decide whether restoration would be a good alternative to punitive actions or not. If they are making the decisions it may be better not to use restorative justice as a concept, but to speak of a victim-oriented criminal law with restorative elements. The reason for this embedding in the criminal justice system is the 'price' of restorative justice. One has to accept inequality with respect to other offenders and one has to accept a degree of mercy (because of the victim's wishes) for very unsympathetic persons – if alternative dispute resolution is to stand a chance. Justice is not the same as equality and sometimes punishment is less important than pedagogy and social efficacy, but this does not mean that one could neglect these negativities.

Restorative justice may work best in minor cases, especially in cases in which the formalism of the criminal trial is unsatisfactory for all persons involved (for example because the trial will be taking place a long time after the event) and/or there are pedagogic reasons or reasons with a view to strengthening social efficacy in a community to look for 'alternatives'.

The question regarding the cases in which we have to opt for restorative alternatives is more difficult to answer in concrete cases than I indicated in the above-mentioned differentiation. Of course, it may not be easy to differentiate between severe, ordinary and minor cases. How to assess a certain case in that perspective? The following thoughts may be helpful, if such an assessment should be made.

Real solidarity with the victim is outside the realm of criminal law. The pragmatic proposals of experts like Groenhuijsen to improve criminal law in a piecemeal way favouring the victims, may be acceptable (see chapter 4). One could think of restorative programs for petty youth criminals and for petty crime in the context of welfare problems in communities. Such developments are to be welcomed.

However, I will monitor such developments with the firm scepticism of someone who was taught that in the drama that is called a criminal trial, there can only be one leading actor. And that is the one who acted, not the one who suffered. No compassion with victims, no disappointment with the current state of criminal justice, nothing can ever change that.

On a fundamental level one has to acknowledge that compassion for the victim because of unjustly inflicted suffering can hardly be reconciled with mercy for the offender. We feel compassionate towards the victim because he suffered an important misfortune he did not deserve. Perhaps we could also be led by mercy for the offender because we – as judges – understand the difficul-

31. J. Blad, 'Strafrecht en bemiddeling' *Recht der werkelijkheid* (2, 2000) may be slightly overstating his case for restorative justice as an alternative.

ties of life of the offender.[32] Thus we have to ask ourselves whether we should limit mercy for the offender because of compassion with the victim, in cases in which we could have done the same thing if we had been in the same situation. It may be exactly in cases where compassion and mercy both demand a non-penal solution that restorative justice may have its best chances.

32. See also M. Nussbaum, *Upheavals of Thought* (Cambridge University Press, Cambridge, 2001), part II as well as *id.*, 'Equity and Mercy' in *Sex and Social Justice* (Oxford University Press, Oxford, 1999).

2. Gearing Justice Action to Victim Satisfaction Contrasting Two Justice Philosophies: Retribution and Redress

Ezzat Fattah*

Victims' bill of rights were enacted, but paled in comparison to enforceable charter rights. They focused on service and information from crime-control professionals without giving victims decision-making powers. In contrast, restorative justice and crime prevention allowed victims and potential victims of crime to make decisions without being subject to adversarial due-process challenges or the false illusion that the criminal law would control crime.

Kent Roach (1999, p. 300)

Introduction

Enhanced awareness of victims' rights and the passage of victims' bill of rights in many countries in the last two decades may give the impression that victims of crime are much better off now than they have ever been. It may suggest that the criminal justice system has finally moved from its singular emphasis on the offender and from its longstanding obsession with punishment to victim-centred or victim-oriented policies and objectives. Alas! The reality is far different from the popular perception and the political rhetoric. Although some progress has been made and some gains have been achieved, the situation of the vast majority of victims has hardly improved. The reasons for this sad state of affairs are not difficult to understand. Actually, the most tangible victories of the victim movement have revolved around the punishment of offenders and their primary focus, as surprising as this may seem, has been a more punitive response to crime. Redress to the victim was only secondary to having the offender severely punished for the offence he has committed, and ultimately both punishment and redress proved to be elusive and unattainable goals. Non-punitive forms of victims' rights were never high on the agenda of those groups that claimed to represent crime victims and to defend their interests. If the real interests of victims are to become the main objectives of the criminal justice system, a fundamental change has to occur. Nothing less than a paradigm shift,

* Formerly Simon Fraser University, Vancouver, B.C., Canada.

a shift from retributive to restorative justice, can truly satisfy victim needs, achieve victim empowerment, and ensure that victims are actively and fully involved in the justice process. This is because restorative justice is justice for victims with the active participation of those victims. It is justice that recognises their plight and affirms their rights. It is justice that ensures that their wishes are respected, their needs are satisfied, and their expectations are met (Fattah, 2000).

Ignoring the victim: The Canadian Sentencing Commission as an example

To illustrate what I mean let me refer to Canada as an example. In the late 1980s Canada had the misfortune of having a so-called 'Sentencing Commission' which I believe was set up by the conservative government of the time in order to move Canada in the same punitive/retributive direction that had already been established in the United Kingdom and the United States. The Commission blatantly ignored the recommendations of critics of retribution, like myself, who wanted to use the opportunity to affirm the superiority of the restorative justice model, and issued a report that was reactionary, flawed, and strongly biased in favour of one specific sentencing philosophy: just deserts. Surprisingly, this was the time when the victim movement was in full swing and there was a growing awareness of victims' plight and of the need to affirm their rights. In such a climate favourable to victim concerns, one would have expected the Sentencing Commission to affirm that the primary goal of sentencing is to repair the harm done to the victim by the offence and to prevent future harm. Instead the Commission (1988) opted for some abstract goals, characteristic of a right-wing philosophy of justice, goals that can only lead to the depersonalisation and dehumanisation of the justice system. It stated that '...the fundamental purpose of sentencing is to preserve the authority of, and promote respect for, the law through the imposition of just sanctions'. (p. 151) Not a mention of victims, their needs and/or their rights, not a word about providing redress to the victims, NOTHING!

Some years later, the Commission's statement was adopted almost verbatim and became part of Section 718 of the Canadian Criminal Code declaring that sentencing has as its fundamental purpose 'to contribute... to respect for the law and the maintenance of a just, peaceful and safe society by imposing just sanctions'.

In a brief submitted to the *House of Commons Standing Committee on Justice and Solicitor General,* in March 1988, I made some comments on the Sentencing Commission's report. I said:

> In an era meant to become the golden age of the victim, there seems to be a growing obsession with punishment, euphemistically called 'just deserts'. *Yet having punishment as the central focus of our criminal justice system is neither morally legitimate nor practically effective.* It can only act to the detriment of the victim. Dispute-settlement, mediation, reconciliation, arbitration, reparation, are concepts

> foreign to a system based on punishment, a system which regards the crime not as a human action but as a legal infraction. The operation of such a system acts to intensify the conflict rather than solving it. And instead of bringing the feuding parties together it widens the gap that separates them.

The point I was trying to make, as far back as 1988, is that the philosophy of 'just deserts' neither serves the interests of crime victims nor satisfies their most obvious needs. Years later, Todd Clear (1994) expressed a similar view when he affirmed that penal harm does not help the victim and cannot make the victim whole again. Instead, the focus on getting even with the offender could in some ways divert the victim from his/her personal path of recovery. Clear adds:

> In this way, the emphasis on penal harm may actually be a disservice to the victim, in that it promises that if the State is only able to impose a penalty severe enough, the victim will be able to overcome the crime. The focus is placed on what happens to the law violator, not what happens with the victims. The victim's victory at sentencing is eventually exposed as a pyrrhic conquest, for the problem faced by the victim does not centre on the offender (1994, p. 173).

The shift from the welfare state to the social control state

In the years that followed the end of the Second World War the social democratic welfare state came into being. Its emergence signalled the dawn of a new era in the history of humanity. In contrast to the oppressive, cruel, bloody and genocidal regimes in Hitler's Germany, Stalin's Russia, and Mussolini's Italy, a very different society was born. It was a more humane and caring society where suffering was reduced and where the least possible amount of pain was deliberately inflicted. The new society was a society that respected its members, came to the rescue of those who needed help, and assisted those in need, whether their plight was the result of poverty, unemployment, economic hardship, social injustice, sickness, disease, or else. A new penal policy was developed whose aims were the humanisation of the penal system and the retrenchment of the system of punishment. Alas, the dream of a just, humane and caring society did not last too long. With the advent of conservative governments led by simple-minded politicians such as Reagan and Bush in the United States, Margaret Thatcher in England, and Brian Mulroney in Canada, we moved from the Welfare State to the Social Control State. Penal philosophy underwent a fundamental change. There was a shift 'from rehabilitation to retribution, from the culpability of society to the culpability of the offender, and from reasoned policy to symbolic gesture' (Cayley, 1998, p. 41). Capitalising on the fear of an unsuspecting and an ill-informed public alarmed by rising crime rates, right wing politicians managed to enact laws that pushed the prison population to record heights. But the futility and the enormous costs of the new wave of repression were bound to call into question the rationality of those punitive policies. The search for less destructive and less costly alternatives became a priority. Inspired by how native and aboriginal communities deal with conflicts and harmful actions, with offences committed by some members of the group against other group members, there were demands for peaceful and reconciliatory means of conflict resolution. Critics of the system wanted to make justice work and to make offenders pay. Restorative justice proponents called for the socialisation and humanisation of justice, for the personalisation and civilisation of conflicts. Victims' advocates demanded that justice be made more sensitive to the victims and more responsive to their needs and their wishes. Soon restorative justice became an attractive option. It is not difficult to understand and explain the irresistible appeal and the growing popularity of restorative justice. Restorative justice calls for restitution not retribution, for redress not revenge, for reconciliation not retaliation, for reparation not incarceration.

The major appeal of restorative justice is that it reconciles the aims of those who demand recognition of, and a voice for, the victim and those who feel that punishment is an abuse of the State's power and a misuse of public funds. What draws people from different backgrounds and different ends of the political spectrum to restorative justice is its ability to satisfy those who are in favour of active victim participation in the justice process and those who believe that offenders need to be sensitised to the pain and suffering they had inflicted upon their victims, those who feel that redress to the victim should be the primary objective of the justice process and those who want to hold offenders accountable for their actions.

Some overlooked benefits of restorative justice

The benefits of restorative justice and the clear advantages it has over the current system of criminal justice have been explained over and over again in the abundant literature on restorative justice. They are well summarised in the preamble to the recommendations made to the Council of Europe by the *Committee of Experts on Mediation in Penal Matters*. Among other things, the Committee (1999) stressed that mediation in penal matters is a flexible, comprehensive, problem-solving, participatory, and viable alternative to traditional criminal proceedings, an alternative that satisfies a strongly felt need to enhance active personal participation of the victim, the offender and others who may have been affected, as parties, by the offence. The Committee also noted that mediation enhances the involvement of the community and recognises the legitimate interest of victims in having a stronger voice in dealing with the consequences of their victimisation, as well as their need to communicate with the offender to obtain an apology and reparation. The committee also emphasised that mediation encourages offenders' sense of responsibility and offers them practical opportunities to make amends which may further their reintegration and rehabilitation. It also has the potential of increasing the awareness of the important role of the individual and the community in preventing and handling crime and resolving its associated conflicts, thus encouraging more constructive and less repressive criminal justice outcomes.

All of those arguments are well known to those with an interest in restorative justice. I personally have discussed them at some length in my writings on the topic (Fattah, 1993; 1995; 1998; 1999; 2000). So is there anything that has not been said or remains to be said about the positives of restorative justice? Are there some hidden benefits that have been somehow overlooked and have not been thoroughly discussed in the fast growing literature on this exciting and promising model of justice? This chapter will briefly mention ten of the less often discussed benefits of restorative justice.

Restorative justice avoids the inherent arbitrariness of retributive punishment and the enormous disparities in its application

Arbitrariness is a structural, innate and irremediable defect in retributive systems. To maintain that a given number of days, months or years in prison is a fair and equitable punishment for offences such as assault, rape, robbery, or else, strikes me as the height of arbitrariness (Fattah, 1982). It is rather difficult to understand how intelligent people: lawyers, scholars, academics and others, could believe and maintain that pain can be measured and dispensed according to some kind of mathematical formula. How could they believe it possible to create some kind of equation that would make a prison sentence fit a crime that has caused physical or psychological injury, material harm or loss? That a seriously flawed concept and a fundamentally defective sentencing model like 'just deserts' could be accepted and implemented for so long is a mystery. When Prof. Graeme Newman of the School of Criminal Justice at Albany suggested some years back, at a meeting of the American Society of Criminology, that carefully measured electrical shocks be used to inflict a just dosage of pain on criminals, those attending the meeting simply laughed at him. And yet his suggestion makes more sense than the arbitrary use of imprisonment as a retributive sanction. Surprisingly, sentencing models that adopt a very similar punishment philosophy, such as the 'just deserts' model, are not greeted with laughter, and more surprising, they are even taken seriously by some scholars and policy makers. Except in a purely theological perspective, retribution is not, and can never be, an instrument of justice. To speak, therefore, of 'retributive justice', is a contradiction in terms. And as it is impossible to establish a fair equation between the punishment and the crime, between the pain to be inflicted upon the offender and the pain caused by the offence to the victim, we should stop associating justice with retribution, as is often done when the popular term 'retributive justice' is used. We should also remove the word 'just' from the sentencing model that is erroneously called 'just deserts' and call it instead 'the arbitrary desert model'.

By settling conflicts through a process and outcome somewhat similar to that of civil courts restorative justice offers a remedy to the arbitrary distinctions between civil and criminal conflicts
Punitive/retributive justice is based on an erroneous premise, the premise that crime is a unique, distinct or exceptional category of behaviour. It is also based on a false dichotomy between the so-called crimes and civil wrongs. Both the premise and the dichotomy are fallacious. A comparison between acts made punishable by the penal law or criminal statutes and similar behaviours that are left unregulated, or are regulated by non-criminal rules or by administrative bodies, reveals that there is no qualitative difference between criminal and non-criminal behaviour. In fact, for every behaviour defined as criminal and sanctioned by law, there are identical or similar types of behaviour that are neither illegal nor punishable (Fattah, 1997). If crime is not qualitatively different from civil torts or civil wrongs, then there is no valid reason to accept redress to the injured or harmed party in the latter and to insist on sanctions of a completely different nature for the former. One also has to wonder why it is that in the case of civil torts the damages ordered by the court go to the victim whereas in criminal offences the penal fine goes to the public treasury. Surprisingly, many of those who oppose the notion of restorative justice and continue to demand retribution, even for non-violent crimes, have no problem accepting administrative or civil remedies for various types of corporate, white-collar and professional crimes, and voice no objection to the civil regulation of corporate wrong doing.

Restorative justice avoids the vagaries of punitive systems
The enormous and inevitable disparities in the application of retributive punishments make a mockery out of what is supposed to be a fair and equitable justice system. No sentencing guidelines, no sentencing model has ever, or will ever, be able to remedy even partially the flagrant punishment disparities. Whether the disparities are a direct outcome of structural flaws in the system, whether they are the result of attitudinal differences, systematic discrimination, or whether they are due to misguided reforms (such as Victim Impact Statements and the right of allocution), the end result is the same. Offenders who commit similar or identical crimes end up receiving enormously different punishments. The disparity in sentencing has become even greater with the introduction of what could only be described as lunatic laws such as 'three strikes and you are out' which make a travesty out of justice. In the American states, which introduced those laws, such as the State of California, a person with two felony convictions who commits an act of shoplifting could be sent to prison for life. Another found guilty of a serious crime, such as forcible rape, and who receives the average penalty for rape is sentenced to five years.

Restorative justice would put an end to the unfair and shameful practice of plea bargaining
Plea bargaining is an unfair and shameful, though popular, justice practice, more common in Anglo-Saxon systems than the justice systems of continental

Europe. In the United States, for instance, 90 per cent of all the cases in which offenders are charged end up with a plea bargain (Ranish & Shichor, 1985). The offender, or more frequently his lawyer, makes an agreement with the prosecutor (sometimes with the blessing of the judge) by which he/she accepts to plead guilty to a lesser charge in exchange for a milder sentence. For obvious reasons, victims are excluded from the negotiation process that leads to the guilty plea. They get surprised, frustrated and resentful when they discover that the charges laid by the prosecutor or the Crown attorney bear no, or little, resemblance to the actual offence committed against them. And when the mild sentence resulting from the bargain is finally pronounced, they become infuriated and feel betrayed by the criminal justice system, by society, and by society's representative, the prosecutor. This sense of betrayal is an inevitable characteristic of punitive justice systems because they promise victims more than they can deliver and create expectations that can never be fulfilled in practice.

Restorative justice encourages and enhances victim reporting

Legalistic interventions usurp the victim's decision-making powers. The current system of criminal justice gives victims no say and no choice. It snatches the conflict from its legitimate owner, the victim, and hands it to the public prosecutor. By so doing it discourages in many instances victim reporting of the offence. Victims who, for one reason or another, do not want the offender punished (either by a prison sentence or a penal fine) are naturally reluctant to go to the police with their complaints. The same is true of victims who are related, in some way or another, to their victimisers. Knowing that the arrest and subsequent punishment of the offender will sever the bond or will strain the relationship beyond repair, they simply refrain from reporting their victimisation to law enforcement bodies. Replacing punishment with a non-punitive conflict resolution mechanism would render those victims less reluctant to report. Restorative justice alternatives also promote the reporting of victimisation by members of disadvantaged social groups that dislike, distrust, or try to avoid the police. Speaking of the promise of restorative justice in the case of wife battering, Presser and Gaarder (2000, p. 186) suggest that restorative justice has the potential to increase victims' likelihood of reporting the abuse. This is because it offers an array of flexible interventions, which can be particularly appealing to women who distrust the criminal justice system such as members of social, ethnic and religious minorities.

Restorative justice minimises the chances of retaliation and the risks of repeat victimisation

This is without doubt one of the most positive aspects of restorative justice. Conflict resolution and dispute settlement are undoubtedly the most effective means to ensure that the violence will not flare up again, that the emotions that fuel the aggression are held in check. Most acts of violence are retaliatory in nature and a very high percentage is committed between people who are related to one another by some family relationship or other personal ties. Unless reconciliation is achieved, the seeds of violence will always remain. Restorative justice aims at restoring the peace and harmony disrupted by the offence, at revitalising the bonds and ties that were severed by the criminal act. And contrary to the retributive system that feeds on vindictiveness and the thirst for revenge, restorative justice promotes forgiveness, understanding and restitution. It gives the victim and the offender a chance to meet face to face, to reach a mutual understanding of one another, to put the past behind them and to come to a fair and just agreement about the future. Restorative justice makes wounds heal and is thus beneficial to the coping process, to the psychological well-being and the satisfaction of the victim.

Restorative justice is the only possible way of dealing effectively with the new blood feuds in modern society

There is a great deal of anecdotal and historical evidence showing that the most effective, perhaps the only way, to settle blood feuds in agrarian societies such as Albania, Sardinia, Sicily, Macedonia, Egypt, etc., is mediation, reconciliation and compensation. Opponents of restorative justice claim that these types of long-standing conflicts and blood feuds no longer exist in modern, industrialised, urbanised societies. They fail to recognise various types of conflict, common in urban centres that have replaced, or are the modern equivalent to, the traditional blood feuds in agrarian societies. Among those are youth gang wars, drug dealers turf struggles, blood battles between organised crime factions, settlement of accounts between members of rival groups, such as motorcycle gangs, etc. Add to this the racial, ethnic and religious conflicts like those between Catholics and Protestants in Ireland, Arabs and Jews in the Middle East, Muslims and Copts in Egypt, Supremacist groups and new immigrants, or ideological conflicts such as between the pro-life and pro-choice groups, environmental conflicts, etc. The only remedy and the most effective solution to violent acts emanating from those conflicts and similar ones are mediation and reconciliation. This is because the attitude that is basically responsible for the violence, and for the conflict in the first place, is INTOLERANCE. Punishment and penal sanctions, whether imprisonment or the death penalty, do not change this attitude. If anything, they are apt to perpetuate the conflict and to contribute to the escalation of violence. Restorative justice designates the prevention of repeat victimisation as one of the primary goals of the process of mediation and reconciliation and as a strategic priority of victim services (Fattah, 2000). It acknowledges that what victims desperately want, even before redress, is the freedom from fear and from the threat of future victimisation. This is why when victims ask for, or seek, imprisonment for the offender, it is not, as erroneously believed or as retributivists claim, to satisfy their thirst for revenge, but to seek some assurances about the threat of future victimisation, a threat that disappears when reconciliation is achieved.

Restorative justice personalises the response
Philosophers who tried to find an acceptable ethical or moral justification for punishment always insisted that for punishment to be just, it has to be personal, meaning that it is inflicted on the guilty person and no one else. But punishment can never be personal. Retributive sanctions punish not only the guilty but the innocent as well, thus contravening one of the fundamental principles of justice. Punishment can never be made personal because its effects inevitably extend to others who have done no wrong. The worst example is undoubtedly the death penalty. But the same is also true of incarceration. A prison sentence is a punishment not only for the offender, but also for the family, the friends, and for everyone who cares about or relies upon the offender. If he is an employer it penalises the employees, if he is a worker the incarceration can cause disruption in his work place, and so forth.

Restorative justice offers some remedy to victims whose offenders have not been identified, arrested, convicted and punished
The attrition in the legal process means that only a very tiny fraction of those who offend are punished. This is because a large number of offences, even serious offences, are never reported for one reason or another. Others are reported but no action is taken. Add to this that the clearance rates, particularly in property offences, are extremely low. In many cases no charges are laid and when charges are laid, a number of the cases end up in an acquittal. All this means that more than nine out of ten victims get no satisfaction and no compensation from the retributive justice system. This is not the case with restorative justice models that provide compensation as well as other help and assistance to those victims whose offender is not known or is not caught. Restorative justice should not be pigeonholed as a diversion or a mediation practice. Restorative justice is much more than just victim-offender mediation, it is about helping victims overcome the economic consequences and the traumatic effects of victimisation, regardless of whether the offender has been identified and arrested or not.

Restorative justice is the most appropriate model for cases of undisputed harm
In the vast majority of criminal cases that reach the court the harm is not disputed. This inevitably raises the question of the criminal justice system's role in cases of undisputed harm. It may be argued that when the basic facts of the case are being disputed there is a need for a neutral, impartial mechanism, an adversarial system to establish what really happened, who is at fault, and what is the extent of the harm or injury that has been caused. But when the harm is undisputed, why should the system impose its own judgement on the parties rather than let them reach their own agreement about the best and fairest way of repairing the harm? Why should the system be allowed to substitute its judgement for that of the victim? Japan is a good example to illustrate this issue because in Japan, in more than 90 per cent of cases with a known offender, there is a freely obtained confession. How can the involvement of a

formal adversarial justice system be rationalised? How can the enormous expenditures of the system be justified? To maintain that the unilateral determination of the punishment is a process of 'doing justice' simply defies logic and rationality. How can such an authoritarian, non-participatory process be preferable to restorative justice practices, be it mediation, sentencing circles, group/community conferencing, or else?

The dangers to, and of, the restorative justice paradigm

The enthusiasm with which the restorative justice paradigm is being adopted and the speed with which it is being implemented should not blind us to some of the real dangers that such a new and promising paradigm is facing. It may be useful therefore to highlight very briefly some of those dangers to, and of, the paradigm.

The danger of hasty and faulty implementation

The history of criminal justice is replete with good ideas that failed and good intentions that never achieved their potential. Unless we proceed carefully and measure our actions circumspectly, the fate of this promising paradigm may not be better than many of those that have preceded it. How many excellent ideas were introduced over the years into the justice system only to fade and die, sometimes a quick death, and other times, a slow death. A good lesson may be learnt from 'diversion'. I was one of the few sceptics when diversion was hailed in the 1960s as the key to the system's salvation. It was going to drastically reduce the courts' caseload, the prison population, and the costs of justice. It was the answer to labelling, stigmatisation, and the continuation of delinquency. Hopes were raised only to be shattered, and the great promises never materialised. Diversion never attained any of the goals that were promised or achieved any of the results that it was supposed to yield. But it remains an excellent example of the system's resistance to change, its strong reluctance to accept and accommodate new ideas, new concepts, and new models. The failure of diversion should serve as a warning, particularly to those who believe that the only hope for restorative justice is to be implemented within or through the existing system of criminal justice.

The danger of failing to secure the support and active involvement of the community

Restorative justice is community justice. It has no chance of succeeding or replacing the existing punitive system unless it is fully endorsed by the community and unless members of that community are actively involved in the resolution of conflicts and the settlement of disputes. Without strong community support and without intensive and extensive community involvement there is a real danger of replacing a State-run bureaucracy and a State-controlled system with yet another bureaucracy and another system under State control.

This is precisely what is happening in some countries, like France, where mediation is now a bureaucracy, run and controlled by State prosecutors.

The danger of widening the net

Because the danger of net-widening is ever present and too well known there is no need to dwell upon it in any great detail. Suffice to refer therefore to the early warnings offered by some of those who assessed the pioneering experiments in restorative justice, like Dittenhoffer & Ericson (1982, 1992, p. 341), who wrote:

> Interests distinct from those of correctional reformers have particularly given credence to the theme that VORP is destined to become part of the widening net of social control, similar to many previous reforms which have enhanced the discretion of various officials in different ways.

The danger of restorative justice being co-opted by the existing agencies of the formal criminal justice system

Vested interests in the present system will do everything to marginalise new ideas, which threaten their basic assumptions (Davis, 1992) or their very existence. If attempts at marginalisation happen to fail, they will try to co-opt the new programs. This should lead to increasing caution about the dangers of compromise, and to reject any strategy based on the naïve belief that the only way of implementing restorative justice is through pilot projects or small-scale experiments conducted within the system. Those who believe that this is the only hope for restorative justice should look at all those mediation programs, in many countries, that had to close down because of lack of referrals from prosecutors.

The danger that restorative justice may develop into an offender- or victim-centred justice alternative rather than having both victim and offender as its central focus

In his insightful analysis of the history of victim initiatives, Paul Rock (1990, p. 408) explained how many of those initiatives were not really meant to help victims but were designed to serve other purposes or some ulterior motives. He said:

> ...criminal injuries compensation was supposed to mollify the reactionary victim-vigilante, and reparation was a device to divert offenders from custody. In both instances, victims were the creatures of penal imperatives, invested with the characters needed to get on with the business of reforming prisons. Compensation and reparation did not have much of a foundation in the declared or observed requirements of victims themselves: they were bestowed on victims in order to achieve particular ends.

When restorative justice practices started in Canada and the United States, spearheaded by the Mennonite Church, redress to the victim prevailed over every other consideration. Although the programs initially called themselves 'victim-offender reconciliation programs' their foremost objective was to ensure restitution by the offender to the victim and to see to it that the offender fulfils the obligations agreed upon in the mediation agreement. They were sarcastically described as 'collection agencies' for the victim. That the programs deviated from their original objectives was highlighted in one of the early evaluations of the programs by Dittenhoffer & Ericson (1982). They stated that:

> This investigation has revealed the manner in which the programme actually does operate, only partially obtaining its goals and departing substantially from the picture painted by most descriptions of the programme.

As the goal of reconciliation became secondary to that of restitution, and as it proved to be an elusive goal, the programs had no choice but to change their name from 'Victim-Offender Reconciliation Programs' to 'Victim-Offender Mediation Programs'. If there is a lesson to be learnt from those early experiences of restorative justice it should be the realisation of how essential and how important it is to maintain a fair and equitable balance between the interests of the victim and the interests of the offender. Those pioneering efforts show how vital it is, for the credibility and the effectiveness of the programs, not to tilt the scale or to favour one party over the other. Those early experiments should also teach us to stick to the defined objectives and not let administrative or pragmatic considerations alter what the programs are set up to achieve.

The danger that restorative justice will become a victim of its own success

Nothing can be more dangerous than success, particularly rapid or quick success. The speed with which restorative justice programs, projects and experiments are being implemented is a constant reminder of the initial success and the instant explosion of diversion programs three decades ago. It should give us reason to pause and to reflect: how long can the interest last? How long can the enthusiasm be sustained before it begins to wane? How long can the state of euphoria be maintained? All this leads to the question: could restorative justice become a victim of its own success? The alliance being formed around, and is currently promoting, restorative justice inevitably raises suspicion about the interests and the motives of the diverse groups that seem to be united in their support of the new model. Restorative justice seems to make strange bedfellows. Both those on the left and the right of the political spectrum seem to find something they like in restorative justice. For those leaning to the left, it is seen as a more humane, less destructive alternative to destructive and debilitating punishments. It is regarded as a way of socialising, decentralising, deprofessionalising and deformalising justice. To those on the right, restorative justice is appealing because it has the potential of reducing State expenditures on the criminal justice system and is guaranteed to shift the financial burden of victim compensation from the State to the offenders. What is difficult to figure out yet are the real motives behind the wholehearted endorsement of police force like the RCMP. In their booth at the 10th International Victimology Symposium in Montreal (August, 2000) the dominant literature was surprisingly about restorative justice! Be this as it may, it remains to be seen what negative, (or positive) influence this diversity of interests, of motives, of ideologies will have on restorative justice. One cannot but fear that different groups will try to gain control of restorative justice programs, claim them as their own creations, and try to gear them in directions that fit their own interests and purposes. This calls for enhanced vigilance and more alertness as well as strong defences to resist any such take-over attempts.

Conclusion

It is often argued that punitive justice provides emotional satisfaction to the victim who has been injured or harmed by the offence. But it is not true that victims are satisfied ONLY when the offender is punished and made to suffer. This is because real justice involves much more than simply quenching the thirst for vengeance. Victims who are absorbed by their hate and obsessed by their desire for vengeance are doomed because they can never regain the peace of mind necessary for a happy existence. Victims who learn how to forgive cope better and heal quicker than other victims. Moreover, forgiveness elevates the victim to new moral heights, whereas retribution lowers the victim and the State to the same level to which the offender has sunk by his crime. It is not difficult to contrast the humanising spirit of restorative justice with the brutalising and demeaning nature of retributive justice, or to compare the healing effects of restorative justice with the agonising and antagonising outcomes of punitive justice. Restorative justice aims at healing and redress rather than violence and duress, it favours the victim's gain over the infliction of pain. Retributive justice is past-based whereas restorative action is present and future oriented. In retributive justice systems there are no winners, only losers. The primary losers are the two major protagonists: the offender gets the punishment and the victim gets nothing. But they are by no means the only ones because in punitive systems there are many other losers as well. And the ultimate loser is society itself.

References

Canada, *Sentencing Commission Report* (Canadian Government Publishing Centre, Ottawa, 1988)

N. Christie, *Limits to Pain* (Martin Robertson & Co. Ltd., Oxford, 1982)

T.R. Clear, *Harm in American Penology: Offenders, Victims and Their Communities* (State University of New York Press, Albany, 1994)

Council of Europe, *Mediation in Penal Matters: Recommendation no. R (99) and Explanatory Memorandum* (Council of Europe, Strasbourg, 2000)

G. Davis, *Making Amends: Mediation and Reparation in Criminal Justice* (Routledge, London, 1992)

T. Dittenhoffer & R. Ericson, 'The Victim/Offender Reconciliation Programme: A Message to the Correctional Reformers' *University of Toronto Law Journal* (Vol. 33, 1983), pp. 315-347, also in E.A. Fattah ed., *Towards a Critical Victimology* (Macmillan, London, St. Martin's Press, New York, 1992), pp. 311-346

E.A. Fattah, 'Making the Punishment Fit the Crime: Problems Inherent in the Use of Imprisonment as a Retributive Sanction' *Canadian Journal of Criminology* (Vol. 24, no. 1, 1982), pp. 1-12

E.A. Fattah, *On Victims, Parole, and the Sentencing Commission* (Brief submitted to the House of Commons standing Committee on Justice and Solicitor General, March, 1988, 33 pages)

E.A. Fattah, 'Beyond Metaphysics: the Need for a New Paradigm: On Actual and Potential Contributions of Criminology and the Social Sciences to the Reform of the Criminal Law' in R. Lahti & K. Nuotio ed., *Criminal Law Theory in Transition: Finnish and Comparative Perspectives* (Finnish Lawyers Publishing Company, Helsinki, 1992), pp. 64-101

E.A. Fattah, 'From a Guilt Orientation to a Consequence Orientation: A Proposed New Paradigm for the Criminal Law in the 21st Century' in W. Küper & J. Welp ed., *Beiträge zur Rechtswissenschaft* (C.F. Müller Juristischer Verlag, Heidelberg, 1993), pp. 771-792

E.A. Fattah, 'Restorative and Retributive Justice Models: A Comparison' in H.H. Kühne ed. *Festschrift für Koichi Miyazawa* (Nomos Verlagsgesellschaft, Baden-Baden, 1995), also in E.A. Fattah & T. Peters ed. *Support for Crime Victims in a Comparative Perspective* (Leuven University Press, Leuven, 1998)

E.A. Fattah, *Criminology: Past, Present and Future* (Macmillan, London, St. Martin's Press, New York, 1997)

E.A. Fattah, 'Some Reflections on the Paradigm of Restorative Justice and its Viability for Juvenile Justice' in L. Walgrave ed., *Restorative Justice for Juveniles: Potentialities, Risks and Problems for Research* (Leuven University Press, Leuven, 1998)

E.A. Fattah, *Mediation in Penal Matters* (Report for Correctional Services Canada, 44 pages, 1999)

E.A. Fattah, 'Victim Redress and Victim-Offender Reconciliation in Theory and Practice – Some Personal Reflections' *Hokkaigakuen Law Journal* (Vol. XXXV, No. 1, July 1999), pp. 155-182.

E.A. Fattah, 'How Valid are the Arguments Frequently Made Against Mediation and Restorative Justice?' in H. Giertsen ed. *Albanian and Norwegian Experiences with Mediation in Conflicts* (Institute of Criminology, Oslo, 2000), pp. 25-36

E.A. Fattah, *Preventing Repeat Victimization as the Ultimate Goal of Victim Services* (Keynote address – Conference on Services for Victims of Crime, Melbourne, Sept. 7-9, 2000)

E.A. Fattah, 'Does Victimology Need Deontology? Ethical Conundrums in a Young Discipline' *Proceedings of the Xth International Symposium on Victimology* (2001)

K.M. Harris, 'Moving Into the New Millennium: Toward a Feminist Vision of Justice' in H.E. Pepinsky & R. Quinney ed., *Criminology as Peacemaking* (Indiana University Press, Bloomington, 1991)

A. von Hirsch, *Doing Justice: The Choice of Punishment* (Report of the Committee for the Study of Incarceration, Hill and Wang, New York, 1976)

G. Newman, *Just and Painful: A Case for Corporal Punishment of Criminals* (Second edition, Harrow and Heston, New York, 1995)

L. Presser & E. Gaarder, 'Can Restorative Justice Reduce Battering: Some Preliminary Considerations' *Social Justice* (Vol. 27, no. 1, 2000), pp. 175-195

D. Ranish & D. Schichor, 'The Victim's Role in the Penal Process' *Federal Probation* (Vol. 49, no. 1, 1985), pp. 50-57, also in E.A. Fattah ed., *Towards a Critical Victimology* (Macmillan, London, St. Martin's Press, New York, 1992)

J. Rawls, *A Theory of Justice* (Belknap Press, Cambridge, Mass., 1971)

P. Raynor, 'Some Observations on Rehabilitation and Justice' *The Howard Journal* (Vol. 36, no. 3, 1997), pp. 248-262

K. Roach, *Due process and Victims Rights: The New Law and Politics of Criminal Justice* (University of Toronto Press, Toronto, 1999)

P. Rock, *Helping Crime Victims: The Home Office and the Rise of Victim Support in England and Wales* (Clarendon Press, Oxford, 1990)

G.M. Sykes, 'The Pains of Imprisonment' in L. Radzinowicz & M.E. Wolfgang ed., *Crime and Justice, Vol. III, The Criminal in Confinement* (Basic Books, New York, 1971)

B. Wooton, *Crime and the Criminal Law: Reflections of a Magistrate and Social Scientist* (Stevens and Sons, London, 1963)

3. Compensation for Victims of Crime

Ian Freckelton*

Introduction

The payment of financial compensation for the non-pecuniary effects of crime, such as the pain and suffering engendered by criminal acts of violence, is a phenomenon of comparatively recent experience. It accompanied the dawning of awareness of the impact of criminal offences of violence upon victims during the 1960s and into the 1970s.

However, what was at first regarded as a breakthrough in community empathy toward victims and the taking of responsibility by governments for the adverse consequences of failed crime prevention was followed in a number of countries by a backlash against the expenditure involved in state funding of criminal injuries compensation schemes. A new era of victim-blaming can be discerned with government-paid lawyers employed to question whether victims contributed to their own victimisation, whether victims' injuries are exaggerated or attributable to causes other than criminal activity, and whether applicants for compensation are deserving recipients of community *largesse* through state-funded schemes. The alternative of criminal injuries compensation schemes in which the principal source for victim assistance is the offender has become swept up in the law and order movement and the movement toward restorative justice.

This chapter focuses upon the Australian experience of criminal injuries compensation, contextualising it within the international experience and highlighting its evolution. The various Australian schemes are selected because of the extent to which they have proved controversial within contemporary western society and because they provide such a stark example of changing governmental attitudes toward the needs of victims. The chapter concludes with reflections about the likely international trends in provision of pecuniary and non-pecuniary assistance to victims of crime.

Statutory compensation schemes for victims in historical perspective

The movement to have the state fund programmes designed to compensate crimes of violence has its roots in the modern era in the rise of consciousness about the long under-recognised plight of victims of violent crime. However, the notion that the lot of the victim of violent crime was remediable or could

* Melbourne University, Monash University, La Trobe University, Melbourne, Australia.

usefully be ameliorated by the provision of pecuniary compensation was relatively novel as recently as the 1950s and 1960s (Miers, 1978; Freckelton, 2001).

It was Margery Fry in England who proved the catalyst for the creation of modern state schemes for compensating victims. She publicly championed the notion that the state owes an obligation to those of its citizens injured through no fault of their own by criminal acts. During the 1950s she argued (Fry, 1950, 1959) from her perspective as a magistrate and social reformer that this was an incident of the government's responsibilities to its constituency. By 1959 there was some institutional recognition of her campaign. A government White Paper, entitled *Penal Practice in a Changing Society*, noted that a defect in changes to criminological theory had resulted in an unsatisfactory anomaly: 'in the public mind the interests of the offender may not infrequently be seen to be placed before those of his victim' (United Kingdom, 1959).

In 1963 in an article in *The Observer* Ms Fry argued in favour of a state-run compensation programme for victims of violent crime, drawing attention to the inadequacies of civil actions for damages. In particular, abandoning the notion which she had earlier embraced on victims being recompensed by offenders (1959), she lamented a 1951 court award of damages of £11,500 to be paid to a man blinded by an assault. Because of the impecuniosity of the defendant, the damages award was ordered to be paid at a rate of 5 shillings per week, a rate which would require 442 years for its total recovery. Ms Fry argued that 'the state which forbids our going armed in self-defence cannot disown all responsibility for its occasional failure to protect.' (1959, p. 207). Her stance was summed up in the final paragraph of her last book:

> We are looking towards a ... system which shall renounce the ideas of weighing wickedness and turn instead to estimating danger, which shall at once acknowledge our ignorance and employ our knowledge to the full; strong enough for gentleness, and wise enough for tolerance.

In 1960 Stephen Schafer of Northeastern University (United States) summarised the functioning of compensation internationally. He published a report commissioned by the English Home Office on restitution and compensation schemes (for a summary see Schafer, 1970). Schafer undertook a comparative survey of 28 countries, in none of which the victim received indemnification from the state for injuries sustained, although he found that in Germany and Finland the state would indemnify the victim if his or her injury were brought about by certain state officials. In short, therefore, there were few available models upon which to draw in 1964 when New Zealand and the United Kingdom implemented schemes of state-funded compensation.

On 1 January 1964 the Criminal Injuries Compensation Act 1963 (NZ) established the Criminal Injuries Compensation Tribunal, allowing New Zealand residents to apply for compensation for criminally-occasioned injuries. It was heralded by the Minister for Justice as an enactment that would 'enhance the reputation of New Zealand for pioneering humanitarian reforms' (New Zealand, *Parliamentary Debates*, 1963, p. 1865; see too Miller, 1996; Cameron, 1963).

The British compensation schemes

Eight months later, by written parliamentary answer, Great Britain established a victims' compensation programme administered by the Criminal Injuries Compensation Board (House of Commons Debates, Hansard, vol. 697, cols 89-94, 24 June 1964). This followed private members' bills that had been introduced in 1959 and 1960 and a 1959 White Paper which had expressed the view that 'the obligation to the victim rests primarily on the society which has failed to protect him against crime and can alone effectively compensate him' (United Kingdom, 1959, para 26.). Under the scheme, compensation was paid from public funds at the level of tortuous damages (see Duff, 1991; Williams, 1972). Duff described the aetiology of the scheme thus:

> ... the existence of public sympathy for victims of violence and, perhaps more important, a well managed campaign documenting this concern, which persuaded the government and Parliament to create the Scheme. Public sympathy was, and still is, the only reason accepted by the state for singling out victims of violence from other victims of misfortune for such preferential treatment (Duff, 1991, p.2).

The Scheme acted in conjunction with the powers of the courts to order an offender to pay compensation either instead of, or in addition to, dealing with an offender by a standard sentencing disposition.

When the Scheme was first announced in the Queen's Speech in November 1963, the Lord Chancellor said that he was hopeful of bringing it into operation without the need for legislation, the advantages of such a process being identified as a combination of flexibility and the Scheme's amenability to administrative adjustment in light of experience. However, from the outset there was considerable malcontent with the informal status of the Scheme. Repeatedly, calls were heard within the bureaucracy and from outside for the Scheme to be placed on a statutory status to place victims' entitlements on a clearer footing. Following a review by an Interdepartmental Working Party in 1978, a revised Scheme was introduced in 1979, the main change of which was to extend the Scheme experimentally to victims of violence within the family. In announcing the changes, the British government ambivalently accepted that the Scheme should be made statutory, that it should continue to be based on tortuous measures of damages and that the Government should consider applying to the Scheme any changes in tort damages which might result from the Royal Commission's other recommendations. It indicated, though, that it proposed to introduce relevant legislation only when there was sufficient experience of the revised Scheme to enable any problems in it to be identified and addressed.

In 1983 a range of important amendments were made to the Scheme, primarily to control costs and allegedly in an attempt to introduce consistency of awards for particular kinds of injuries (Williams, 1986). In due course, these would provide the inspiration for the South Australian scheme. Guideline figures were promulgated for specific injuries. Included amongst these were £2,500 for rape; £12,000 for loss of vision in one eye; and £32,000 for total loss of hearing. Again, the changes were controversial, with argument about the fairness of the amounts of money arbitrarily assigned to particular designations of injury.

After 24 years of a non-statutory arrangement, the Criminal Justice Act 1988 (UK) finally put the Scheme on a statutory basis, receiving Royal Assent in the same year. After much toing and froing, the legislation ultimately only came into effect on 1 February 1990. The Scheme did not alter the basic principles on which criminal injuries compensation had been payable since 1964, namely for personal injury or death directly attributable to a 'crime of violence' or to a variety of attempts to enforce the law or prevent crime. The Scheme retained an aspect of the earlier *ex gratia* element of the making of awards in that victims did not have the right to sue the Crown or the Board for a failure to award compensation but 'eligible victims' for the first time did have statutory rights to compensation within the terms of the legislation. (For early United States schemes, see Meiners, 1978.)

The next phase of British reform to the statutory scheme was the introduction in 1994 of a tariff scheme for 186 named injuries valued at between £1,000 and £250,000. It prompted acrimonious debate in both the House of Lords and the House of Commons, Lord Ackner for instance proclaiming that the Government's contention that the system would provide a better service to victims was characterised principally by hypocrisy: 'This is a cost-cutting exercise.'(House of Lords Debates, Hansard, vol. 554, col 1072) The Labour Leader, John Smith described the exercise as 'humbug' (*The Guardian*, 5 March 1994); the Liberal Democrats spokesman said that the Scheme represented a 'grave injustice' (*The Times*, 29 March 1994); and the Parliamentary representative of the Police Federation described the Scheme as a 'betrayal of victims' (*The Times*, 29 March 1994). It was clear though that it was going to save a great deal of money.

Unfortunately for the Government, the Scheme was found to be unlawful by a 3:2 decision of the House of Lords (*R v Secretary for the Home Department; ex parte Fire Brigades Union, 1975*) on the basis that the Home Secretary had improperly precluded himself from exercising the statutory power for the purposes and on the basis which Parliament intended. The Government responded by hurriedly introducing the Criminal Injuries Compensation Bill 1995 (UK) which reconstituted the Scheme in a revised and more complicated version, this time incorporating no fewer than 310 descriptions of injury! The Minister of State proclaimed that:

> Its aim is to provide statutory backing for the payment of compensation to blameless victims of violent crime. The Bill will provide the framework for an enhanced tariff scheme. That new scheme will concentrate on a simple tariff approach for the majority of victims, while ensuring that generous compensation is paid to those most seriously affected by their injuries. In this way we believe that the enhanced tariff scheme provides the right balance between the needs of victims while

> protecting the interests of taxpayers (House of Lords Debates, Hansard, vol. 566, col 292, 19 July 1995).

Victims and their entitlements have become a seriously politicised issue in Britain, as in many other countries, and the debate in the House of Lords was emotional and vitriolic (see Freckelton, 2001). The Scheme is predicated on the notional creation of 25 levels for awards for pain and suffering, level 25 representing the maximum amount payable for any single injury, awards also being able to be made for loss of earnings and loss of earning capacity and for special expenses. It remains highly controversial, a number of commentators arguing that it presents an incoherent picture. Compensation is now generally limited to the standard payment constituted by the tariff whereas under the previous scheme the focus was upon the impact that the crime had had on the particular victim, an impact that can vary dramatically from one person to another:

> the decision to adopt a restitutionary model [under the previous scheme] may not have been particularly logical but it did provide a clear framework around which the material and symbolic functions of compensation could operate. ... [W]hile the original Scheme suffered from shaky theoretical foundations, the familiar yardstick of common law damages helped to reduce the confusion over the level of compensation resulting from the Scheme's lack of a clear rationale. ... [However] the abandonment of the common law model and the adoption of a tariff, will bring further confusion to the Scheme (Duff, 1998, p. 140).

The most significant difficulty is that the concept of restitution with its victim-centred orientation no longer generates the ideology underlying the Scheme but no other clear ideology has replaced it, simply arbitrary numerical designations of compensation. In addition, the bureaucracy of the scheme means that for the most part decisions are made behind the scenes of the criminal justice system by 'claims officers' and 'assessors', rather than in any form of open hearing.

The New Zealand experience

The specially created rights of victims of crime in New Zealand were subsumed under the general entitlements of victims under the Accident Compensation Act 1972 (NZ). The result of this was that victims of crime ceased to be entitled to pain and suffering compensation *per se*, instead being eligible for earnings-related compensation, lump sums and counselling. The Criminal Justice Act 1985 (NZ) addressed this to some degree by enabling reparation orders to be issued against offenders so as to compel them to compensate victims for emotional harm and property loss and damage. However, this is rarely helpful because of the impecuniosity of most offenders. Further changes in 1992 resulted in persons with pure psychiatric injuries, other than rape victims, not being covered. Calls continued for the reintroduction of a criminal injuries compensation scheme in New Zealand (see Tobin, 1994; Mackenzie, 1993). By 1999 the Labour Party incorporated in its election platform a partial reintroduction of criminal injuries compensation payments up to a ceiling of $NZ10,000.

In August 2000, though, Cabinet vetoed the return to pecuniary payments, so law reform in New Zealand remains on hold.

The United States experience

Attempts at securing statutory entitlements to criminal injuries compensation in the United States commenced in the 1960s. They were particularly championed by Arthur Goldberg (1964), a justice of the United States Supreme Court. He argued that the lot of the victim had been under-recognised, excessive concentration having been devoted to the rehabilitation of offenders:

> Whenever the government considers extending a needed service to those accused of crime, the question arises: But what about the victim? We should confront the problem of the victim directly; his burden is not alleviated by denying necessary services to the accused. Many countries throughout the world, recognising that crime is a community problem, have designed systems for government compensation of victims of crime. Serious consideration of this approach is long overdue here.

The first state to implement a victims compensation program was California in 1966, followed by New York and Maryland. The models for the programs varied considerably, New York, for instance, setting up an independent administrative board while the Massachusetts scheme was administered through the courts (see Edlhertz and Geis, 1974). In due course all 50 states of the United States, plus the District of Columbia, the Virgin Island and Guam set up victims compensation programs providing financial assistance to victims of violent crime. Overwhelmingly, they do not compensate for pain and suffering suffered by victims but provide assistance for crime-related expenses such as lost wages and medical, counselling and funeral costs.

An important initiative commenced in March 1973 when the United States Senate passed the Victims of Crime Bill 1973 (US) whose aim was to establish a program for compensating victims of crime in territorial areas of direct federal concern (Lamborn, 1972). The purpose of the Bill was to create a Violent Crimes Compensation Board, composed of 3 members to be appointed by the President. The Bill provided for dependants of the victim of criminal homicide to be eligible for compensation but pain, suffering and property damage were not compensable. Nor were personal injuries suffered by virtue of the operation of motor vehicles compensable unless the injuries were intentionally inflicted. Its principal focus was upon compensation for loss of earnings and loss of support for dependants. It contained a ceiling of $US50,000. However, the legislation had a chronically foundering progress through the legislature (Lamborn, 1979; a Committee of the NSW Parliament, 1997) not becoming law until the passage of what became the Victims of Crime Act 1984 (US). This created a fund administered by the Office of Victims of Crime within the United States Department of Justice. Its primary function is supplementation of state compensation programs for crime victims. Its revenue arises from funds deposited from fines, forfeited bail bonds and special assessments collected by the United States Attorney's Office, Courts and the Bureau of Prisons.

By dramatic contrast with the British scheme, the average amount paid to victims of violent crime is $2,000, in the order of $200 million being paid to about 100,000 victims per year. The eligibility for criminal injuries compensation payments varies amongst states but the maximum amounts payable generally vary between $10,000 and $25,000. In all states 'primary victims' are eligible for payments and in an increasing number 'secondary victims' are also eligible. In few jurisdictions are amounts payable for pain and suffering experienced by victims at the hands of impecunious assailants.

The Canadian experience

Compensation for criminally caused injuries is a state matter in Canada. A number of different models for compensation exist and are controversial. In British Columbia a full compensation scheme exists for victims of violent crime under the provisions of the Criminal Injury Compensation Act 1996 (BC). Compensation can be awarded by the Workers' Compensation Board for (a) expenses actually and reasonably incurred or to be incurred as a direct result of the victim's injury or death; (b) pecuniary loss or damage incurred by the victim as a result of total or partial disability affecting the victim's capacity for work; (c) pecuniary loss or damage incurred by immediate family members as a result of the victim's death; (d) maintenance or a child born as a result of rape; (e) other pecuniary loss or damage resulting from the victim's injury and any expense that it is reasonable to incur; (f) non-pecuniary loss or damage for pain, suffering, mental or emotional trauma, humiliation or inconvenience.

Compensation is payable from the consolidated revenue and can be paid in a lump sum or in periodic payments as the Board deems appropriate. In determining whether to make an award and in determining the amount of such an award, the Board is specifically directed to have regard to 'all relevant circumstances, including any behaviour of the victim that may have, directly or indirectly, contributed to his or her injury or death'. An award must be made within a year of the date of injury or death, unless the Board extends the time frame. The amount awarded by the Board for injury or death of a victim cannot exceed $C50,000.

By contrast, under the Ontario Compensation for Victims of Crime Act 1990 (Ont), compensation is awardable by the Criminal Injuries Compensation Board where a person is injured or killed by any act or omission in Ontario resulting from the commission of a crime of violence, but not including the use of a motor vehicle other than assault by means of a motor vehicle, from lawfully arresting or attempting to arrest an offender or suspected offender for an offence against the person or from preventing or attempting to prevent the commission of a crime or suspected crime against the person (see too Victims of Crime Act [Alberta]). Compensation may be awarded for:

- expenses actually and reasonably incurred as a result of total or partial disability affecting the victim's capacity for work;
- pecuniary loss incurred by the victim as a result of total or partial disability affecting the victim's capacity for work;
- pecuniary loss incurred by dependants as a result of a victim's death;

- pain and suffering;
- support of a child born as a result of rape;
- other pecuniary loss resulting from the victim's injury and any expense that, in the opinion of the Board, it is reasonable to incur.

Application must be made within one year of the date of the injury or death although the Board within the 12 months can extend the time for such further time as it deems appropriate. 'Injury' is defined to include actual bodily harm and includes pregnancy and mental or nervous shock. Decisions about eligibility are made by the Board. Orders for compensation can be made whether or not a person is prosecuted for or convicted of the offence giving rise to the injury or death. In deciding whether to make an order for compensation and the amount of the award, the Board is obliged to have regard to all relevant circumstances, including any behaviour of the victim that may have directly or indirectly contributed to his or her injury or death. The Board has a discretion to refuse to make an order for compensation or order a reduced amount of compensation where it is satisfied that the applicant has refused reasonable co-operation with, or failed to report promptly the offence to, a law enforcement agency. The amounts awarded by the Board to be paid in respect of the injury or death of one victim cannot exceed $C25,000 in the case of lump sum payments; and $C1,000 in the case of periodic payments. The total amount awarded by the Board to all applicants in respect of any one occurrence cannot exceed $C150,000 in the case of lump sum payments; and cannot exceed $C250,000 in the case of periodic payments.

European crimes compensation schemes

This section of the chapter reviews a number of the schemes applying in Europe; it does not purport to be exhaustive. One of the international trends discernible in relation to compensation of victims is the encouragement of schemes in which victims can obtain court orders that they be recompensed from the pockets of the person who has caused their pain and suffering. A model for such compensation is the *voeging als benadeelde partij*, the joining procedure, in The Netherlands (see Maguire & Shapland, 1997). If the accused is found guilty of criminal conduct, and when it has been proved that the criminal conduct caused damage to a victim, the sentencing court can order the offender to pay for the losses. However, there is a qualification, as in Australia, Canada and England – the case must be reasonably straightforward. As of 1995 the 'Terwee Act' introduced provision for a compensation order (*schadevergoedingsmaatregel*) whose aim it is to restore the legal situation that existed prior to the commission of the crime (Malsch & Carrière, 1999). The party eligible to seek the compensation order is the public prosecutor. The order can be made when the court has determined the accused person guilty of a crime and when the offender is liable to pay damages to the victim under the civil law of The Netherlands. Under the order of the court, the offender is obliged to pay compensation to the State which, in turn, refunds the money directly to the victim.

However, a problem experienced under the Terwee Act, with the orders that function as an adjunct to the imposition of dispositions at sentencing, is that they are only as effectual as the offender is moneyed. If the offender is without assets, or at least without substantial assets, even should he or she be prepared to cooperate in an order, reparation from the wallet or purse of the offender cannot be made. Herein lies the deficit in individual accountability as promulgated as a solution to the state's exposure. Forty years later, it is the same flaw that led Margery Fry to campaign for the state to step into the shoes of the offender, not out of sympathy or generosity toward the criminal, but out of a recognition that if the state did not do so, the victim would be disadvantaged. Otherwise only the small proportion of victims 'fortunate' enough to be raped, beaten or otherwise brutalised by a propertied offender would have access to rights.

The French system encompasses both state compensation in limited measure and facilitation of civil actions against those found guilty of criminal violence. Article 706-3 of the *Code de Procedure Penale* allows compensation to be awarded from the state by a commission similar to a criminal injuries compensation tribunal. However, it applies only to crimes causing personal injury of a kind which subsists for at least more than one month (Bell, Boyron & Whittaker, 1998). This facility co-exists with the ability of a victim to involve themselves in the criminal process by institution of an *action civile*. This allows the award of damages directly against the assailant for harmful consequences directly caused to the victim. The procedure is viewed as both compensatory and punitive. It results in many delictual claims being brought as an adjunct to the criminal process (Bell, Boyron & Whittaker, 1998; Dadomo & Farran, 1996, p. 201).

In Sweden it is common for the prosecutor also to claim pecuniary compensation on behalf of the victim. However, if the compensation issue is complicated, the court can separate the actions, leaving the victim to institute a civil action after the completion of the criminal proceedings. This happens sometimes, but not often. Regardless of how the compensation issue is handled, the problem for the victim is that the convicted person frequently has little by way of money or other assets. For this reason a special board has been constituted, called the *Brottsskadenämnden*. On application, it pays the victim a certain amount of money, the amount depending on the extent of the damage or loss suffered by the victim. However, the compensation is and has always by tradition been small. If the civil case is separated from the criminal, compensation cannot be claimed from the *Brottsskadenämnden*. Instead the normal procedure in civil cases applies. Thus, if the defendant lacks money, the victim must go to the Execution Office and hand over the judgement with the obligation to pay compensation. Then at a later date there will be an attempt to enforce the order with an execution officer functioning as a sheriff and selling available assets of the defendant to meet the judgement debt. Often they will not find anything of value, having had to resort to assets such as the home insurance. In practice this often means that the insurance company will institute the action against the defendant in civil cases and sometimes also enter into criminal cases.

By order of German law, all citizens have health insurance which pays for health costs when people are injured by criminal actions or omissions. The key access to compensation for victims of violence is via the Federal War Victims Maintenance Act, the *Bundesversorgungsgesetz*. Victims of violent acts are entitled to the same compensation as are victims of war. This has been provided for by the Victim Compensation Act which provides financial awards to victims of violent crimes who have suffered physical and financial hardships. Monthly pensions are payable for medical treatment and vocational rehabilitation. There are eligibility requirements. A report must be made to the police within a year, although exceptions are made where the interests of justice so demand. Victims of crime and dependants of homicide victims can make claims. There is no maximum award limit. Compensable costs include medical expenses, psychological care, vocational rehabilitation, pensions for disabled victims if their earning capacity is reduced by at least 25 per cent for six months or more, benefits for dependants of homicide victims, physical therapy, funeral expenses, lost support for dependants and services to replace work in the home previously performed by the victim. Compensation is not payable for pain and suffering *per se* arising from a violent assault. Moreover, compensation is not payable if there are public policy reasons to the contrary, for instance, because of the victim's conduct or if the person has failed to assist in the police investigation.

Provision also exists for sentencing judges to order offenders to compensate their victims. Article 153a of the German Code of Criminal Procedure permits the prosecutor to dismiss the case against an offender on the condition that the offender pay restitution to the victim. The Victim Protection Law 1986 (Germany) obligates sentencers to consider the attempt made by the offender to compensate the victim in assessing the severity of the disposition that should be imposed.

International instruments

In 1983 the member states of the Council of Europe became signatory to the European Convention on the Compensation of Victims of Violent Crimes. Article Two of the Convention prescribes that when compensation is not 'fully available' from other sources, the State shall contribute to compensate those who have sustained serious bodily injury or impairment of health directly attributable to an intentional crime of violence and the dependants of persons who have died as a result of such crime. Compensation is obliged to be paid in such cases even if the offender cannot be prosecuted or punished. Under Article Four the compensation must cover at least 'loss of earnings, medical and hospitalisation expenses and funeral expenses, and, as regards dependants, loss of maintenance'. Article Five provides that compensation schemes may, if necessary, set for any or all elements of compensation an upper limit above which and a minimum threshold below which compensation shall not be granted. It can be reduced or refused on account of the applicant's financial situation. Under Article Eight, compensation can be reduced or refused:

- on account of the victim's or the applicant's conduct before, during or after the crime, or in relation to the injury or death;
- on account of the victim's or the applicant's involvement in organised crime or his membership of an organisation which engages in crimes of violence; and
- if an award or a full award would be contrary to a sense of justice or to public policy.

Article Ten provides that the State may be subrogated to the rights of the person compensated for the amount of compensation paid.

Article Twelve of the United Nations Declaration of Basic Principles of Justice for Victims of Crime and Abuse of Power provides that:

> When compensation is not fully available from the offender or other sources, States should endeavour to provide financial compensation to:
> 1. Victims who have sustained significant bodily injury or impairment of physical or mental health as a result of serious crimes;
> 2. The family, in particular dependants of persons who have died or become physically or mentally incapacitated as a result of such victimisation.

Article Thirteen states that the establishment, strengthening and expansion of national funds for compensation to victims 'should be encouraged', while Article Fourteen provides that 'Victims should receive the necessary material, medical, psychological and social assistance through governmental, voluntary, community-based and indigenous means'.

Article 75 of the International Court of Justice legislation prescribes that:

> 1. The Court shall establish principles relating to reparations to, or in respect of, victims, including restitution, compensation and rehabilitation. On this basis, in its decision the Court may, either upon request or on its own motion in exceptional circumstances, determine the scope and extent of any damage, loss and injury to, or in respect of, victims and will state the principles on which it is acting.
> 2. The Court may make an order directly against a convicted person specifying appropriate reparations to, or in respect of, victims, including restitution, compensation and rehabilitation. Where appropriate, the Court may order that the award for reparations be made through the Trust Fund provided for in article 79.
> 3. Before making an order under this article, the Court may invite and shall take account of representations from or on behalf of the convicted person, victims, other interested persons or interested States.

Under Article 79 a trust fund is established by decision of the Assembly of States Parties for the benefit of victims of crimes within the jurisdiction of the Court, and of the families of such victims. The Court can order money and other property collected through fines or forfeiture to be transferred, by order of the Court, to the Trust Fund. The Trust Fund is managed according to those criteria determined by the Assembly of States Parties.

The Australian schemes

In a number of Australian jurisdictions, prior to the implementation of statutory schemes of compensation, provision had long existed for a sentencing court to order a sum to be paid from the offender's property as 'compensation' to the victim. However, the provisions related to property loss and damage and were scarcely ever used (Chappell, 1970; Freckelton, 2001).

Different phases in the provision of pecuniary compensation to victims of violent crime can be discerned in Australia:

Phase One: the pre-legislative phase where courts had power to order offenders to pay compensation or restitution to their victims. In addition, individual victims could apply for *ex gratia* compensation from the state but specific schemes of compensation had not yet been established;

Phase Two: the early legislative phase in which courts were given power to make a determination at or around the time of sentence that a victim should be compensated by the offender or by the State, up to a certain amount, the Treasury generally determining the quantum;

Phase Three: the next legislative phase starting in 1972 in Victoria and extending into the late 1970s and early 1980s in which specialist machinery was set up, assessors and tribunals, for the most part, having responsibility for quantifying the compensation that should be awarded and the circumstances in which applicants were entitled to awards;

Phase Four: the increasingly legalistic and expensive phase, commencing in the early 1990s when schemes started to attract high numbers of applicants and to cost substantial sums of money for the public purse. Appellate proceedings generated significant amounts of case law and technical difficulties; delays in awards began to increase;

Phase Five: the backlash of governments against the costs and technicalities, in which New South Wales and Queensland introduced complex Tables of Maims and Victoria and then the Australian Capital Territory radically cut back their schemes' liability. The phase was characterised too by an increasing focus upon orders directly against offenders and the sophistication of machinery for the State to recoup compensation payouts from offenders;

Phase Six: a *further re-evaluation period*, characterised first by the partial re-introduction in Victoria of a state scheme of financial compensation for pain and suffering as a result of acts of criminal violence, hand in hand with provision for court orders against offenders; toughening of eligibility criteria in South Australia; and attempts in the ACT to liberalise entitlements to pain and suffering compensation.

1. *The pre-legislative phase*

In the pre-legislative, pre-victim consciousness era, namely prior to 1967, there was little by way of a perception on the part of the community, or of the courts, that curial or other processes should be used to redress the harm done by criminal behaviour inflicted upon victims. This was an era that preceded significant community acknowledgement of the direct and indirect effects of criminal violence. Victim blaming and stereotyping were prevalent – to the particular detriment of women and children – but mostly victims were outside community consciousness (Jenkins-Hall & Merlatt, 1989). In Australia especially they were expected to get over it and get on with it. As Miers (1978) put it: 'Overall, the victim was portrayed as a social and economic pariah whose needs were neglected by a society which excused criminal behaviour and comforted the offender.' There was little understanding of psychiatric injuries such as those that ensued subsequent to traumatic incidents and even less sympathy.

Victims had little say in the criminal justice system, save as witnesses, and civil actions were virtually never initiated by victims against offenders. For offenders' accountability for their actions, victims had only the criminal courts to look to and for the most part courts' sensitivities to the psychological injuries suffered by victims were very limited. Understanding of the *sequelae* of crime was largely confined to property and somatic damage.

Under a series of long-existing legislative provisions, most jurisdictions in Australia did have provision for courts to order that offenders pay compensation to victims (Lanham, 1986; Crimes Act 1914(Cth), s21B; Crimes Act 1900 (NSW), s437; Criminal Law Consolidation Act 1935 (SA), s299; Crimes Act 1958 (Vic), s83); Penalties and Sentences Act 1985 (Vic), s92; Criminal Code (Qld), s685A; Criminal Code (WA), s719(1); Criminal Code (Tas), s425A; Criminal Code (NT), s393). However, applications for such compensation were seldom made and less often granted. Mr Sheahan, the Member for Burrinjuck in New South Wales, in the debates on the first of Australia's criminal injuries compensation schemes drew the attention of Parliament to the fact that, although s437 of the Crimes Act 1900 (NSW) had been amended to double the amount of compensation that could be ordered from the offender from $A1,000 to $A2,000, this still did not encourage judges to utilise it. In fact, he said:

> In all my long association with the criminal law I remember only one judge making a direction under that section, and [that was] many years ago. I do not know why the judges are reluctant to use this section. It may be that they have always held the view that it was wasting judicial and administrative time to make an order of this nature. It is most extraordinary that only one such case has occurred in many years (NSW Legislative Assembly, Hansard, 8 March 1967, p. 3214).

In short, the pre-legislative phase enabled sentencers to order an offender to pay to the victim a modest amount of compensation. However, the facility was little availed of, partly because of limited focus upon the entitling provisions, even where the offender had assets, but no doubt primarily because of the inability of most offenders to pay. In this phase, victims were left to rely upon their resources individually to lobby the Attorney-General of the government of the day for an *ex gratia* payment to ease their situation. Few such applications were made and fewer found favour with the controllers of the public purse. Much depended on the notoriety of the case and the political advantage that was perceived by the Attorney-General to be likely to flow from individual and occasional public manifestations of largesse.

2. *The early legislative phase*

In the late 1960s and early 1970s in Australia, consciousness of the effects of crime upon victims came into being. Encouraged by the efforts of Margery Fry and other reformers, the victims movement commenced. Deeper into the 1970s, feminism shone a light upon the particular effects of criminal violence upon women and also upon children (Egger, 1997). Awareness of the incidence of sexual assault and of domestic violence started to filter into public consciousness.

At first, though, the victims movement was fuelled by middle-class neo-conservatives, dominated by representatives of church groups and characterised by value judgements and expectations about 'deserving' and 'real' victims. To fit into the category which should receive compensation, victims had to conform to traditional stereotypes. Their victim status came under a cloud as soon as they departed from the image of the morally blameless 'solid citizen'. This was particularly problematic for the substance dependant, the unemployed, the homeless, those living 'alternative' lifestyles, those with criminal records, the mentally ill, the intellectually disabled, those sexually active outside marriage and so on. Nonetheless, the popular media began to acknowledge the broader effects of criminal violence and public awareness of the disenfranchised status of the victim emerged. With media involvement political interest began to flower.

Under the first phase of legislative intervention, more formalised arrangements for compensation were initiated, permitting the ordering of compensation by courts. Boards and tribunals were eschewed and the already existing court model was built upon. Where no criminal trial took place, the victim remained able to throw him or herself on the mercy of the government of the day and to apply directly for an *ex gratia* award. Still, though, governments were far from receptive to such overtures.

In 1967 New South Wales became the first Australian jurisdiction to enact a scheme to compensate victims of crime (Criminal Injuries Compensation Act 1967 [NSW]). Subsequently in 1968, 1969 and 1970 respectively Queensland (Criminal Code Amendment Act 1968 (Qld), South Australia (Criminal Injuries Compensation Act 1969 [SA]), and Western Australia (Criminal Injuries [Compensation] Act 1970 [WA]) implemented schemes which bore a relationship to that which had preceded them in New South Wales. The first schemes also empowered courts to order convicted defendants to pay sums of money to their victims up to a specified (and very low) amount (in New South Wales $A2,000 until 1972 when it became $A4,000; in South Australia initially only

$A1,000). What was new, as was pointed out in parliamentary debate about the New South Wales initiative, was that:

> ... a court after hearing a trial of a crime which caused injuries to another party, makes a determination under [the new legislation], the Treasury is authorised to pay the amount of compensation from public funds. This does not mean to say that the guilty person is freed from his obligation to pay compensation for the injuries caused by him and the State will stand in the shoes of the aggrieved person as regards his civil and other rights against the offender. The advantage of this principle is that the injured party receives his compensation in any event and at a much earlier stage than if he had to rely on his civil remedy against the offender (New South Wales Legislative Council, Hansard, 14 March 1967, p. 4006).

However, the schemes were not well known for a long while. In fact, only modest attempts were made to publicise them. Few applications were made at first and even fewer awards of compensation were forthcoming. Duncan Chappell (1972) noted that only a very small amount ($A55,000 in total) was paid to 59 successful applicants in New South Wales during the first three and a half years of the program.

The early rhetoric in favour of establishment of the schemes is interesting to analyse in historical perspective. The Minister introducing the Criminal Injuries Compensation Bill to the Legislative Council in New South Wales noted the existence of a three-person tribunal in New Zealand to assess applications and a six-person board in England. He proudly proclaimed that in New South Wales the government would save the administrative expense in such formal processes by using its existing courts (The Hon AD Bridges, New South Wales Legislative Council, Hansard, 14 March 1967, p. 4005). He observed that legislative provisions had long existed to permit courts to order compensation to be paid by the offender but that they had been far from extensively used on the basis that many offenders were 'men of straw' unable to meet such orders. He stated that the function of the court would be not to sit as a compensation tribunal but to deal with the application for compensation as a normal incident arising from the conviction of a person tried before it. He was explicit in stating that, as in England and New Zealand:

> It is not intended that the State undertake responsibility to provide compensation for all victims of crimes against the person or against property and in considering the measure now before this House the Government paid special attention to the necessity for providing means of distinguishing the deserving claimant from the undeserving or fraudulent. No one would suggest that the State should compensate the victims of gang warfare. Other vital considerations for the Government were that the costs of administering the scheme should not be disproportionately high and that the work of determining whether compensation should be paid and the amount of compensation should not throw an undue burden on the courts or the police of the State.

A significant part of the Minister's preoccupation in establishing the political advantage of setting up the scheme was in convincing the electorate that while the scheme had an inherent vulnerability to exploitation by the vulnerable, a process had been set in place to sift out spurious claims effectively. By the late 1990s and into 2000 it was the perceived failure of later versions of the scheme to accomplish the sifting exercise effectively that was placing it under extreme pressure (Select Committee, 1997b, 2000).

In South Australia, too, the government was at pains to emphasise the unlikelihood of people misusing the scheme, the ceiling of $A1,000 being advanced as a means of dissuading those tempted to engage in such conduct. The major controversy in relation to the legislation was in relation to the discrepancy between compensation amounts available under the workers' compensation scheme and the $A1,000 cap on the crimes compensation scheme. Criticism was also made of the lowness of the compensation available under the crimes compensation model.

Support for the new exercise of 'responsibility' on the part of the State was not uniform. The Law Society of South Australia, for instance, voiced significant concern about the concepts underlying the legislation: 'This Bill involves a departure from a fundamental concept of our administration of justice, namely, that criminal proceedings should be concerned solely with the guilt and punishment of persons charged with crime and that civil proceedings should be concerned solely with the protection of individual rights and compensation for the infringement of rights'. (Legislative Council of South Australia, Hansard, 27 November 1969, p. 3358). The government rejected the Law Society's contention, arguing that it was merely building upon a pre-existing statutory model whereby sentencing courts could make limited orders for compensation in favour of adversely affected victims (Legislative Council of South Australia, Hansard, 12 November 1969, p. 3360).

The early statutory schemes were little utilised, in spite of the optimism expressed by the parliamentarians implementing them. As early as 1974, Edelhertz and Geis (1974, p. 237) were moved to be cynical, commenting that early Australian court-connected victim compensation schemes had shown that 'endeavours can be nothing more than public placebos, tranquillising showpieces aimed at placating the public and protecting the politician, all for a negligible price'.

3. *The specialist decision-maker phase*

In the 1972 Victorian legislation, a different model was employed. It was somewhat derivative of the 1963 New Zealand legislation. A one-person tribunal was constituted. The initial expectation was that it would not operate full-time (Freckelton, 2001). Australia's first Crimes Compensation Tribunal sat in private, although it could open its hearings if it thought proper. It was obliged to act informally, without being fettered by technicalities of evidence law. It was able to make awards of compensation when satisfied on the balance of probabilities that a victim was injured or killed by the criminal act or omission of another. However, conviction of an offender was not a prerequisite to the award of compensation.

The Tribunal was stipulated to be unable to make an award if the application for compensation was lodged more than a year after the event, unless the Tribunal specifically extended the period. It could not make awards for less than $A50 as the legislation explicitly discouraged 'small and minor claims'. Significantly, too, there could be no award where the victim was a member of the household of the offender and parliamentary debate did not even acknowledge the phenomenon of domestic violence.

Compensation was payable for a variety of matters, including expenses incurred, loss of wages, other pecuniary loss, as well as for pain and suffering. The ceiling for awards was low ($A3000), although this prompted debate in parliament, opponents of the government proclaiming that the sum made available was seriously inadequate by reference to both common law damages and to what a victim of serious criminally-caused injury would need.

Funding of the scheme was suggested in the initial Victorian debate to have the potential to come from recovery of money from persons convicted of crimes or from a percentage of fines imposed upon those convicted (Freckelton, 2001). As it turned out, this was never accomplished. Recovery from the offender was adverted to in the second reading speech:

> Naturally it is in the public interest that, wherever practicable, the offender shall, in the long term, foot the bill. Even if no proceedings are taken by the victim against the offender, the Under Secretary may himself take proceedings against the offender and orders may be made against the offender for repayment of the amount (The Hon A.J. Hunt, Victorian Legislative Council, Hansard, 5 December 1972, p. 2850).

However, as it transpired, such an action was all but unknown after the scheme came into operation, the state bearing the burden of compensation payments.

4. *The increasingly expensive and technical phase*

With the 1980s came an increasingly organised and activist victims movement. The 'ripple effect' of criminal violence well beyond direct victims of criminal acts started to be acknowledged (see Corns, 1996). Scholars and community representatives lobbied government for substantive recognition of the disempowerment of victims. Mental health professionals, sexual assault centre workers, domestic violence refuge workers, youth workers, criminologists and a new class of academics who called themselves 'victimologists' drew attention to the direct and indirect effects of criminal violence – especially on women and children. Pressures built upon governments to be seen to respond to the effects of crime (see Sumner, 1987). The focus shifted from rehabilitating offenders to 'law and order' policies which recognised the plight of victims by dealing more punitively with offenders. At the same time, services started to be made available for victims. Pressures built for rape law reform to reframe the law relating to consent and to change court processes so as to alleviate unfair pressures upon complainants. Provision was made for victims to have a say in the sentencing phase of trials by creating the facility for victims to provide accounts of the impact that crimes of violence had upon them – victim impact statements. Pressures grew too for victims to be given formally recognised entitlements. Ultimately, this found recognition, for instance, in New South Wales in the Victim Rights Act 1996 (NSW) which mandated instruments of government to treat victims 'with courtesy, compassion and respect' and entitled victims to provision of information about the progress of criminal investigations, trials and important decisions about the trial of offenders.

With the 1980s, too, came international pressures for Australian states and territories to ensure greater access by victims to state compensation where offenders were unable to pay. It was a time when victims became politicised and the plight of victims became a vote-winner. New South Wales set up a Taskforce on Services for Victims of Crime. It reported in September 1986 and particularly took account of the principles endorsed by the General Assembly of the United Nations in 1985:

> When compensation is not fully available from the offender of other sources, States should endeavour to provide financial compensation to:
> (a) Victims who have sustained significant bodily injury or impairment of physical or mental health as a result of serious crimes;
> (b) The family, particularly dependants of persons who have died or become physically or mentally incapacitated as a result of such victimisation.
> The establishment, strengthening and expansion of national funds for compensation to victims should be encouraged. Where appropriate, others funds may also be established for this purpose including those cases where the State of which the victim is a national is not in a position to compensate the victim for the harm (New South Wales Task Force on Services for Victims of Crime, 1986).

The pressures exerted by victim advocates resulted in the political imperative to spend public moneys. This meant increasing funding of sexual assault centres and women's refuges, although this was slow and often had the appearance of being grudging. Lingering stereotypes of 'deserving victims' meant that governments could limit their financial exposure by tapping into community reservations about whether a percentage of victims, especially women, placed themselves imprudently or recklessly at risk of assault by their behaviour (see Elias, 1986; Fitzroy, 1995, pp. 82-83). Governments also queried whether a new class of pseudo-victims had emerged which tried to take advantage of the community's generosity, colluding in criminality with their assailants or faking acts of violence, pretending injury where it had not occurred. In this way, victim blaming took on a new role, legitimising the imposition of checks and balances upon those seeking to draw on the public purse and requiring a suspiciousness about the claims of victims not conforming to expectations about victim behaviour before and after alleged assaults.

Another aspect of this phase of victim-consciousness was the pressure for governments to acknowledge the injuries of 'deserving victims' financially to an extent that provided effective compensation for the losses that victims had suffered and for the pain and suffering that had been caused to them. Increases in amounts of compensation were implemented throughout the 1980s in most jurisdictions and the diversity of scheme models became pronounced (see

Freckelton, 1996, 2001). In jurisdictions such as the Australian Capital Territory (ACT), amounts of up to $A50,000 could be awarded for pain and suffering compensation.

At the same time, no doubt related to the potential for substantial amounts of money to be awarded via criminal injuries compensation, a new phenomenon became noticeable: plaintiff lawyers commenced to engage with the process. Solicitors and barristers specialising in criminal injuries compensation applications and in appeals against first instance decisions emerged. As long as they handled sufficient cases, there was money to be made from servicing the needs of victims in the criminal injuries compensation process. This meant that expert medical and psychological reports needed to be procured in ever-increasing numbers. The personal injuries side of medico-legal practice, of course, was well used to such demands but criminal injuries compensation applications in New South Wales and Victoria introduced a source of work for clinical, counselling and forensic practitioners as never before. This coincided with the 1980s international recognition of post-traumatic stress disorder as one of the serious *sequelae* to exposure to life-threatening or frightening stressors (see e.g. Mendelson, 1987, 1988, 1999; Van Der Kolk & Weisaeth, 1996).

In addition, the existence of the schemes was better advertised and commenced effectively to percolate community consciousness. Numbers of applications rose dramatically, in particular in the sexual assault area. For instance, in Victoria the number of awards for sex-related offences had increased from 139 in 1988-89 to 1,207 in 1993-94, the cost having risen from $951,000 in 1988-89 to $13.2 million in 1993-94, the average amount awarded for sex offences having risen from $6,841 in 1988-89 to $10,900 in 1993-94. The changes were a function of a number of different social phenomena. The sexual assault centre movement and the women's refuge movement professionalised and commenced to receive government funding during the 1980s. So did victim support organisations. Victims, especially victims who were women, commenced to have a voice and to have a source of support. The stigma of being a victim of crime, including of sex crimes and crimes of domestic violence, started to dissipate somewhat. Police commenced routinely to provide victims with application forms for crimes compensation. Victims were often referred to support groups who also encouraged them to make application for their entitlements in relation to compensation.

All in all, the public purse was placed under considerable strain in the 1980s and the 1990s by the 'success' of the schemes. Decisions in Western Australia, the ACT and Victoria (Freckelton, 2001) apparently opening the way to multiple awards to people who had been repeatedly victimised threatened to impose even more pressure on the schemes. Plaintiff lawyers succeeded in persuading appellate courts to permit late, even very late, applications for criminal injuries compensation, the clock only starting to run, as in the civil law, not at the time of the assaultive act, nor at the time when the injuries manifested, but at the time when the victim associated the current disability with the act which, objectively viewed, had caused it. This resulted in large numbers of applications for compensation from people assaulted sexually and/or physically many years previously and from women who had been raped or attacked by their partners within their own houses.

Governments started defending appellate actions in the name of the public purse. They began to express concern about dubious initial decisions at first instance permitting compensation or permitting 'too much' compensation. They queried whether police and emergency services personnel were taking too large a slice of the compensation pie. Decision-making appointments became politicised as governments looked to place a curb on what they started to view as profligacy and irresponsibility in awards.

However, those options that did exist to recoup from offenders were still little availed of. It was almost unknown for offenders to be civilly sued by their victims and it was rare for courts to make orders for compensation against persons being sentenced for property crimes and crimes of violence.

5. *The backlash*

By the 1990s a backlash can be discerned within governments and on the part of a number of commentators about the emerging role of victims in the criminal justice system (see Hughes, 1993; Dershowitz, 1995; Ashworth, 1993). A number of different measures were adopted to reduce state exposure to victims' claims for compensation (mostly for pain and suffering) in the late 1990s. This mirrored developments in Canada and The United Kingdom with tightening up of schemes being prominent so as to close off access to those classified as 'undeserving victims' (Sheehy, 1994; Langer, 1991). In Queensland and New South Wales Tables of Maims were introduced, based upon the British model, specifying particular amounts of money which victims were eligible to receive for particular injuries. In South Australia a 'tariff' system was inserted into legislation, although without any of the relative financial generosity within the British scheme. The advantage of such mechanisms was that they enabled better prediction by victims and their legal representatives of the quantum of their entitlements. Their disadvantages were their inflexibility, their insensitivity to the particular responses to injury of some victims, and some of the internal relativities and inconsistencies which made them appear arbitrary and unfair. There was also the limited extent of the compensation available for victims and the increasing hurdles which victims and their legal representatives were required to jump in order to qualify for what was becoming the 'privilege' of compensation.

Victoria The most dramatic backlash, however, occurred in Victoria where, without public consultation, the Conservative Government of the day enacted the Victims of Crime Assistance Act 1996 (Vic). It abolished awards of crimes compensation for pain and suffering, thereby removing the heart of what had been the compensation scheme in that state since 1972. The practical result for Victorians was that those who were physically or psychiatrically injured in the sense of suffering, for instance, a long-term post-traumatic reaction to a rape or some other form of assault, ceased to be eligible to receive compensation from the state unless they had actually lost money as a result of their injury. If the person was seriously injured but happened to be unemployed, or of a pre- or post-employment age, or intellectually disabled, or on a pension, their suffering was not compensable unless they could sue their assailant – most unlikely in light of the removal of legal aid assistance for civil actions, and the impecunious character of most offenders. The only exception was that in 'exceptional circumstances' (undefined) an award could be made for other expenses actually and reasonably incurred, or reasonably likely to be incurred to assist the victim of crime to recover from an act of violence. Perhaps not surprisingly, few applications for such compensation were made.

One of the changes under the new legislation was the division of victims and their entitlements into different categories. In general, entitlement to compensation from the state was generally confined to awards for expenses actually incurred or reasonably likely to be incurred by 'primary' and 'secondary' victims for reasonable counselling services or medical expenses. Primary victims were stipulated to be entitled to up to $A20,000 for loss of earnings suffered or reasonably likely to be suffered as a direct result of an act of violence, while secondary victims in 'exceptional circumstances' could be awarded a comparable amount for loss of earnings as a direct result of witnessing or becoming aware of the act of violence. The legislation abolished the previous Crimes Compensation Tribunal and constituted a new Victims of Crime Assistance Tribunal, still staffed by Magistrates and still holding hearings on the rare occasions when they were pressed to do so into victims' alleged entitlements.

Another significant aspect to the new Victorian regime was its transfer of the principal port of call for victims injured by criminal acts from the state and so the public purse to offenders. Important amendments were made to sentencing procedures (Sentencing Act 1991 (Vic), s85B) enabling a court at the time of sentencing or within 12 months to order compensation, not just for loss or damage to property, as had previously been the case, but also for pain and suffering. It constituted a significant return to court-ordered compensation, a refocusing away from state liability to pay, to offenders' liability to compensate their victims. However, the facility for sentencing orders in favour of victims is only viable when an offender is a person of means, against whom a court order is realistically enforceable.

The Attorney-General announced that 'The State will be given the right to pursue offenders or other relevant parties at common law for civil damages if victims agree to assign their rights. Victims will receive any money recovered which exceeds the assistance they receive under [the legislation]. This could include compensation received by way of pain and suffering recovered through the civil procedure'. (Victorian Legislative Assembly, Second Reading Speech, Hansard, 31 October 1996, 1023). Exactly what this was intended to mean in practice and how enthusiastic the government was going to be to fund civil litigation against suspected perpetrators of criminal violence was never able to be tested owing to the Conservative government unexpectedly losing office at the next election in 1999.

The Bill was the subject of passionate opposition in Parliament. The shadow Attorney-General, Mr Hulls, three years later the Labour Attorney-General, attacked it as 'perhaps the most insidious piece of legislation to come before this house in many years'. (Victorian Legislative Assembly, Hansard, 21 November 1996: 1436). He argued that it was important that society not forget that

> ... [it] has a duty of care generally but in particular to those most vulnerable members whom we simply cannot walk away from in their hour of need. ... A civilised society has an obligation to look after its victims and ensure that the public purse pays them for the pain and suffering they have endured as a result of serious assaults and other offences (Victorian Legislative Assembly, Hansard, 21 November 1996, pp. 1440-1441).

The savings made by the state as a result of the changes were dramatic, applications for any kind of 'assistance' slowing to a trickle and tens of million dollars being saved (Freckelton, 2001). Some $A10 million was expended on a victims' health scheme, run by a body named the Victims Referral and Assistance Service. The Service made available through a database of psychologists, social workers and therapists counselling services to a wide variety of crime victims.

The ACT In the ACT in 1998/1999 criminal injuries compensation entitlements also became overtly subject to political controversy. The process of public consultation was facilitated by the public exposure of the Victims of Crime (Financial Assistance) (Amendment) Bill 1998 (ACT) and by the holding of public hearings by a multi-party committee of the ACT parliament. The Bill proposed to initiate thoroughgoing changes to victims' entitlements to criminal injuries compensation in the ACT. The ACT government explained the objectives of the legislation thus:

> Given the high and increasing costs of the current scheme ... and the large areas of unmet victims' needs as identified in the Working Party's Report, it is reasonable to conclude that the Territory is not getting 'value for money' from the scheme in the Criminal Injuries Compensation Act 1983 (ACT). The fundamental challenge for the Government and the Assembly is to deliver a scheme which contains costs at an affordable level while providing better assistance to a greater number of crime victims each year (Standing Committee on Justice and Community Safety, ACT Parliament, 1999, 3).

The proposed legislation, which ultimately was substantially enacted (Freckelton, 2001), confined the entitlement to compensation of a 'primary victim' to '(a) the expense reasonably incurred by or on behalf of the victim as a consequence of the injury; (b) the pecuniary loss suffered by the victim as a consequence of total or partial incapacity for work due to the injury; and (c) the expense incurred in making application for financial assistance, other than by way of fees paid to a legal practitioner.' In addition, 'special assistance' may be awarded by the Magistrates Court to a 'primary victim' but only where the criminal injury involved is 'an extremely serious injury', as defined, and where 'the victim has obtained such assistance from the victims services scheme as is reasonably available, unless the person is physically incapable of benefiting from the scheme'.

The sting, and the extent to which the availability of 'special assistance' became a chimaera under the new legislation, lay in the definition of 'an extremely serious injury', prescribed in s11 of the Victims of Crime (Financial Assistance) Act 1983 (ACT), to be '(a) a permanent impairment of a bodily function that is extremely serious and will remain so permanently; (b) a permanent loss of a bodily function that is extremely serious and will remain so permanently; (c) a permanent disfigurement that is extremely serious and will remain so permanently; (d) a permanent mental or behavioural disturbance or disorder that is extremely serious and will remain so permanently; (e) the loss of a foetus.' The category of persons, for whom a psychiatrist would be prepared ethically to say that their PTSD, for instance, is extremely serious 'and will remain so permanently' is so small as to guarantee the ACT government almost complete indemnity against compensation payments for psychiatric injury applications. It would be a rare psychiatrist who would abandon hope in respect of the efficacy of treatment for disorders such as depression, anxiety, adjustment and post-traumatic stress.

A proposal from the ACT government, ultimately not enacted, was also that lawyers be removed from the application process, further disempowering applicants from assistance which would otherwise apprise them informedly of the residual rights which they would retain under the reforming legislation.

The Standing Committee on Justice and Community Safety (Standing Committee on Justice and Community Safety, ACT Parliament, 1999, 13) found that there was no conclusive research 'which clarifies whether it is the experience of hearing a judge make an award, or the official nature of the compensation payment, which gives the victims the feeling that the State has acknowledged the victim's experience' but found that the issue of 'pain and suffering' compensation was of particular significance for victims of sexual assault and domestic violence: '[it] represents acknowledgement by the State of the horrendous violation which these victims have suffered'. The Committee found that a number of the arguments advanced by the ACT Government to justify its dismantling of the compensation payment system contained 'logical flaws'. It rejected the proposition that there was evidence to link victim dissatisfaction with the availability and receipt of financial payments, concluding instead that victim dissatisfaction 'appears to be linked, instead, with inadequacies in the compensation schemes'. The Committee found no evidence of rorting of the existing scheme and rejected this as a justification for cutting financial payments.

However, the Committee provided some support to the ACT Government's proposal to remove the provision of compensation payments for pain and suffering for the majority of victims eligible under the current system: 'This proposal is justified on the grounds of cost-effectiveness, to improve access and equity, and to facilitate the rehabilitation of victims of crime.' (Standing

Committee on Justice and Community Safety, ACT Parliament, 1999, pp. 15-16). However, in respect of the Government's stated objective of targeting financial assistance to sexual assault victims, the Committee expressed the strong view that the requirement of proof of 'permanent psychological damage' should be removed. It recommended that financial assistance continue to be available for victims of sexual assault and also of domestic violence. It proposed that the ACT scheme be more liberal than the 1996 Victorian scheme, permitting recovery for financial expenses likely to be incurred in the future. It recommended that victims of sexual assault, murder and violent crimes in the workplace continue to have access to lump sum financial payments for pain and suffering.

The ACT Government's response to the recommendations of the Committee was largely to repudiate them and to proceed with the proposed legislation. The result is that only very narrow categories of 'extreme-end victims' as of 2002 are eligible for pain and suffering compensation in the ACT.

6. *The re-adjustment phase*

In 1999 the governments of South Australia and Victoria commenced inquiries into their crimes compensation systems, an object of which was to evaluate the desirability of the changes initiated in Victoria in 1997. In speaking of the inquiry in his state, the South Australian Attorney-General noted in particular a survey of victims conducted on behalf of the government:

> Feedback from the victims survey shows that the most important justifications for state funded victim compensation are:
> a means of helping to hold the offender accountable (86.0 per cent) (even though the offender frequently did not contribute);
> compensation for physical injury (74.3 per cent);
> helping the victim adjust (69.8 per cent);
> compensation for emotional and mental distress (63.5 per cent);
> to recover financial loss (64.9 per cent); and
> finally the state acknowledging its responsibility (43.7 per cent).
> (Griffin, 2000, p. 22).

He drew attention too to the fact that victims themselves differentiate amongst different categories of victims. Eighty per cent of victims responding to the South Australian survey had said that they regarded sexual assault victims as especially deserving, followed by victims of personal violence (64 per cent), and family members of a primary victim of violent crime:

> When victims were asked about the scope of any compensation scheme, 75 per cent of victims considered payment to cover the costs of a physical injury was very important, and a further 16 per cent said this was quite important. Almost 67 per cent of victims considered payment to cover mental injury was very important ... On the controversial issue of pain and suffering, about 56 per cent considered payment to cover this was very important and a further 24 per cent said this was quite important (Griffin, 2000, pp. 22-23).

The results of the Victorian inquiry were manifested in a dramatic turn-around in criminal injuries compensation entitlements. The new Labour government implemented an electoral commitment to bring back pain and suffering compensation entitlements for victims. By the Victims of Crime Assistance (Amendment) Act 2000 (Vic) it overturned the abolition of pain and suffering compensation and replaced it with a new, lean system of modest entitlements to 'special financial assistance'. The amounts for which victims are now eligible are of smaller dimensions than those existing anywhere else in Australia – the maximum is a mere $A7,500. However, the Victorian turnaround in historical terms is quite dramatic, honouring as it does an election promise to re-institute an abolished form of compensation, and recommitting a further $15 million per year to compensation to victims of violent crime. Significantly too, constraints were placed on the Victims Referral and Assistance Service which provided counselling and allied health services to victims, a tighter cap being placed on permissible sessions with therapists and more stringent eligibility criteria being imposed.

The other distinctive characteristic of the Year 2000 Victorian scheme is that it consolidated the Conservative government's focus upon facilitating victims' capacity to recoup from offenders at the time of sentencing and by 2001 had cut back significantly on the victims' health scheme, which had been a cornerstone of the previous government's initiatives.

Meanwhile, in New South Wales the Victims Compensation Act 1996 (NSW) created a significantly revised scheme of compensation for acts of violence, commencing in the second quarter of 1997. 'Acts of violence' legitimising the making of awards are now more tightly defined. The Act entitles 'primary' and 'secondary' victims to compensation for what are prescribed to be compensable injuries, as well as to financial loss up to the sum of $A10,000. The maximum amount of compensation available for victims injured by a single act of violence is limited to $A50,000, a figure that applies both to the primary victim and to all other victims applying through the victim. Numbers of applications have been curtailed by the imposition of a threshold of injuries of $A2,400 before compensation becomes payable to any victim, other than a 'family victim'. Significant restrictions are imposed in relation to the categories of persons eligible to receive awards. Compensation is determined by 'compensation assessors' from whose assessments an appeal may be made to the Victims Compensation Tribunal. Sexual assault victim entitlements have been made the subject of complex levels of regulation. Compensation is available for injuries arising from indecent assault or assault with violence in the course of attempted sexual intercourse in the sum of $A2,400-$A10,000; for injuries from unlawful sexual intercourse or a pattern of indecent assault at $A10,000-$A25,000; for injuries arising from a pattern of unlawful sexual intercourse at $A25,000-$A50,000.

The status of the New South Wales scheme is far from static, however. A series of reports from the New South Wales Joint Select Committee on Victims' Compensation (Joint Select Committee on Victims' Compensation, 1997a, 1997b, 2000) between 1997 and 2000 recommended the adoption of measures to reduce the government's financial exposure to mounting costs of provision of criminal injuries compensation. One assessment suggested that if changes were not made to the scheme, the payments which in 1995-1996 had climbed from $66.7million to $A82.9 million would have grown to $A295 million by the year 2000 (Stewart in Joint Select Committee, 1997b). For instance, it was proposed that consideration be given to deleting the categories of 'shock' other than for permanent injuries, homicide and sexual assault and that the minimum threshold to receive compensation be raised to $A5,000.

The future for criminal injuries compensation schemes in Australia

The impetus for major government cutbacks to pain and suffering compensation for victims has dissipated somewhat with the loss at the polls of the Conservative government in Victoria and the partial reinstitution of such benefits by the succeeding government. However, in the ACT most victims still have few entitlements to pain and suffering compensation as a result of that Territory's implementation of Victorian-inspired legislation.

A positive aspect of the community debates engendered by the 1997 Victorian reforms was a recognition that the needs of victims are not met by the mere payment of money. Improved health and counselling services for victims of crime were instituted in Victoria and then copied in a number of other Australian states. However, the recognition that ensued was that health and counselling facilities also do not constitute a comprehensive answer to the difficulties experienced by victims of violent crime. A combination of the two forms of response is necessary if victims are to be assisted to resume their previous levels of functionality within the community.

The consequence in Victoria has been a partial reintroduction of compensation for pain and suffering but a concomitant reduction in the therapeutic services made available for victims. This is likely to be the pattern for the short term for other Australian jurisdictions.

What appears to have emerged in the debates about the Victorian and ACT initiatives has been a recognition that financial compensation for pain and suffering, as well as for direct financial losses suffered by victims of criminal violence, has a constructive place in victim recovery. One of the issues yet to be resolved, though, is whether it is the provision of money *per se* that has the potential for a therapeutic impact or whether such potential lies within the circumstances in which money is provided by the state. In a number of jurisdictions in Australia, such as Victoria, South Australia, the ACT and Queensland, compensation for pain and suffering has been awarded by a court or a tribunal. This enables an overt message to be delivered by the magistrate, tribunal member or judge – often to the effect that the community has real concern for the victim, accepts that the crime that has harmed them was not their fault and that it wishes to make a meaningful gesture to show its concern. It may well be that the provision of pecuniary compensation without such personal articulation is less therapeutically efficacious.

Another component of current Australian political responses to the awarding of pecuniary compensation, especially for pain and suffering experienced by victims of crime, has been a new stringency. Legislation has been altered in South Australia, for instance, to make it difficult for victims who were injured while engaged in criminal conduct of any form to obtain compensation. In a number of other jurisdictions, increased rigor has been applied to determining whether a victim, by reason of their background or the conduct surrounding their being injured, should be regarded as disentitled from receiving compensation or undeserving to draw upon the public purse. A range of moral judgements has accompanied such designations, including those which are antagonistic toward persons receiving the fruits of state compensation if they have at any stage been involved in criminal activity, if they have failed to leave abusive relationships or if they had been slow in complaining or reporting to police or other authorities.

The funding of agencies providing state-administered treatment and counselling has also come under new pressures. Within four years of its creation, the Victorian scheme was substantially downscaled with a new demand for transparency, accountability and moderation in making costly facilities available. It is likely that in the future the same kinds of questions that have been posed of the critical incident stress debriefing industry (see e.g. Wessely, Rose & Bisson, 1997; Freckelton, 1998; Raphael & Wilson, 2000) will be asked of services that provide prompt state-funded access for victims to counselling: is the counselling actually reducing the incidence of psychiatric illnesses; is it effectively facilitating victims' reintegration into the community; can the objectives of the service be achieved by reduced expenditure; is there a clear treatment plan whose objectives are being met; is the bureaucracy running the services in a lean enough way; are professionals exploiting the services; are people injured in non-criminal ways taking advantage of the system?

It is likely that the increasing focus upon restorative justice will give a further fillip to the primary responsibility for compensating victims being placed upon offenders, wherever that is possible. Eyes will be cast upon the success with which the amended version of the Victorian Sentencing Act 1991 succeeds in offenders actually compensating victims, with the state taking secondary responsibility. Ironically, though, the substantial awards starting to be made by courts against offenders in Victoria may well prompt a new form of compensation litigation in which convicted offenders regularly query the claims to victimisation or the extent of victimisation made by applicants. Such hearings are likely to become more seriously and professionally contested, thereby causing significant levels of secondary traumatisation for victims. Saving money by the state may well come at a therapeutic price for many victims.

It is clear that the day of substantial payments by the state of 'solatium', 'compensation' or 'assistance' to victims of crime is passing for the present in Australia. However, there are considerable political pressures to retain some meaningful level of state assistance for 'genuine' victims of violent crime. There will continue to be a difficult tension between the expectation of the community that 'innocent' victims should be recompensed out of state funds, if necessary, for the financial losses that they have incurred and for the suffering that they have endured by reason of criminal acts, and the imperative on the part of governments to control their exposure to victims' claims for compensation. It is likely that the Victorian compromise will provide a model for other jurisdictions but that public pressure will lead to governments following the Victorian example to upgrade to some degree the amount of compensation made available to victims.

Concerningly, Australia has entered a divisive phase of 'victim blaming' in which it will only be those victims who are accounted as acceptably 'deserving' who will be regarded as worthy recipients of state-funded compensation. Clear indicia of what constitute forms of behaviour that render victims ineligible for compensation need to be prescribed. They need to be humane and reasonable as well as such as to find community favour. An incident of fiscal accountability will continue to be clear satisfaction by applicants for state compensation of the criteria for eligibility. These criteria may well become increasingly stringent and even moralistic.

Compensation for victims: looking toward the future

Across different countries the victims movement has consolidated the awareness that victims of violent crime deserve to receive formal recognition that they have been wronged and in many cases have suffered pathological *sequelae* from criminal conduct directed at them or from which they have become harmed albeit without the exercise of malicious intent directed specifically toward them. However, instruments such as the European Convention on the Compensation of Victims of Violent Crimes do not mandate payments of financial compensation for victims' pain and suffering.

The restorative justice movement has resulted in an increasing inclination on the part of governments to locate the responsibility for addressing victims' suffering in the pockets of offenders. Proponents of therapeutic jurisprudence too have identified a potential for healing in the victim being compensated by the person who has been the author of their misfortune.

However, therapeutic jurisprudence principles also suggest that one of the consequences of crime can be the alienation of citizens from a community that has failed to protect them and thereby played a role in an ongoing sense of injustice and vulnerability on the part of victims. Hence the assertion that the state's recognition of the consequences of crime for victims can constitute a therapeutically symbolic gesture of collegiality and concern, articulating the assumption of responsibility by the general community for the welfare of the victim and thereby reaffirming the fact that many victims of crime are in no way responsible for the crimes committed against them. Such formal recognition can be cathartic and facilitate the movement of victims beyond the crimes committed against them and the suffering and other adverse pecuniary, vocational and personal consequences of the criminal conduct. It also enables victims of impecunious offenders, and many offenders fall into this category, to receive compensation which otherwise would not be available to them.

However, real concern for the victim, where either offenders cannot be identified, or where offenders are not sufficiently moneyed to be able to pay compensation, has led to a number of developments internationally. The first is a recognition that money alone, whether its provenance be the coffers of the state or the pockets of an offender, can only accomplish so much by way of assisting victims of violent crime to reintegrate into the community and to resume their lives in a way comparable to how their lives would have been had the criminal conduct not been committed. This has led to an improvement in the provision of health services, in the broadest sense, for victims of crime. However, the question has arisen whether provision of health services alone is sufficient and is enough of an acknowledgement by offenders or by the State of their level of responsibility for the plight of victims of violent crime. Ironically, too, the cost of such services can be surprisingly substantial; it is apparent that the consequences of crime often extend well beyond post-traumatic stress, anxiety and adjustment disorders. All manners of non-pathological *sequelae* of crime deserve recognition and should be acknowledged as caused by crime.

A characteristic of the demise or attenuation of early-phase schemes has been 'blow-outs' in state liability for financial compensation and provision of health services. On occasion, this has resulted in suspicions of fake and embellished claims by applicants for compensation, and also in attacks on lawyers and experts who have facilitated such applications. It has even been claimed that the 'lawyerisation' of the compensation process has been counter-therapeutic. Often the measures to dismantle or diminish state schemes have been couched in identification of the limits in pecuniary intervention and proposals for a shift in emphasis away from money and toward health services – money has been proclaimed not to be the answer or even to be the obverse of the answer.

The fruits of the victims, women's, therapeutic jurisprudence and restorative justice movements is disuniformity of international approaches toward the needs of victims who have been harmed by violent crimes. This is exacerbated by the financial outlays made by governments which have committed themselves to payment of financial compensation of significant dimensions to victims of crime; such an initiative has commenced to expose the 'dark figure' of crime, especially in relation to sex offending and child abuse, and to draw out victims whose complaints had not previously been heard and whose needs had not been recognised. Ironically, we have learned much about the incidence and consequences of crime by the different models employed internationally to provide support to victims of crime. What has become increasingly apparent over the past decade is that genuine attempts to facilitate the recovery of victims cannot be confined to the payment of financial compensation or to the provision of enhanced and empathic health services to victims. Those who have been harmed by violent conduct have a variety of needs which should be met by the state at a symbolic level, via provision of therapeutic services and the creation of opportunities for victims of crime of which they have been deprived by their experiences. As much as possible, too, such measures should involve contribution by offenders, at both a financial and a symbolic level. This has the potential to bring home to offenders what has ensued from their violent conduct but can also facilitate the restorative processes for victims. What is now clear is that there is no one answer to healing the wounds of violent criminal behaviour. A complex and personalised response is necessary from government and offenders alike to meet the multi-factorial needs of victims. This is neither cheap nor easy but it is worthwhile.

References

A. Ashworth, 'Victim Impact Statements and Sentencing' *Criminal Law Review* (1993), pp. 498 ff.

J. Bell, S. Boyron & S. Whittaker, *Principles of French Law* (Oxford University Press, Oxford, 1998)

B. Cameron, 'Compensation for Victims of Crime: the New Zealand Experiment' *Journal of Public Law* (1963), pp. 367 ff.

D. Chappell, 'The Emergence of Australian Schemes to Compensate Victims of Crime' *Southern California Law Review* (43, 1970), pp. 69 ff.

D. Chappell, 'Providing for the Victim of Crime: Political Placebos or Progressive Programs?' *Adelaide Law Review* (4, 1972), pp. 296 ff.

C. Corns, 'Victims of Crime Assistance Act 1996' paper presented to Leo Cussen Seminar, *Victims of Crime Assistance* (Melbourne, 1997)

C. Dadomo & S. Farran, *The French Legal System* (Sweet and Maxwell, London, 1996)

A. Dershowitz, *The Abuse Excuse* (Little Brown & Co, New York, 1995)

P. Duff, *Criminal Injuries Compensation* (Butterworths, Edinburgh, 1991)

P. Duff, 'The Measure of Criminal Injuries Compensation: Political Pragmatism or Dog's Dinner?' *Oxford Journal of Legal Studies* (18, 1998), pp. 105 ff.

H. Edelhertz & G. Geis, *Public Compensation to Victims of Crime* (Praeger Publishers, New York, 1974)

S. Egger, 'Women and Crime Prevention' in P. O'Malley & A. Sutton, *Crime Prevention in Australia: Issues in Policy and Research* (Federation Press, Sydney, 1997)

R. Elias, *The Politics of Victimization: Victims, Victimology and Human Rights* (Oxford University Press, New York, 1986)

L. Fitzroy, '"Right or Privilege" in Victorian Community Council Against Violence' in *Bringing it Together: A Victim Support Strategy: Proceedings of the Conference* (VCCAV, Melbourne, 1995)

I. Freckelton, 'Criminal Injuries Compensation for Domestic Sexual Assault: Obstructing the Oppressed' in C. Sumner, M. Israel, M. O'Connell & R. Sarre, *International Victimology: Selected Papers from the 8th International Symposium* (AIC, Canberra, 1996)

I. Freckelton, 'Critical Incident Stress Debriefing and the Law' *Journal of Law and Medicine* (6, 1998), pp. 105 ff.

I. Freckelton, *Criminal Injuries Compensation: Law, Practice and Policy* (Law Book Co, Sydney, 2001)

M. Fry, *Arms of the Law* (Victor Gollancz, London, 1951)

M. Fry, 'Justice for Victims' *Journal of Public Law* (8, 1959), pp. 191 ff.

A.J. Goldberg, 'Equality and Government' *New York University Law Review* (39, 1964), pp. 224 ff.

D. Greer, *Compensation for Criminal Injuries* (Sweet and Maxwell, London, 1991)

K.T. Griffin, 'Righting the Wrong, Minimising the Risk' (paper presented to the 2000 Victimology Conference, Toronto)

R. Hughes, *The Culture of Complaint: The Fraying of America* (Oxford University Press, Oxford, 1993)

Inderdepartmental Working Party, *Review of the Criminal Injuries Compensation Scheme* (HMSO, 1978)

K.D. Jenkins-Hall & G.A. Merlatt, 'Apparently Irrelevant Decisions in the Relapse Process' in R. Laws ed., *Relapse Prevention with Sex Offenders* (Guilford Press, New York, 1989)

Joint Select Committee on Victims Compensation, Parliament of New South Wales, *Report of the Study* (Tour of Interstate and Overseas Jurisdictions, Sydney, 1997)

Joint Select Committee on Victims' Compensation, Parliament of New South Wales, *Second Interim Report: The Long Term Financial Viability of the Victims Compensation Fund* (Sydney, 1997)

Joint Select Committee on Victims Compensation, Parliament of New South Wales, *Report: Ongoing Issues Concerning the NSW Victims Compensation Scheme* (Sydney, 2000)

L.L. Lamborn, 'The Propriety of Governmental Compensation to Victims of Crime' *George Washington Law Review* (41, 1972), pp. 446 ff.

L.L. Lamborn, 'Reparations for Victims of Crime: Developments and Directions' *Victimology* (4(2), 1979), pp. 214 ff.

D. Lanham, 'Criminal Fraud and Compensation Orders' *Criminal Law Journal* (10, 1986), pp. 297 ff.

R. Langer, 'Battered Women and the Criminal Injuries Compensation Board' *Saskatchewan Law Review* (66, 1991), pp. 453

R. Laws ed., *Relapse Prevention with Sex Offenders* (Guilford Press, New York, 1989)

R. Mackenzie, 'Lump Sums or Litigation? Compensation for Sexual Abuse: the Case for Reinstatement of a Compensation for Criminal Injuries Scheme' *New Zealand Universities Law Review* (15, 1993), pp. 367 ff.

M. Maguire & J. Shapland, 'Provisions for Victims in an International Context' in R.C. Davis, A.J. Lurigio & W.G. Skogan ed., *Victims of Crime* (2nd edition, Sage Publications, London, 1997)

M. Malsch & R. Carrière, 'Victims' Wishes for Compensation: The Immaterial Aspect' *Journal of Criminal Justice* (27(3), 1999), pp. 239 ff.

R.E. Meiners, *Victim Compensation* (Lexington Books, Lexington, 1978)

G. Mendelson, 'The Concept of Post-traumatic Stress Disorder: A Review' *International Journal of Law and Psychiatry* (10, 1987), pp. 45 ff.

G. Mendelson, *Psychiatric Aspects of Personal Injury Claims* (Charles C. Thomas, Springfield, Illinois, 1988)

G. Mendelson, 'Forensic Psychiatry: the Civil Practice' in I. Freckelton & H. Selby ed., *Expert Evidence in Family Law* (LBC Information Services, Sydney, 1999)

D. Miers, *Responses to Victimisation: A Comparative Study of Compensation for Criminal Violence in Great Britain and Ontario* (Professional Books, Oxford, 1978)

J. Miller, 'Compensating Crime Victims Within New Zealand's No Fault Accident Compensation Scheme: the Advantages and Disadvantages' in C. Sumner, M. Israel, M. O'Connell & R. Sarre ed., *International Victimology: Selected Papers from the 8th International Symposium* (AIC, Canberra, 1996)

New South Wales Task Force on Services for Victims of Crime, *Criminal Injuries Compensation in New South Wales* (Govt Printer, Sydney, 1986)

B. Raphael & J.P. Wilson, *Psychological Debriefing: Theory, Practice and Evidence* (Cambridge University Press, Cambridge, 2000)

R v Secretary for the Home Department; ex parte Fire Brigades Union [1995] 2 AC 513

S. Schafer, *Compensation and Restitution to Victims of Crime* (2nd edition, Patterson Smith, Montclair, NJ, 1970)

E. Sheehy, 'Compensation for Women Who Have Been Raped' in J.V. Roberts & R. Mohr ed., *Confronting Sexual Assault: A Decade of Legal and Social Change* (University of Toronto Press, Toronto, 1994)

Standing Committee on Justice and Community Safety, ACT Parliament, *Report on the Inquiry into the Victims of Crime (Financial Assistance) (Amendment) Bill 1998 (ACT)* (Report No 2, ACT Govt, Canberra, 1999)

C.J. Sumner, 'Victim Participation in the Criminal Justice System' *Australian and New Zealand Journal of Criminology* (20, 1987), pp. 195 ff.

C. Sumner, M. Israel, M. O'Connell & R. Sarre ed., *International Victimology: Selected Papers from the 8th International Symposium* (AIC, Canberra, 1996)

R. Tobin, 'Reinventing the Wheel: Criminal Injuries Compensation?' *New Zealand Law Journal* (1994), pp. 378 ff.

United Kingdom, *Penal Practice in a Changing Society* (Cmnd 645, London, 1959)

B.A. Van Der Kolk, A.C. McFarlane & L. Weisaeth, *Traumatic Stress* (The Guilford Press, New York, 1996)

S. Wessely, S. Rose & J. Bisson, 'Psychological Debriefing: A Systematic Review of Brief Psychological Interventions ("Debriefings") for the Treatment of Immediate Trauma Related Symptoms and the Prevention of Post Traumatic Stress Disorder' *Cochrane Collaboration Electronic Library* (25 November 1997)

D.B. Williams, *Criminal Injuries Compensation* (Waterlow Publishers, London, [1972,] 1986)

4. Victims' Rights and Restorative Justice: Piecemeal Reform of the Criminal Justice System or a Change of Paradigm?

Marc Groenhuijsen*

1. *Introduction*

During the past two decades, nearly all modern criminal justice systems have been reformed on behalf of victims of crime. In most jurisdictions change has been achieved by introducing new procedural rights for individual victims. It is striking to observe the similarities of victims' rights which have been introduced or expanded in criminal justice systems which are otherwise hardly comparable. In this way, the Anglo-American adversarial systems on the one hand and the more inquisitorial systems on the European continent on the other have come to harbour nearly identical provisions with respect to the interests of crime victims. In countries of both legal families law enforcement officers are now required by law to treat victims with respect for their dignity. Nowadays, the police and the prosecutor's office must supply the victim with information and explanation about the progress of the case. In many jurisdictions the victim has acquired a right to provide information to officials responsible for making decisions relating to the offender. Victims furthermore have often been granted the right to have legal advice available, regardless of their means. Attention has also been paid to the right to protection, both of their privacy and of their physical safety. Finally, many nations have improved systems in order to promote reparation to be paid by the offender or – in cases where this proves to be impossible – State compensation.[1]

* Tilburg University, The Netherlands.

1. It is no coincidence that these are the legal rights which have most frequently been introduced in various national criminal justice systems. The examples mentioned reflect the standards set by documents adopted by the international community. See for example the United Nations Declaration on the Basic Principles of Justice for Victims of Crime and Abuse of Power (1985); the Council of Europe Recommendation on the Position of the Victim in the Framework of Criminal Law and Procedure (1985); and the Statement of Victims' Rights in the Process of Criminal Justice (by the European Forum for Victim Services, 1996).

A number of years after the widespread introduction of these reform measures, at least two general problems remain unsolved. The first one is about implementation.[2] As has been asserted many times before, it is relatively easy to pass legislation, but it is infinitely more difficult to actually make the new provisions work as intended. This point has been proven by experience in almost every jurisdiction involved.[3] The second issue which remains to be addressed concerns the precise theoretical nature of the reform efforts on behalf of crime victims. Are the recently introduced victims' rights mere refinements of the currently existing criminal justice systems, or should they be considered as expressions of a new way of thinking which is incompatible with the basic structure of the traditional model of administering criminal justice? This question is also triggered by the fact that the introduction of new victims' rights is quite often presented as being part of the wider movement under the umbrella label of *restorative justice*.[4]

In this chapter it will be argued that the two remaining problems referred to above are interconnected. The question of effective implementation cannot be fruitfully tackled without developing a well-reasoned notion of the precise theoretical status of reform efforts in this area. In the final analysis, the question about the epistemological status of modern-type victims' rights is tantamount to a dispute about whether or not *restorative justice* is to be considered as a new paradigm in the technical meaning of the term (as used by Kuhn).[5] In the subsequent section, the position of those who do feel this is the case will be outlined. Section 3 then moves on to critically assess this view. It will be argued that the main properties of restorative justice can to a large extent be incorporated in modernised features of traditional criminal justice systems. Finally, in section 4, it will be demonstrated that a strategy aiming at piecemeal reform of the current system offers a strategy which is superior to the compet-

2. M. Brienen, M. Groenhuijsen & E. Hoegen, 'Evaluation and Meta-Evaluation of the Effectiveness of Victim-Oriented Legal Reform in Europe' *Criminologie* (vol. 33, no. 1, 2000), pp. 121-144.
3. To acknowledge and remedy this deficit, many tools have been designed. On a global level I may refer to the *Handbook on Justice for Victims: On the Use and Application of the Declaration of Basic Principles of Justice for Victims of Crime and Abuse of Power* (United Nations Office for Drug Control and Crime Prevention, Centre for International Crime Prevention, New York 1999) and its corollary: *Guide for Policy Makers: On the Implementation of the United Nations Declaration of the Basic Principles of Justice for Victims of Crime and Abuse of Power* (United Nations Office for Drug Control and Crime Prevention, Centre for International Crime Prevention, New York 1999).
4. A wealth of material is collated and commented on by D. Miers, *An International Review of Restorative Justice* (Crime Reduction Research Series Paper 10, London, 2001).
5. One of the compelling reasons for phrasing the question this way is that many advocates of restorative justice actually claim they are proposing this kind of new paradigm. A different (for other purposes equally useful) 'typology of models' is presented by J. Dignan & M. Cavadino, 'Towards a framework for conceptualising and evaluating models of criminal justice from a victims' perspective' *International Review of Victimology* (1996), pp. 153-182.

ing one with the objective of replacing the existing paradigm of criminal justice with the brand new paradigm of restorative justice.

2. *Analyses of what hampers effective implementation of modern victims' rights in traditional systems of criminal justice*

According to a powerful school of thought, it is the paradigm underlying the present criminal justice system which is responsible for its fatal flaws. This paradigm – the *retributive paradigm* – is condemned as being counterproductive. It is accused of serving neither the best interests of the State (because it does not effectively stop or reduce crime) nor those of its primary 'clients', the perpetrators of crime and their victims. From a victimological point of view it is contended that adopting new victims' rights in a system based on the retributive paradigm can never be regarded as more than paying lip-service to the ideals of restorative justice. The existing legislative policy is criticised as 'going through the motions' of victim care, while at the same time neglecting the underlying interests which are really at stake. Introducing victims' rights in the traditional repressive system of criminal law is considered to be a *contradictio in terminis* because the system itself does not allow any additional perspective to be taken seriously outside the scope of the battle between the prosecutor and the defendant.

Ezzat Fattah is one of the most prominent leaders of this school of thought.[6] His profound criticism of the current model of criminal justice – and its underlying paradigm – is remorseless, even devastating. He claims that the conventional system is 'in a state of crisis' because the retributive paradigm is 'obsolete', it relies on 'inadequate old concepts' and hence it is in 'a state of Anachronism'. These defects are beyond repair, so Fattah concludes: 'All this points to the urgent need for the western nations to rethink, reassess, and modernise the archaic and antiquated criminal codes of the 19th century to bring them to the standards and requirements of the space age and to prepare them for the challenges of the 21st century'.[7] Real progress can only be achieved by abandoning the retributive paradigm of criminal justice. Victims' rights can only be effectively implemented within the framework of a comprehensive new para-

6. E. Fattah, 'From a Guilt Orientation to a Consequence Orientation: A Proposed New Paradigm for the Criminal Law in the 21st Century' in W. Küper & J. Welp ed., *Beiträge zur Rechtswissenschaft*: *Festschrift für Walter Stree und Johannes Wessels zum 70. Geburtstag* (Müller, Heidelberg, 1993), pp. 771-792, and E. Fattah, 'Some reflections on the paradigm of restorative justice and its viability for juvenile justice' in L. Walgrave ed., *Restorative Justice for Juveniles: Potentialities, Risks and Problems* (Leuven University Press, Leuven, 1998), pp. 389-401. Another leading representative of this approach is R.E. Barnett, 'Restitution: A New Paradigm of Criminal Justice' *Ethics: An International Journal of Social, Political and Legal Philosophy* (87/1, 1977), pp. 279-301.
7. *Op. cit.*, p. 773.

digm. Indeed, Fattah announces that the stage seems to be set for a scientific revolution or a paradigm shift in the sense proposed by Kuhn.[8]

A paradigm shift involves a complete and total overthrow of concepts, values, objectives and principles within an academic discipline. Fattah confirms this by outlining the stark contrast between the current system and the model he envisages for the future. His sketch of some basic elements of the proposed new paradigm comprises several compartments.[9]

The first concerns different conceptualisations of crime. In the traditional paradigm of criminal justice, crime is viewed as wrongful, sinful, immoral wicked behaviour that must be punished. An essential element of crime also resides in the fact that it is considered to be an offence against the State; crime is a violation of the public order, affecting society at large. Because crime is defined as an offence against the State, it is obvious that there is no room for interference by the victim in the aftermath of crime: the victim is by definition an outsider who could never be accepted as a serious player during the course of a criminal procedure.[10] Crime is furthermore perceived as a unique, exceptional category of behaviour which is qualitatively different from civil torts and other non-criminal types of behaviour. In other words: there is an ontological reality of crime. Alternatively, in the proposed new paradigm crime is viewed as a harmful, injurious behaviour that needs to be redressed in the present and prevented in the future. Crime is not seen as a manifestation of the wickedness of an individual fellow citizen, but as a social risk, one of the many hazards of life in modern, industrial, technological society. Crime is no longer seen as an offence against the State, but as a human conflict, a dispute between two parties. If this is the case, then it makes sense to also involve both parties on an equal basis in subsequent legal proceedings. Also, there is no recognition of the ontological reality of crime: it is exemplified by behaviour which is neither exceptional nor unique; it is not qualitatively different from tort; it can well be less serious, less injurious and less dangerous than many other types of behaviour outside the scope of criminal law.

The second part deals with fundamental concepts and principles. This touches on the core essence of the difference between the old *guilt-oriented paradigm* and the proposed new *consequence-oriented paradigm*. According to Fattah, the conventional system is based on theological, metaphysical and abstract concepts, whereas the new model is founded on concepts of a sociological, positivist and secular nature. Among the former category he ranks moral guilt, *mens rea* (intent and negligence), malice and wickedness. The latter cate-

8. T. Kuhn, *The Structure of Scientific Revolutions* (2nd edition, University of Chicago Press, Chicago, 1970).

9. See the summarising tables, *op. cit.*, pp. 791-792.

10. Likewise: H. Zehr, *Changing Lenses: A New Focus for Crime and Justice* (Scottdale, Pennsylvania/Waterloo, Ontario 1990), p. 82: 'Since the state is defined as victim, it is not surprising that victims are so consistently left out of the process and that their needs and wishes are so little heeded. Why should their needs be recognized? They are not even part of the equation of crime.'

gory is about harm, injury, loss and endangerment. In the traditional paradigm moral responsibility is the key concept, which is based on the presumption of the free will of the actor. Conversely, the consequence-oriented paradigm focuses on social responsibility which goes hand in hand with the principle of strict liability.

The definition of crime and the fundamental concepts and principles have far-reaching implications for the characteristics and goals of criminal law and procedure: the third and final analytical compartment. According to Fattah, the current system is moralistic and stigmatising. In the new model, this should be replaced by a neutral, objective approach. The present system is idealistic in nature (i.e. its presumptions and vocabulary does not always correspond to social realities) whereas its alternative is based on realism. Traditional criminal law is repressive, retributive and punitive. In the new paradigm, these properties are to be replaced by characteristics such as being regulatory, distributive, utilitarian, restitutive, restorative and preventive. Instead of a depersonalised, authoritarian and adversarial attitude, a personalised and conciliatory approach should be promoted. It is wrong to always look backward, to be oriented to the past; instead, the system should be oriented to the present and the future and thus ought to look forward. Finally, there is a huge difference in the role of – and the connection between – those who have been directly involved in the criminal act. Criminal law as we know it places the discretion in the hands of third parties and distances the feuding parties, and in doing so widens the gap that separates them.[11] In the proposed alternative model the discretion is left in the hands of the parties involved, which brings them together in order to effect reconciliation.

3. *The capacity of the criminal justice system to be responsive to new demands and changing circumstances*

I happen to agree with most of the critical observations made by Fattah and his intellectual companions. There is no doubt that the traditional system of criminal law, as we have known it for a long time in most western jurisdictions, has serious shortcomings. It is highly questionable whether it has served society well; and it is undeniable that it has not served the best interests of the principal parties, namely the offender and the victim. The system has unduly focused on the past and has been insufficiently oriented to the future. Furthermore, it has equally indisputably been preoccupied with allocating blame and inflicting pain instead of aiming at providing amends for the harm that was done to the victim.

So the need for reform is obvious and this has been the case for quite a long time. The real question, then, is about strategy. What appears to be the most effective way to bring about the changes we are aiming for? This issue of

11. The most famous criticism of this aspect was expressed by N. Christie, 'Conflicts as property' *British Journal of Criminology* (17/1, 1977), pp. 1-15.

strategy cannot be disconnected from a reflection on the epistemological nature of the process in which change needs to be brought about. Do the proposed new objectives really call for a new paradigm of criminal justice? If restorative justice promises to be the answer to many of the defects of the current system, does that automatically require that we abandon all basic concepts, values and objectives of the criminal justice system that we grew up with? I am ill-convinced. I feel that the goals and methods of restorative justice can to a large extent be pursued by gradually adapting the traditional system of administering criminal justice. I will argue that for methodological reasons they can even be *more effectively* attained by adopting a piecemeal approach. In short, it will be argued that the prevailing system of criminal justice is much more flexible – much more responsive[12] – than writers like Fattah seem to assume.

Before moving on to answer the question as to whether it is desirable or even inevitable to opt for a new paradigm of criminal justice, it is useful to make some preliminary remarks on the nature of a paradigm. In this chapter the concept of a paradigm is used in the technical sense of the word.[13] That means a paradigm is more than just a sweeping new idea. It is different from just any 'grand design', blueprint or master plan. The concept is used here as elucidated by Kuhn, from the perspective of the history of science.[14]

It has been pointed out that an initial difficulty is caused by Kuhn's multiple definitions of a paradigm. Margaret Masterman, for instance, counted no less than twenty-one different descriptions.[15] For the sake of brevity, I quote only a few significant examples:

> - [Paradigms are] universally recognised scientific achievements that for a time provide model problems and solutions to a community of practitioners.
> -... some accepted examples of actual scientific practice – examples which include law, theory, application, and instrumentation together – provide models from which spring particular coherent traditions of scientific research. The study of paradigms (...) is what mainly prepares the student for membership in the particular scientific community with which he will later practice.
> - To be accepted as a paradigm, a theory must seem better than its competitors, but it need not, and in fact never does, explain all the facts with which it can be confronted.
> - So long as the tools a paradigm supplies continue to prove capable of solving the problems it defines, science moves fastest and penetrates most deeply through

12. The concept of responsive law is used as elaborated by Ph. Nonet & Ph. Selznick, *Law and Society in Transition: Toward Responsive Law* (Harper & Row, New York / Hagerstown / San Francisco / London, 1978).
13. Hence the present discussion does not pertain to the views expressed by writers who use the word 'paradigm' in a more casual way: see for example M. Young, 'Restorative community justice in the United States: a new paradigm' *International Review of Victimology* (1999), pp. 265-277.
14. See footnote 2 *supra*.
15. M. Masterman, 'The Nature of a Paradigm' in I. Lakatos & A. Musgrave ed., *Criticism and the Growth of Knowledge* (Cambridge University Press, Cambridge, 1970), pp. 59-89.

> confident employment of those tools. (...) As in manufacture so in science – retooling is an extravagance to be reserved for the occasion that demands it.

And so on, and so forth. The bottom line of these descriptions – in the sociological sense – is that a paradigm is the sum total of the sources of problem-solving methods and standards which are at a given point in time generally accepted by a given scientific community. Being a general epistemological viewpoint, a paradigm is also an organising principle which can govern perception itself.[16] It is important to notice that this concept of a paradigm cannot be fully understood apart from the way it works in various stages of development of science.[17] To this end two stages must be distinguished: a period of 'normal science' and the revolutionary stage.

During a period of normal science, the paradigm both generates problems and serves as a source of tools and devices to solve these problems. Problems are inescapable. There are always new and unexpected situations which are – at first sight – inconsistent with the theoretical framework provided by the obtaining paradigm (in technical jargon they are called 'anomalies'). It is then considered to be the task of the scientific community to reconcile the prevalent theory with the apparently contradicting data. This is what Kuhn refers to as finding a way out of a 'puzzle'. It is important to note that the existing paradigm determines which puzzles are worth looking into. On top of that, a normal-scientific puzzle always has a solution, which is guaranteed by the paradigm, but it takes ingenuity and resourcefulness on the part of researchers to find it.[18] Another part of the period of 'normal science' consists of elaborating the paradigmatic theories and generating answers to questions which have up to then only been raised by the paradigm.[19] The key-insight which we need to keep in mind is that the mere fact that there are anomalies – discrepancies between theory and observed facts – is in itself neither unusual nor disturbing. Quite often it turns out that after a while an explanation is discovered or the paradigmatic theory can be adapted in a way which reconciles it with the problematic empirical findings. Also, even persistent and generally acknowledged anomalies do not always lead to a crisis in the cycle of normal science.

The picture only changes when the paradigm starts to show a continuous inability to solve normal-scientific puzzles. Even then, the deep commitment to

16. In Popperian language this would be called 'the searchlight theory of science'. See K. Popper, *The Open Society and its Enemies, Part II, The High Tide of Prophecy: Hegel, Marx and the Aftermath* (5th edition, Routledge and Kegan Paul, London, 1966), p. 260, and *Conjectures and Refutations* (4th edition, Routledge and Kegan Paul, London, 1972), pp. 45 ff.
17. M. Masterman, *op. cit.* p. 70: '(I)f we ask what a Kuhnian paradigm is, Kuhn's habit of multiple definition poses a problem. If we ask, however, what a paradigm *does*, it becomes clear at once (assuming always the existence of normal science) that the construct sense of "paradigm", and not the metaphysical sense or metaparadigm, is the fundamental one'.
18. Th. Kuhn, *op. cit.* p. 36, p. 60, p. 131.
19. Th. Kuhn, *op. cit.* pp. 46-50.

tradition will inhibit many members of the scientific community to abandon their previously held beliefs and values. It is only when an alternative paradigm has surfaced, that fundamental change can be contemplated. The intellectual competition between a dominant paradigm and its potential successor is not completely governed by rational considerations. For the most part, Kuhn describes the eventual transition process in near-religious terms. Transferring allegiance to a new paradigm is like an act of faith; it comes close to being converted to a different denomination. An existing paradigm never loses its prominence because it clashes with a single anomaly. It can only perish – over time – in competition with a succeeding paradigm.[20] Yet the alternative paradigm has to meet at least two standards in order to be acceptable for the community of professional researchers. First, the new candidate must hold a promise to provide a solution for a vitally important and generally acknowledged problem which cannot be tackled in any different way.[21] And secondly the emerging new paradigm must retain a substantial part of the problem-solving capacity of the competing old paradigm. Only if and when these conditions are met, a paradigm shift may be in the air. When successful transition has been completed, Kuhn speaks of a scientific revolution.

For the purposes of the present contribution, it is important to keep in mind that the battle between competing paradigms is a struggle for life. There can only be one winner. Because of the 'incommensurability' of the theoretical frameworks, there is no room for compromise. One cannot have it both ways by picking preferred bits and pieces from two competing paradigms. Against this background we can now turn our attention again to the epistemological status of restorative justice.

Back to restorative justice: the basic question to be addressed in this section is whether it is desirable – or even necessary – to pursue the objectives of restorative justice within the framework of a completely new legal paradigm. Taking into account the information collated in the preceding paragraphs, the first step towards an answer could be that it is most certainly *possible* to position restorative justice as a new paradigm in the technical sense of the word. The exposition by Fattah *cum suis* makes it abundantly clear that the quest for restorative justice can be shaped in a way which is 100 per cent incompatible with the traditional criminal justice system. The next question then appears to be: is this *the only* viable way of looking at restorative efforts in the aftermath

20. J.O. Wisdom, 'The Nature of "Normal" Science' in P. Arthur Schilpp ed., *The Philosophy of Karl Popper*, Vol. 14 in *The Library of Living Philosophers* (Open Court Publishing Company, La Salle, Illinois, 1974), p. 829: 'Such facts give a sociological basis for the idea that scientific theories do not get refuted; like old soldiers, they only fade away. This is the sort of impression Kuhn conveys'.

21. M. Masterman, *op. cit.* p. 82: '*not* just an incidental counter-argument to the theory, or an awkward fact, which Kuhn correctly characterizes as merely an "irritant". Neither is it an extra-paradigmatic novelty, nor a problem which used to exist within the field at an earlier stage, but which the developers of the paradigm have now suppressed and rendered invisible, because it is incompatible with the paradigm's "basic commitment". The anomaly, to be a true anomaly, has to be produced from within the paradigm'.

of crime? Furthermore: would this be *the most fruitful approach* when we try to balance expected advantages and unexpected drawbacks of such a move? Again, I do not feel this to be the case. When restorative justice is positioned as a brand new comprehensive paradigm, the capacity of the currently prevailing paradigm of criminal justice to adapt to new circumstances is seriously underestimated. The potential of our traditional system to meet new standards and additional demands deserves more credit than it is given by its critics. *Quod erat demonstrandum.*

On a conceptual level, Fattah contends that the first obstacle to change resides in the definition of crime. According to conventional wisdom, crime is defined as an offence against the State, a breach of the public order. This explains why the prosecutor acts as the representative of society in a criminal trial, and it has also led to the expulsion of the victim from these proceedings. In my view, however, this line of reasoning rests upon a dysfunctional reading of the definition of crime. From the indisputable starting point that the State is indeed affected by criminal acts – because crime is a disruption of the *public* order – some writers incorrectly infer that the State is *the real victim*[22] or even *the only victim*. There is no compelling logic supporting this inference. Crime is clearly *more* than just an offence against the State, or against society. In quite a few modern jurisdictions it is explicitly recognised that, although the State is actually affected by criminal acts, the crime still is first and foremost a violation of the individual victim's rights. There is no single dogmatic obstacle towards acknowledging this basic fact. If and when the definition of crime is then expanded (or interpreted more broadly) in this way, it opens up new avenues to take the victims' interests into account in the aftermath of the victimising incident. It offers a dogmatic justification for additional victims' rights in criminal procedure, as well as providing a solid basis for taking victims' interests into account when determining which punitive response can be regarded as adequate.[23]

There is more than just that. We have to be cautious not to take things upside down. When Fattah and Zehr criticise the one-sidedness of the definition of crime, they tend to overstate their case. They substitute the State by the victim as *the sole* entity affected by crime. In my view, this is clearly a bridge

22. H. Zehr, *op. cit.*, p. 82.

23. B.-D. Meier, 'Restorative Justice: A New Paradigm in Criminal Law?' *European Journal of Crime, Criminal Law and Criminal Justice* (6/2, 1998), pp. 125-139, p. 127: '... historically the necessary abstraction and institutionalisation has led to a diminution of the role of the victim in the criminal justice process, a reduction of the real-life person stricken with injury, loss and fear to that of the bearer of a specific function in an abstract, institutionalised and depersonalised procedure. The objective of the idea of restorative justice, therefore, is to bring the personal and individual levels of the offence, the experience of the harm and the consequences of the offence for the lives of the victim and others, back to light and reintegrate these aspects into the process of criminal justice. The aim of restorative justice is not (...) the abolishment of criminal justice, but an amendment to and perhaps the completion of the criminal justice system by drawing the attention to elements which have for a long time been rather neglected'.

too far. Crime is still more than just a dispute between two private parties; it involves more than a quarrel between two individuals.[24] Because of the nature of the infraction, the victim has a legitimate right to claim the full support of the legal order in the aftermath of crime. He is entitled to the solidarity of society, precisely because the violation of his private interests also constitutes a breach of the public order. From this perspective it is only appropriate – as well as beneficial for victims – that the State acts as a representative of society in general and of the victim in particular when it prosecutes crime. This point is particularly well articulated in a policy-document issued by the European Forum for Victim Services:

> Throughout Europe, the State has assumed responsibility for prosecuting offenders and has removed from the victim the burden of responsibility for determining any action to be taken in respect of the offender. The acceptance of responsibility by the State should be recognised as a fundamental right of victims of crime, and no attempts should be made to erode this by returning the responsibility for decision making to victims.[25]

The point may be underscored by means of a few remarks on the relevance of the particular institutional framework in which restitution is being awarded to a crime victim. Empirical evidence confirms that reparation paid by an offender to the victim within the framework of a *criminal* trial has more impact than the same amount of money being transferred as a result of a claim for damages – based on tort – in a *civil* court.[26] The moral support for this kind of financial amends by the constitutional authority of institutions like the public prosecutor and the trial judge enhances justice. It fortifies the conviction that financial compensation for victims is not only a private affair, but is also to be regarded as serving demands of public interest.

Fattah further argues that criminal law is by nature moralistic, stigmatising, oriented to the past or even exclusively looking backward. It would require a completely new system to be realistic, utilitarian, oriented to the present and the future. In my view, however, the dogmatic separation of punishment on the one hand and financial reparation or restitution on the other, is a historical contingency. The fundamental distinction between punishment and reparation is a dogmatic aberration; it clearly constitutes a conceptual misunderstanding which can and should be remedied within the current paradigm of criminal justice.

24. I am not particularly referring to petty crime. The following comments are basically about more serious instances of crime.

25. European Forum for Victim Services, *Statement of Victims' Rights in the Process of Criminal Justice* (London, 1996), p. 5 (under the heading 'Principles for the establishment of victims' rights').

26. See J.J.M. van Dijk, 'Strafrechtshervormingen ten behoeve van het slachtoffer in internationaal perspectief' *Justitiële Verkenningen* (9, 1988), pp. 7-27 and J. Shapland & al., *Victims in the Criminal Justice System* (Hants, Gower, Cambridge, 1985).

Quite a few jurisdictions have already proven that it is feasible as well as fruitful to transcend the distinction between punishment and court-ordered restitution. The most obvious example of this is the successful introduction of the *compensation order*.[27] The rationale behind the compensation order – and similar penal sanctions which have surfaced in other jurisdictions under different names – is that forcing an offender to pay restitution to the victim will serve all of the well established goals of traditional types of punishment.[28] A very brief clarification of this point has to suffice.[29] In a way, this type of restitution can be considered as the most literal form of *retribution*. With regard to special prevention or *rehabilitation*, it is likely that the awareness that one has to pay for the damage one has inflicted will at least have the same dissuasive effect on possible re-offending as the imposition of a fine to be paid to the government. The same is true – *mutatis mutandis* – for general prevention, or *deterrence*. Finally, the goal of *conflict resolution* is only on a very high level of abstraction promoted by traditional forms of punishment; the compensation order probably has more tangible effects in this respect.

Of course, the main argument against this has always been that punishment must be strictly understood as intentional infliction of pain. In the traditional retributive paradigm, the occurrence of a crime is supposed to trigger an automatic response. The guilty state of mind of the offender (*mens rea*) calls for *just deserts*. This is regarded as a basic principle of justice, irrespective of the anticipated beneficial or detrimental effects of the imposition of such a penalty. Within the framework of this perspective, forced reparation to the victim could never count as real punishment. There are supposed to be two main reasons why a compensation order could not be accepted as punishment *per se*. One is that there is a pre-existing obligation (emanating from civil law) to reimburse the victim for damage, so that forced reparation does not add anything in terms of adverse consequences of the crime. The second reason is that even when the compensation order would be accepted within the framework of a criminal trial, it could never be imposed with the intention of inflicting pain on the perpetrator and hence it would still have to be excluded from the list of available punitive sanctions.

27. D. Moxon, J.M. Corkery & C. Hedderman, *Developments in the use of compensation orders in magistrates' courts since October 1988* (London: HMSO 1992), and the general overview in M.E.I. Brienen & E.H. Hoegen, *Victims of Crime in 22 European Criminal Justice Systems*, (Wolf Legal Publishers, Nijmegen, 2000), ch. 26, pp. 1057-1101. This study clearly shows that the compensation order-model (restitution as *penal* sanction) is much more beneficial to victims than the partie civile-model (restitution following a *civil* claim for damages during the criminal trial).

28. See J.W. De Keijser, *Punishment and Purpose: From Moral Theory to Punishment in Action* (Thela Thesis, Amsterdam/Leiden, 2000).

29. More on this is provided by B.-D. Meier, *op. cit.* pp. 130 ff., H.-J. Albrecht, 'Kriminologische Perspektiven der Wiedergutmachung: Theoretische Ansätze und empirische Befunde' in A. Eser *& al.* ed., *Neue Wege der Wiedergutmachung im Strafrecht* (Max-Planck-Institut, Freiburg i.Br., 1990), pp. 43-72, and M. Cavadino & J. Dignan, 'Reparation, Retribution and Rights' *International Review of Victimology* (1997), pp. 233-253.

In my view, these objections reveal a remarkable lack of sociological or empirical consciousness. Plausible as they may look from a narrow perspective of legal doctrine, they completely ignore the reality as experienced by the principal clients of the system: the victim and the offender. For the offender, there is no difference between the imposition of a fine on the one hand and an obligation to pay (the same amount of) restitution on the other. The proceeds of the crime have usually long been spent, thus the financial burden is equal in both situations. For the offender, the hardship – the pain – is neither affected by the recipient of the financial offer he has to make (the state or the victim) nor by its legal origin (tort/civil law vs. crime/punishment). This is the main justification for a steadily increasing number of jurisdictions in elevating compensation orders to the same legal status as the more traditional types of financial punitive sanctions.

Even when this is persistently rejected on dogmatic grounds, as is the case in many German speaking environments, it does not automatically follow that reparation is beyond the scope of criminal law. Löschnig-Gspandl, for instance, holds the opinion that there remains a fundamental gap between the goals of punishment and the goals of restitution. In a carefully reasoned argument, though, she further stipulates that efforts to promote reparation by the offender to the victim do coincide with the objectives of the criminal justice system and hence can and must be incorporated into the penal process.[30]

Quite a few advocates of restorative justice complain about the theological and metaphysical nature of the basic concepts of criminal law. The moral type of guilt is a case in point. However, this type of criticism begs the question of what damage could be done – and to whom – by entering a moral aspect in the equation. The moral dimension of the decision on guilt (*mens rea*) seems to be one of the key parts of the justification of state interference in the aftermath of crime, and this is not entirely without reason. When the state has failed to protect its citizens against criminal victimisation, the least it can do is to show solidarity with the victim in the aftermath of the crime. This acknowledgement of victimisation includes the allocation of moral blame: part of the process is about determining to what extent the offender is responsible for the criminal act and for the damage it has caused. The public display of disapproval of the criminal act helps to restore the victim's sense of order. It contributes to the victim's belief in a just society. And it assists victims in the process of coping with the effects of crime.

Thus from the perspective of the victim there is very little wrong with some of the fundamental moral elements in the dogmatic superstructure of crime and punishment. On the contrary, experience shows that it is quite often the narrow legal definitions of tort law which prove to be beyond understanding for the victim of crime. The pioneering study of Brienen and Hoegen concludes that the 'first technical impediment that commonly frustrates the general realisation of compensation for the victim through the adhesion model is the *strict adher-*

30. M. Löschnig-Gspandl, *Die Wiedergutmachung im österreichischen Strafrecht: Auf dem Weg zu einem neuen Kriminalrecht*? (Verlag Österreich, Vienna, 1996), pp. 71 ff.

ence to the principle of civil liability'.[31] Civil law is not a promising solution for crime victims, it is one of the historical roots of their problems.

Returning to the main question of this section: what about the capacity of the criminal justice system to be responsive to new demands and changing circumstances? Zehr is ruthless in his final judgement:

> Over time dysfunctions begin to develop as more and more phenomena do not fit the paradigm. However, we keep trying to rescue the model by inventing epicycles, reforms, which piece it together. Eventually, though, the sense of dysfunction becomes so great that the model breaks down and is replaced by another.[32]

According to Zehr, victim compensation and assistance may be viewed as another such epicycle, vainly trying to improve things within the malfunctioning framework of criminal law as it still exists today. As Zehr puts it, this approach seeks to remedy a problem in the existing paradigm but it does not question basic assumptions about the state's and the victim's role in justice: 'They recognise a legitimate problem but not the root source of the problem.'[33] I respectfully disagree. In the preceding paragraphs I have tried to demonstrate that the criminal justice system – and its underlying conceptual framework – can be reformed step by step, in order to better serve the needs of all individuals concerned.[34] In the terminology used by Thomas Kuhn: those who argue for restorative justice as a new paradigm apparently underestimate the problem-solving capacity of the currently prevailing paradigm.

4. *Two strategies for effecting change*

The result of the preceding sections is that there appear to be two strategies available for improving the status of victims' rights within the legal system. One is to aim for a change in paradigm; the other is to opt for piecemeal reform of the current paradigm of criminal justice. These strategies are mutually exclusive. So we are compelled to determine which one looks most promising from the point of view of effectively promoting victims' interests. My own

31. Brienen & Hoegen, *op. cit.*, p. 1070: 'The strict adherence to the principle of civil liability should be slackened to allow the criminal court to (a) estimate, rather than establish accurately, the level of damages, and (b) take the means of the offender into consideration so that a realistically enforceable amount is awarded rather than a castle in the air'.
32. H. Zehr, *op. cit.*, p. 92.
33. H. Zehr, *op. cit.*, p. 93.
34. Perhaps this is the best moment to emphasise that 'piecemeal' reform and acting 'step by step' do include possibilities of *fundamental reform*, and can easily go hand in hand with remarkable boldness, as may have become evident in the preceding exposition on the changing concepts of crime and punishment. The word 'piecemeal' is to be understood in the limited meaning of referring to 'non-paradigmatic'.

preference is for the piecemeal approach. There are two sets of arguments supporting this position.

The first cluster of arguments is derived from the nature of a paradigm, as explained in the previous section. A paradigm refers to a complete 'world view'. It comprises all convictions, concepts, values, priorities and principles prevalent in a given academic discipline. It also entails objectives, goals and standards of success. The comprehensive – all encompassing – nature of a paradigm has far-reaching theoretical and practical implications. The most striking one is that competing paradigms are, in Kuhn's words, 'incommensurable'. The incommensurability of different paradigms means there is an 'incomplete logical contact' between them. In ordinary language this means that advocates of different paradigms can hardly engage in a productive dialogue. Success and improvements within the framework of one paradigm are regarded as irrelevant or futile within another. Thus arguing for a new paradigm manifestly limits room for rational debate. There is no common ground to serve as a basis for communication, let alone for persuasion.

The features of the theoretical concept of a paradigm yield two specific arguments against a strategy of paradigm change in favour of restorative justice. First, the absence of any room for compromise leads to a final choice between either criminal justice or restorative justice. If the inevitable decision is presented in this binary way, it seems extremely unlikely that a general sentiment will swing in the latter direction. It does not seem realistic to expect that a majority in the academic community will be prepared to completely abandon all the existing basic propositions of criminal law and procedure. On top of that, it has to be kept in mind that there are many more stakeholders in the operation of the criminal justice system.[35] Legislators, politicians, professionals like judges, prosecutors and defence attorneys, as well as the public at large, they all have ideas, opinions and quite often even strong feelings about crime and the best ways to respond to crime. The point here is that academic discourse in this area does not prosper in a social vacuum. It is – by contrast – strongly interconnected with cultural circumstances prevailing in society at a given period in time. Taking this kind of socio-cultural intangibles into account, it looks all the more unlikely that there will be a radical – indeed: a revolutionary – shift in world-view leading to the overthrow of all previously held convictions surrounding the concepts of crime and punishment. In this sense, legal doctrine is different from, for instance, the domain of theoretical physics.

The second argument is closely linked to the first one. It points to the problem that there is *no way of managing the transition process* from one paradigm to another. The transition process is described as a quasi-religious experience, a collective conversion to a new belief. Since there is no opportunity for rational debate between the converted and the not-yet-converted (see above),

35. Specific attention to the various constituencies of restorative justice is also given by K. Roach, 'Changing punishment at the turn of the century: Restorative justice on the rise' *Canadian Journal of Criminology* (2000), pp. 249-280.

there are no guidelines on how to effectively advocate a dominant status for the new paradigm. This only compounds reservations concerning the possibility that restorative justice could ever prevail at the expense of the traditional system of administering criminal justice.[36] In this light, aiming for a new paradigm does not even come close to a potentially successful strategy for promoting victims' rights.

The second set of considerations supporting my preference for a strategy of piecemeal reform is also based on the allegedly comprehensive nature of the alternative model of restorative justice. Let me first recall the basic conditions which have to be met in order for a potential new paradigm to be acceptable to the scientific community. According to Kuhn, the new paradigm must hold a promise to leave a major part of the problem-solving capacity of the old paradigm intact. And on top of that it should offer a solution for a major and generally acknowledged problem which cannot be overcome in any other way.

In my view, it is highly questionable whether these standards are met by restorative justice as a paradigm candidate. During the Ninth International Symposium on Victimology, Weitekamp correctly observed: 'Even if we would come close to [a system of restorative justice] we still need parts of the current system in order to guarantee the rights of offenders and foremost of victims who do not want to participate in programs of restorative justice. Further on we will have offenders for whom this approach will not work and who have to be incarcerated in order to protect citizens, communities and societies.'[37] No doubt this point ought to be generalised. We need a punitive criminal justice system for the large number of cases where restorative justice just does not work. The existing system of criminal justice is indispensable, for instance, in cases of 'victimless crime', such as trafficking in illegal narcotics.[38] Furthermore, we could not do without traditional criminal law in instances where a larger group of citizens is victimised, in such a way that individuals are not affected to an extent that justifies mediation or other types of restorative interventions: environmental crime or economic crime are obvious examples of this. And last but not least, some cases of hard-core crime are so serious that it would – for the time being – be inconceivable to consider them as a private affair between the offender and the victim. Murder and rape leap to mind, of course.[39] Adding to

36. It must be noted that when restorative justice is presented as a new paradigm, it can only succeed by eliminating criminal law as we have known it for centuries. In this sense, it cannot be denied that the movement pressing for a new paradigm is essentially abolitionist in nature.

37. E.G.M. Weitekamp, 'The Paradigm of Restorative Justice: Potentials, Possibilities and Pitfalls' in J.J.M. van Dijk *& al.* ed., *Caring for Crime Victims: Selected Proceedings of the Ninth International Symposium on Victimology* (Monsey, New York, 1999), pp. 122-123.

38. This point has been made before by, among others, L. Zedner, 'Victims' in M. Maguire *& al.* ed., *The Oxford Handbook of Criminology* (Clarendon Press, Oxford, 1994), p. 1239.

39. B.-D. Meier, *op. cit.*, p. 131: 'There are good reasons to assume that somewhere there is a border beyond which the general public is not willing to accept restorative justice as

this is the problem that in a majority of cases the perpetrator is never found or arrested. In all of these instances the concept of restorative justice as advocated in a new paradigm loses much of its meaning. Yet even when the offender is not apprehended, the victim is still in need of some assistance and support by law enforcement agencies. His interests must be taken care of. Thus he needs information and other rights against the government during the investigation.

It is important to be aware of the fact that these limitations cannot be presented or interpreted as exceptions to the rule. Restorative justice is not a promising new paradigm which is – because of the infant stage of its development – confronted with some challenging anomalies (in the examples just referred to) which will disappear in due time. Quite the opposite appears to be the case. Criminal law in its traditional structural form will *at least* remain *part of* our conception of justice in the extended future. To recognise this inevitable fact is by definition incompatible with the claim that restorative justice is a new paradigm in the true sense of the word.

5. *Concluding remarks*

Restorative justice is a great idea, a convincing philosophy and a wonderful inspiration. But it is not a new paradigm. The idea is being used – as it ought to be – to reform and improve the criminal justice system step by step. These steps need not be small or insignificant ones. Quite the contrary: piecemeal reform can actually take the form of the proverbial giant leap.[40] As Martin Wright remarked before, it is better to think not of alternatives but of a continuum, and to work to move the centre of gravity from the repressive towards the restorative.[41] In this sense, restorative justice can be a guiding principle.[42] The concepts and objectives it has yielded can lead to carefully planned and evaluated experiments aimed at improving the position of victims in the criminal

---

the only form of reaction to the offence but calls for retribution and punishment', with additional references.

40. Examples of this have been outlined in the preceding sections, where redefinitions of the concepts of crime and punishment have been discussed *within* the framework of the currently existing system.

41. M. Wright, 'Can Mediation be an Alternative to Criminal Justice?' in B. Galaway & J. Hudson ed., *Restorative Justice: International Perspectives* (Monsey, New York & Amsterdam, 1996), pp. 227-237. Idem: C. Pelikan, 'UN draft resolution on restorative justice programmes in criminal matters' *Newsletter of the European Forum for Victim-Offender Mediation and Restorative Justice* (Vol. 3, Issue 1, February 2002), p. 7: 'Great emphasis was put on the fact that RJ programmes are complementary to the CJS, not an alternative and not at all intended to replace the conventional system'.

42. The same conclusion was reached by B.-D. Meier, *op. cit.*, p. 139: 'The assessment that the idea of restorative justice stands for a "paradigm shift" in the criminal law system is certainly too euphoric. Instead, it seems more appropriate to describe restorative justice as a new perspective in the criminal law system.'

justice system. This is the most responsible – and effective – way of shaping reform.

Just a final remark on the practical relevance of the basic question addressed in the present exposition. It may seem somewhat academic to explore the technical meaning of the concept of a paradigm and to see how restorative justice fits into that concept. Why not allow a more casual use of the word paradigm? After all, it can hardly be contested that restorative justice is a relatively new, broad, appealing idea.

In my view it is important to understand the exact epistemological status of restorative justice, because this also has significant practical implications. When university students are educated on the virtues of restorative justice, they are usually interested and perceptive. The same is true for law enforcement officials such as police and public prosecution officers. They only turn apprehensive when they are being told that the only way to take restorative justice seriously is to abandon all beliefs, concepts and objectives attached to the traditional system of criminal law. For most people, this just goes too far. So in order to promote interest in the potential of restorative justice it is important to state the exact nature and extent of the proposed reform efforts. Victims' rights are about improving a system, not about abolishing a system and then starting from scratch.

Thomas Kuhn's book on scientific revolutions has been extraordinarily influential. It has also been misinterpreted. After the book was published, some thinkers felt that the only way to really contribute to academic discourse is to propose or conduce to a scientific revolution. Kuhn meant something different. Progress is usually achieved during periods of 'normal science'.

5. Against the Pain of Punishment: Retribution as Reparation through Penal Servitude

Hendrik Kaptein*

1. *Introduction*

Not too long after restorative justice ideas and ideals took the scholarly world of crime studies by storm (and even led to restorative practice, however scattered), uneasiness about things restorative is rising. Typical restorative justice measures like victim-offender meetings may be more or less adequate in dealing with lesser crime, for example street robbery without lasting physical (and hopefully, mental and emotional) consequences. In such cases, restorative justice may do good to everybody concerned, while punitive measures may be superfluous or even counterproductive. But how would restorative justice look like in cases of murder? Apart from a few exceptions, talking with surviving relatives seems just as senseless as talking to the dead themselves.

Or: petty crime only may be dealt with by restorative justice, serious crime cannot be but punished in a real sense, it seems. That is, even if conferencing with relatives would lead to victim satisfaction in a few cases, still punishment as infliction of pain for public purposes seems inescapable. But then restorative justice in its turn is strongly motivated by all too well known theoretical and practical problems and shortcomings of current punitive systems, even in highly developed legal orders.

How to get out of this predicament? A common theme in restorative justice approaches is the incompatibility of restorative justice and retribution. Adequately dealing with offenders is seen as something at odds with or at least completely different from adequately dealing with victims. This may be a fundamental misunderstanding, the solution of which may well lead to integration of justice for victims and punishment. *Retribuere* originally means: to pay back, to restore, in contrast to its current 'meaning' in terms of hitting back in kind or worse. Or: offenders are to completely compensate for what they did wrong.

Such retribution suitably reinterpreted is not at all at odds with justice for victims. It is at the core of it, starting from the basic principle that what one does wrong, one ought to redress oneself. This may be called civilised criminal

* Faculty of Law, University of Amsterdam.

law in two senses. First, civil law concepts of damage are suitably reinterpreted and integrated in criminal law and punishment. Second, it is civilisation in a wider sense, in doing away with suffering as the essence of punishment. Criminal procedure and punishment need to be reoriented toward full restitution, compensation and reparation as the main sanction. Thus civilised criminal law aims at integration of restorative justice on the one hand, and criminal procedure and punishment on the other. Retribution as complete compensation for victims by offenders themselves is to replace punishment as suffering.

Compensation for crime victims is not new, of course. In theory and increasingly in practice, however scattered, many criminal and/or civil law compensatory measures for crime victims are to be found. The conception to be developed here differs from this in aiming at complete integration of forfeiture, punishment and compensation, on the basis of a conception of compensation for harm transcending criminal law. Criminal law and punishment attempting to offer humanly acceptable answers to crime cannot be but based on conceptions of acceptable answers to harm in general.

Discussion of this will proceed as follows. § 2 offers one more critical overview of standard attempts to justify punishment as suffering, their sometimes painful failure and their unexpected potential in backing a better view of punishment. § 3 explains outlines of moral psychology of wrongful harm, resentment and reparation as not just a basis for meaningful personal relationships, but also for state intervention in order to make criminal offenders pay for what they did wrong. In § 4 this moral basis for reparation by offenders is translated in terms of penal servitude on behalf of victims. Offenders going free or judged to be not responsible for their criminal conduct are not to stand in the way of victims' compensation (§ 5). § 6 outlines a few basic advantages of what may be called civilised criminal law in more than a few senses. But of course even with civilised criminal law not all is well, as will inconclusively appear in § 7. § 8 outlines principles of civilised criminal procedure, partly determined as it is by roles and rights of crime victims. More specifically, rules of criminal evidence and proof may be reformed in the light of victims' rights and interests (§ 9). § 10 contains an attempt to outline the future of civilised criminal law.

2. *Pressing problems and hidden powers in popular attempts to justify punishment as infliction of pain*

The need for rethinking criminal law and punishment is not just a consequence of attention to victims' rights and interests. The human costs of punishment by imprisonment are huge on all accounts, even in contemporary legal orders under the rule of law. Though this has been stressed many times before in vain, a brief summary of suffering under current criminal procedure and punishment may still be apposite. Marginalising and criminalising effects of imprisonment are evident, still apart from undeserved suffering of inmates' relatives. Not for nothing, consequences of state punishment have been compared to the ravages of war, famine, pestilence and other disasters beseeching mankind. Some of these disasters have been more or less overcome by much human effort.

Criminal law and punishment, on the other hand, are inevitably felt and judged to be indispensable. This at least seems to be the state of mind of democratic majorities, backed by ever more punitive electorates. But of course this cannot come down to any real justification at all, if only because few if any legislators, never having been in prison for any length of time, really know what they are deciding about. The same holds good for the majority of law-abiding citizens. The prison system (and capital punishment in a few morally underdeveloped 'legal orders') is a sad symbol of the modern state's failure to deal with violation of the rules. Reasonable rules galore, but as soon as citizens seriously violate them, they are simply put away in cages, by want of any idea what really to do with them.

Of course, there is an abundance of attempts at theoretical justification of criminal law and punishment as infliction of pain, in terms of retribution and/or special and general prevention of crime. No doubt both prevention of crime and retribution, requiring that crime is reacted to in some or other way are both deeply plausible. Everything ought to be done to prevent crime in the first place, just as no crime may pass without any consequences for the offender. On the other hand, apologetic attempts to apply both kinds of justification to punishment as infliction of pain lead to well-known and seemingly insuperable difficulties.

Thus preventive theories cannot really explain why large scale petty crime and its social costs may not be countered by setting terrifying examples, like hanging a few loiterers in order to effectively scare the hell out of the rest. Special prevention is effectively served by such and like measures as well, but again locking petty offenders up for life or worse does not seem to be justifiable on any count. This still apart from the well-nigh universally accepted fact that none too great preventive effect is to be expected from the promise or even reality of harsh punishment against serious crime. (More or less effective social control through fines against traffic violations and comparable offences is an exception of course.)

One more strange quality of preventive theories is the lack of any direct connection between the offence committed and the punishment meted out against it. Once committed, the offence itself is no more than one of many relevant considerations. Or: for this reason as well, offenders are reduced to social engineering factors. Adding to this is the real possibility that even highly developed systems of criminal law and punishment will not lead to a positive balance of human good by prevention of crime over the sum total of the cost of criminal procedure and punishment. Offenders and so many others suffer greatly for the purpose of a marginally safer society at best.

Against this, it may be objected that offenders' suffering is less important than increase in well-being for other parts of the population. Added to this may be the idea that victims of crime may feel satisfaction as a consequence of offenders' pain through punishment. True, but then prevention is no longer the essence of punishment. Retribution comes to the fore, then: offenders presumably deserve to be punished and for that reason alone their suffering is deemed irrelevant in any balancing of social costs. Their suffering is the essence of their deserved punishment, it is contended. Objections to this interpretation of retribution are obvious again. How can still more suffering undo the pain of crime? Religious and profane metaphors depicting retribution as purification of sinners' souls or interpretations of retribution as 'signals of society indicating that wrongdoing will not be tolerated' cannot salvage retribution through infliction of pain.

It may be clear by now that both prevention and retribution (and so many attempts to combine them) got stuck in their usual apologetic roles. Behind this is the strangely unquestioned assumption that punishment cannot be but infliction of pain. In as far as this is taken to be true by definition, all fruitful discussion is forestalled beforehand. But neither prevention nor retribution need be limited to this. Prevention may be more effectively served by so many measures apart from punishment, at less human cost (but see also § 6 on preventive effects of civilised criminal law).

Retribution does not necessarily imply infliction of suffering either. Again, *retribuere* means: to restore, to pay back, which is what people expect from wrongdoers in general, whether criminal or not. A more fundamental discussion is apposite here: what is to be done by victims and offenders outside the confines of criminal law, in the daily life and times of individuals, inevitably and sometimes intentionally harming each other at times? May there be any sensible generalisations on this issue and if so, that are implications for dealing with criminal offenders and their victims?

3. *Moral psychology, or how to reverse the course of history*

In contrast to a lot of not always fruitful theory and philosophy of meaning and justification of criminal law and punishment as answers to crime, relatively little is found in criminal legal theory (and in modern moral philosophy, for that matter) on humanly acceptable answers to harm in general (apart from recent discussion of truth and reconciliation issues and other special subjects). This may be an important reason for the relative lack of plausibility and practical importance of such criminal legal theories. (Tort law may fare better in these respects: see for example Coleman, 1992.) Here an attempt will be made to develop a kind of 'internal essentialism' of meaningful answers to the infliction of harm (on the methodological idea of internal essentialism see Nussbaum, 1992). Basic mental and emotional facts of human life and human interaction may suggest principles guiding ways out of harmful predicaments.

Main concepts of infliction of harm, resentment, expression of guilt, apologies, reparation, forgiveness and reconciliation may be clarified by an example from everyday life: a conflict arises between two people, in the company of others. Anger rises and after exchange of ever nastier invectives one of them hits the other in the face. The victim and the rest of the company are startled and feel resentment about this seemingly outrageous misconduct. No good reason for the assault was apparent at all. This is communicated to the actor, who is taken to task. 'I hit him in anger' the actor retorts. But this cannot bring resentment felt by the victim and by the others to rest. Thus the offender is made clear that he failed to justify his conduct.

What is such an offender to do next, on the basis of reasonable expectations of the victim and the bystanders? If resentment and further explanation make clear to him that there was no justification for his assault indeed, he may apologise in the first place. If such apologies are to make any real impression, the actor ought to do something in favour of his victim, at his own expense. He may even do so publicly, in order to abate bystanders' resentment as well. Thus he may buy his victim a drink, or even a substantial present, in order to symbolise both regret and respect and to make up for wrongful losses inflicted. What was unjustly taken away is given back again. This way the victim 'returns to his original position', as things were before harm was done. Forgiveness and reconciliation may be positive end results. Forgiveness may even become superfluous, as there is nothing left to be forgiven after the offender fully compensated for wrong done, through his own effort.

Reactions to harm done are to restore respect and self-respect. Victims may feel lack of respect by being wrongly harmed. Respect may be restored by offenders taking seriously what they did, acknowledging responsibility and repairing wrongs as much as they can. Bystanders' resentment may motivate them all the more to do so. Such bystanders may respect offenders in their turn again, if they accept full responsibility and act on it. Though of course not just depending upon acceptance of responsibility and its consequences, such respect and self-respect are the primary goods of man and society (see Rawls, 1999).

This sequence of human communication and conduct may even be regarded and experienced as a kind of changing the past for the better. Harm was done and undergone, but is restored by constructive retribution, undone in the sequence of apology, reparation and reconciliation. Indeed this is quite unlike retribution in the usual sense as infliction of pain through hitting back in kind. Nothing else than still more harm is the result, then. Still, offenders may suffer under their reparative burdens as well. But then such suffering is a by-product and certainly not the core of retribution.

Essential here are notions of personal and moral resentment. Personal resentment is felt and expressed by victims themselves, moral resentment is felt and expressed by fellow human beings, as a kind of compassion with victims. Such resentment is a complex of judgement, feeling and emotion, made up of normative judgement prohibiting harm, antipathy toward offenders regarded as responsible for what they did, claims to some kind of compensation and desire for communication of all this to offenders and others. Thus there can be no justified resentment against rightful harm, as caused by fair competition, or against clearly compulsory offenders, like epileptics inadvertently striking somebody. In the same way, resentment may be more or less abated when offenders make clear that they did not really mean what they did, and so on.

Still, never feeling and expressing resentment with its attendant expectations seems well-nigh impossible or at least highly undesirable. Victims without any resentment cannot but be regarded as imposing no limits at all to what others may do to them. Thus such victims in more than one sense will not be taken seriously, not even by themselves. It goes without saying that mental and emotional health and well-being depend on expression of personality by making clear what may be done and what may not be done to oneself. In the same way, offenders causing harm without accepting and realising any attendant responsibilities cannot be respected at all, again not even by themselves, though they may be so mentally and emotionally disordered as to know and feel nothing of it.

Expression of resentment is essential for human communication. Without such expression, people will not even understand each other. They cannot know what is important or harmful to them and what is not. In the same way, gratitude, as the positive counterpart of resentment, is a basic precondition for human understanding and community as well. (Strangely enough, few contemporary communitarian conceptions pay attention to resentment and gratitude related to individual responsibility as basic preconditions for community.)

Moral resentment is a basic precondition for community too. Expression of moral resentment by relatives, friends and other fellow human beings is both an expression of solidarity with or even love for victims and a signal to offenders, compelling them to take responsibility for and to repair what they did wrong. Moral resentment makes fellow human beings come to the rescue of more or less powerless victims, threatening offenders with expulsion or worse if they do not take their reparative responsibilities. Moral bonds between all concerned are thus restored. Without compassion in moral resentment, victims, offenders and in fact all concerned are condemned to collective loneliness. George Sand wrote about wrongdoing (see Mason ed., 1955, p. 166):

> Humanity is outraged in me and with me. We must not dissimulate nor try to forget this indignation which is one of the most passionate forms of love.

Of course, sequences of human experience and conduct as explained here are idealisations, to follow upon the less than ideal fact of harm done. To begin with, perceived harm may be no real harm at all, at least not for normal human beings. Narcissist complexes and related illnesses of the mind may make people react forcibly against conduct that was not only unintentional as far as harm was concerned, but also completely harmless to mentally healthy persons. Or victims wrongly ascribe freedom of action to offenders who were in fact unable to prevent what they did. Or real harm may not be wrongful harm after all. (Thus deserted lovers do not tend to keep in mind that there is nothing like a right to be loved by somebody.) Or victims forget about their own responsibilities for harm done to them. Thus the person hit in the face may have been pestering his opponent for quite some time, no longer eliciting an oral response but provoking a manual answer. Though this may not justify offender's conduct, it may still lead to lessening of personal and moral resentment and its consequences.

Next, expression of such resentment may take many different and not always constructive forms, from facial expression and other body language to directly hitting back in active or passive ways, for example by simply walking away. Indeed, one well-known reaction to perceived harm, real or otherwise, is to keep shy of the actor, for example by breaking pre-existing bonds of friendship, family ties or even bonds of love. Also, people hurt may indeed communicate their resentment by simply hitting back in some or other way, harming supposed malefactors in their turn. The same holds good for bystanders' reactions.

Apart from petty cases, such simply hitting back cannot be all of it. No doubt, some or other forceful expression of resentment and even temporarily shunning offenders without further explanation may have positively preventive effects. But of course it should not be the end of things, enlarging expression of resentment and its consequences to punishment as infliction of pain. On the other hand, more than a few (non-criminal) offenders seem to leave no other option, as they do not act upon their responsibilities. More than a few offenders do not even apologise. Even if they do, adequate reparation is not always forthcoming.

A basic problem of modern society (if not only of modern society) is not taking responsibility for one's own conduct. Reasons and causes for this may range from narcissist complexes again to vanity and general lack of interest in other human beings. The concept of guilt is not very popular in contemporary culture anyway. Partly for very good reasons of course, as negative guilt feelings do not add to anybody's quality of life. But a society free from guilt in the sense of feeling and being responsible for one's own conduct and acting to it cannot but be a lonely crowd indeed.

Such responsibility presupposes basic differences between what people do to each other on the one hand, and what happens to them on the other. What is perceived as deliberate conduct causing harm elicits resentment, whereas mere accidents causing harm and suffering cannot understandably lead to any such resentment, though such accidents may lead to many different kinds of human thoughts, judgements, feelings and emotions. Of course, harmful consequences of mere accidents are to be repaired as well. But then there are no specific actors to be held liable and to be put under the obligation to repair harm done. (Imagine the social fate of somebody never ever taking responsibility for his own conduct, like: 'It just happened, there is nothing to be done about it.' In a way, he thus indicates his non-existence as a fellow human being, ranking himself with the accidents and ravages of nature. Respect and self-respect may be incompatible not only with absence of personal responsibility and resentment, but with strong determinism as well.)

In this sense, discussion of resentment and reparation touches upon the free will-determinism issue. Indeed, Strawson (1962, 1985) famously tried to refute determinism by appealing to the unalterable human facts of personal and moral resentment. Unless there are basic differences between free choice and deliberate action on the one hand and what happens as a consequence of whatever causes on the other, there can be no resentment at all. Or human beings were to undergo whatever was done to them or happened to them as just unhappy twists of fate. But such a stance, however much aspired to by ascetics and other otherworldly beings, cannot be the normal attitude, mode of being, of human beings enjoying some sense of respect and self-respect: see among others Butler, 1726, Sermon VIII, § 8 and Hart & Honoré, 1985, pp. lxxx-lxxxi for an unequalled account of this:

> The idea that individuals are primarily responsible for the harm which their actions are sufficient to produce without the intervention of others or of extraordinary natural events is important, not merely to law and morality, but to the preservation of something else of great moment in human life. This is the individual's sense of himself as a separate person whose character is manifested in such actions. Individuals come to understand themselves as distinct persons, to whatever extent they do, and to acquire a sense of self-respect largely by reflection on those changes in the world about them which their actions are sufficient to bring about without the intervention of others and which are therefore attributable to them separately. This sense of respect for ourselves and others as distinct persons would be much weakened, if not dissolved, if we could not think of ourselves as separate authors of the changes we make in the world. If we had to share the authorship of such changes with numerous prior agents, of whom it could be said that, had they not acted as they did, we should not have been able to bring about the change, we could no longer think of ourselves as separate authors in the way we now do. This would be true even if the responsibility of the prior agents was only a prima facie responsibility, which might be excluded, for example, by the absence of some mental element required by law or morality (e.g. intention). For the allocation and apportionment of responsibility for the changes which human action brings about would in that case be inherently a matter of dispute; there would be nothing that we could unequivocally claim to be *our doing*.

The argument from harm, resentment and reparation developed here is, in a sense, Strawsonian anti-determinism put on its head and then next extended. The core of Strawson's argument comes down to free will or actorship as a necessary condition for irreplaceable personal and moral resentment. The argument developed here starts from infliction of harm leading to resentment, to be undone by apologies, restitution and reparation and to be concluded by forgiveness and reconciliation. Whichever way round, this kind of argument relies on resentment as a basic given in human life. As such, concepts of resentment plays all kinds of roles in philosophy and psychology (see Wallace, 1994, Baldwin, 1999, rudimentarily about relationships between resentment and criminal law and Probst, 1992 for an overview). Such resentment is to be distinguished from *ressentiment* and related Nietzschean negative notions. *Sklavenmoral* is the complete opposite of acting upon resentment as an expression of autonomous self-respect.

Against essential relationships of harm, resentment and compensation it may be adduced that resentment, appeal to guilt and the need for reparation of harm done by offenders are culturally relative. Thus it may be thought that some or other real or imaginable society and culture could do without. The possibility of such imagination is not to be denied here. But even a staunch relativist like Posner (1999) asserts the universality of resentment. To this it may be added that the universal occurrence of resentment and related notions may be further explained in terms of universal basic human needs or even in evolutionary terms (see Mackie, 1999). If such descriptive universalism holds good, epistemological relativisms seem to lose interest.

On the other hand, Posner rightly notes that subjects of resentment vary widely, within and between different cultures. Apart from the question whether there may still be common elements, like resentment against wanton killing of people and associated prohibition of it, it may come as no surprise that contents of norms prohibiting harm and consequently of material criminal law may not be completely identical in different societies. So what?

4. *Retribution redefined: penal servitude as integration of forfeit, compensation and punishment*

The essence of handling harm is repairing it. Victims' suffering is to be undone, offenders may suffer resentment and burdens of reparative efforts in their turn. But such offenders' suffering (if it may be called suffering at all) is not the main issue of course. Thus regarded, current punishment is enlargement out of all bounds of just one element in the whole sequence of handling harm: infliction of resentment. Surely offenders may be forcibly made clear that they did wrong. But this cannot be the end of it. Though Duff (1986) and others tried to explain infliction of punishment as a kind of communication, locking up offenders and leaving things at that (for a long time) is a far cry from constructively dealing with harm done.

Remember that relationships of harm, resentment, reparation and reconciliation are presuppositions of respect and self-respect, the primary goods of man and society. Thus such respect and self-respect is to govern reaction to criminal harm as well, with full compensation for crime victims as the main objective.

The core idea in translation of such relationships in terms of criminal procedure and punishment is penal servitude. Offenders' own efforts are to compensate for all material and immaterial consequences of what they did wrong. Thus thieves may pay their debts to victims by performing penal servitude not only covering the costs of material harm done, but also covering mental and emotional harm, however difficult it may be to express such harm in material terms (see also § 7). The symbolic value of such complete payment for victims may be more important than any exact determination of immaterial harm done. Though penal servitude may lead to hardship for offenders, such attendant suffering is not at all the main objective of civilised punishment, if it still deserves that name.

Restorative justice in informal senses, presupposing co-operation of all concerned, may be the optimal expression of this. Unhappily (but naturally) enough, in the real world of crime not all real criminals will ever even join in with such restorative efforts. If they get arrested at all, few of them will freely offer apologies and reparative efforts. Apart from this, crimes against general interests do not seem readily amenable to such informal solutions. Adding to this are real dangers of inequality between mediated and unmediated cases (and between different mediation efforts with possibly rather different results) and possible lack of satisfaction of public moral resentment through mediation. Results of restorative justice through informal efforts may be acceptable to some victims and offenders, but not to other citizens.

Criminal law, then, ought to deal with harm against which victims may not, cannot and/or need not come up themselves. First, prohibition of taking the law in one's own hands is essential of course (though it is a kind of theft from victims as well). Second, in more than a few cases, crime victims are unable to bring offenders to task, if only because more than a few offenders run away with their crimes. Third, victims need not handle criminal harm themselves (of course apart from offences against general interests, to be handled by the state anyway). Moral resentment implies public coercion of reparation whenever possible. Such moral resentment entertained by all is the main motive and force behind public criminal law as solidarity with crime victims. Society, represented by a public administration not having forestalled criminal harm in the first place, is to do everything to undo consequences of crime for victims.

Three kinds of resentment come to the fore, then. First, personal resentment of crime victims. Second, moral resentment in an anonymous sense, as not just expressing solidarity of immediate bystanders, but also public solidarity of all citizens with crime victims. Third, a kind of generalised personal and moral resentment elicited by harm against general interests. Citizens partly identify themselves with such general interests, thus feeling and expressing a kind of generalised personal resentment. There may be moral resentment involved as well, in as far as citizens may resent offences against general interests not directly touching their personal rights and interests (think here of specific conduct crimes like not buckling up).

Indeed, criminal law, suitably civilised or not, deals with more kinds of offences than wrongful harm against individuals. Thus there may be criminal prohibition of harm against general interests, like tax dodging (probably eliciting more than a bit of resentment because of free riding involved). Also, risky activities like carrying firearms are liable to punishment. Harm caused by such offences includes public fear for consequences. Or conduct is criminalised for ordering purposes in the first place: think of traffic regulations (see Feinberg, 1984-1988 for extensive discussion of kinds of criminal harm).

What is to be done, in order to make offenders undo harm and let victims enjoy compensation and satisfaction as far as possible? (Of course, criminal law plays 'prospective', public order, preventive and repressive roles as well. Prevention of crime comes first, punitive reaction to crime, civilised or not, ought to be *ultimum remedium*. But such aspects are not the subject here, though it may be noted that restorative measures against offenders may well have ordering, preventive and repressive side-effects as well: see § 6.)

In the very first place, it goes without saying that penal servitude and other reparative sanctions to be enforced against offenders ought to be codified, at least in terms of minimum and maximum payment related to specific offences. Next, petty offences violating public order regulations without causing any direct harm may be dealt with in purely administrative ways, by imposing petty fines, restoring balance in favour of public interests (to hopefully good preventive effect as well again). More or less the same applies to minor offences directly causing public harm, like littering.

On the other hand, serious and systematic offenders may be sentenced by independent courts to penal servitude like sweeping the streets, as temporary members of cleaning gangs. In such a way, there is both (hopefully educational) confrontation with consequences and restoration by offenders' own efforts. Offenders' suffering through penal servitude (if it may be called by that name at all) is a not unwelcome by-product, then.

In this and in related general interest cases, civilised sanctions may consist of offenders' efforts in restoring harm done in some or other direct way, in more than a few cases. In cases of individual harm things may be rather different. Even apart from mediation not all individual crime victims are looking forward to direct confrontation with offenders' restorative efforts, if possibly effective at all. Thus more than a few rape victims do not want to be confronted with 'their' offenders ever again. This brings to light a fundamental and unavoidable limitation of translation of principles of personal reparation to public spheres of criminal law. Apart from special cases, the only reparative medium available between anonymous people is: money.

Strangely unacceptable as this may seem at first sight, there is no alternative at all. Monetary payment is the main option, just as it is in most cases of civil law damages. In general, nothing else but money is available to restore justice of distribution of goods and services in society, whether based on contract, tort or indeed criminal liability.

On the other hand, crime ought to be paid for from the proceeds of penal servitude. Reparation of wrong done is to happen through offenders' own efforts, if such reparation is to be meaningful in material and in symbolic senses. Crime victims enjoy mental and emotional satisfaction in retribution through offenders' own efforts, leading to real costs and real disadvantages or even suffering for offenders as a not unwelcome by-product again. Mere payment for consequences of serious crime will strike victims as carelessness. Indeed, such mere payment is no option in cases of serious crime. Penal servitude is the principle.

Still, payment of insurance money to victims may be apposite in borderline cases. Such payment may not even be limited to petty offences. Thus involuntary manslaughter may be related to a minimum of negligence, excluding any serious penal servitude to be performed by offenders. Victims may be entitled to both material compensation, to be paid by insurance companies, and a symbolic minimum of payment by offenders themselves in such cases.

Next, payment by offenders themselves may indeed be just payment. But serious crime against individual victims may not just be answered by mere payment from offenders' own means. Again, a basic principle not only of civilised criminal law but also of reparation of any wrong done holds it that offenders are to make good what they did wrong themselves, so as not to get away with it and in order to assuage victims' and others' resentment.

Thus offenders may be sentenced to payment from their wages, as distinct from payment from the whole of their capital. Also, offenders may choose themselves whether to pay by earnings from existing jobs or from extra work. Parts of offenders' earnings may be withheld by employers, to be handed over to the state, analogous to tax systems. A certain freedom of choice in kinds of penal servitude may motivate offenders to do their jobs properly, just as they may work harder to earn compensation if it frees them from penal servitude in less time.

Still, it may be difficult to distinguish between payment from wages and payment from capital, as wealthy offenders may still have paid jobs, if not really in order to cover their living costs. Also, special penal servitude may serve more special purposes, like confrontation, penance or even constructive shaming. (Though civilised criminal law is not about shame in any sense, it does not exclude some or other positive effects of shaming either, for example in confrontation with consequences of what was done wrong. About shaming see Braithwaite, 2002 in the first place.) Thus offenders against physical integrity without lasting consequences may be ordered to be *brancardiers* for some time, rewards of which are to go to their victims again.

Serious or even deadly crime against life and limb may be more or less compensated for by long term special penal servitude only (in as far as such compensation and reparation is possible at all, of course: penal servitude is no panacea for victims' pain: see § 7). In more than a few cases, such penal servitude is to be performed in some or other kind of confinement, for special prevention and/or other reasons (to be discussed later in this paragraph). Confrontation and education effects are not always to be hoped for, then. Still, every offender is to be put to work, however marginal material rewards may be. The symbolic force of making good for what was done wrong remains in force. Such penal servitude contrasts favourably with idle imprisonment anyway.

Public funds covering the costs of crime may be put between offenders and victims. (In current legal orders, such more or less recently instituted funds play relatively marginal roles only, though both theory and practice of such funds are much older: see Brienen & Hoegen, 2000 and Schafer, 1970.) This not only precludes possible problems with any undesirable communication between offenders and victims. Public funds may also be paid for more by the rich and well-earning than by the poor and/or by offenders without much earning power, as criminal justice implies equal burdens for identical offences. Supplements to such funds from public means are probably unavoidable, if there is to be any decent standard of payment to victims, if only for symbolic reasons.

Such funds are also to cover the cost of crime in a wider sense. The necessity of the whole of the criminal law apparatus is offenders' fault only. So the same offenders are to pay for its costs (though civilised criminal law may be much cheaper than current practice: see § 6). Still, offenders' payments may not suffice to cover all costs of crime. The necessity of public supplements to funds covering for the costs of crime acquires a special meaning here. It is the public administration's primary responsibility to protect citizens against each other, not just because of the prohibition of taking the law into one's own hands. If the same public administration fails to prevent crime, it is responsible for all consequences as well. This is related to public administrations' responsibility for covering the costs of crime in cases in which the same public administration did not bring in offenders to perform any penal servitude (see § 5).

Of course, compensation for crime victims is not new (see for example Braithwaite & Pettit, 1990 for a 'republican' view of criminal justice reminiscent of civilised criminal law, Zehr, 2002, and Barnett, 1998, Barnett & Hagel ed., 1977 and Morimura, 2002, to mention a few less well-known contemporary sources). However, civilised criminal law may differ from other proposals and practice in at least three fundamental respects (but see also Schafer, 1970, for an overview of the history of elements of civilised criminal law). First, restorative justice approaches well-nigh universally start from an unbridgeable gap between retribution and reparation (see for example Schafer, 1970, Cavadino & Dignan, 1998, notwithstanding attempts at 'a principled compromise between retribution and reparation' and De Keijser, 2000, pp. 28-31 for an overview). Understandable though this may be, it still is a basic misunderstanding, much fostered by the deep-rooted misunderstanding that retribution cannot be but infliction of pain. Real retribution is something quite different. It is reparation by offenders on behalf of victims.

Second, complete integration of forfeit, compensation and punishment in penal servitude is the core idea of retribution as reparation. Forfeit is realised by offenders' work and payment: offenders lose what they hoped to earn through their crimes. Compensation is realised through payment and through victims' knowledge that offenders did not just pay but had to work for it. Moral resentment of all others is abated in the same way. Lastly, penal servitude has punitive aspects too, in the sense of infliction of pain or at least of extra hardship. Though this pain is not essential, it still is an unavoidable and not unwelcome by-product of the same penal servitude.

Third, civilised criminal law is an attempt to translate essential elements of human relationships to public institutions. If offenders' compensation for wrongful harm is the thing to do between human beings in general, then penal servitude may be the best approximation of such compensation in criminal law. On the other hand, personal reconciliation between victims and offenders is not to be expected in all cases of crime. Victims may simply want to be left alone. Still, full performance of penal servitude restores offenders' full citizenship. Having made good what they did wrong, they are on equal footing with other citizens again.

Indeed, essential for civilised sanctions is their inclusive nature. Nobody is to be locked out of community and society by way of punishment. (Performance of penal servitude as part of a normal job may be a good thing for such reasons as well.) In personal relationships, separation from real or imaginary offenders may be the only answer to perceived harm, or just the only way to end it. Civil society however ought to be everybody's community, offenders included. Locking out wrongdoers in personal life leaves open alternative communities for all concerned. Locking out offenders by condemning them to solitary confinement leaves them with no community at all.

Still, imprisonment and other forms of bodily coercion cannot always be avoided. Such coercion may never be punishment in itself, as in current criminal law. Infliction of pain is an unavoidable by-product of civilised coercion. If only for reasons of proportionality and subsidiarity, as much use ought to be made of electronic and other means of surveillance limiting convicts in freedom of movement and/or monitoring their progress in penal servitude. Imprisonment ought to be really *ultimum remedium*, instead of the standard sanction against serious crime.

First, as in current criminal procedure, some suspects and criminal defendants are to be temporarily detained if there is to be trial in their presence (or even on behalf of possible negotiations on behalf of victims, under the supervision of the public prosecution). Other reasons may have to do with safeguarding evidence and so on, again as in current criminal procedure. Second, offenders unwilling to co-operate in realisation of their conviction may face the alternative of (long-term) detainment. Third, special prevention reasons may lead to separation of dangerous offenders from society, whether combined with some kind of treatment or not. Fourth, offenders may be detained in order to guarantee not only victims' safety, but also their peace of mind. Some victims of serious crime may find the thought of offenders walking freely around intolerable, even if such offenders may have become harmless in the meantime.

Probably more so than the first two reasons mentioned, the last two reasons require careful consideration and weighing of interests. Still, even the need for victims' peace of mind may in the end lead to long-term detainment. On the other hand, detainment need not always be lone isolation. Much more so than in current penal practice, attempts ought to be made to institute some kind of society or even community within prison confines. For some inmates, such community building may offer a first opportunity in their lives to earn respect and feel self-respect, simply by being listened to and being able to speak out. Such community building may even involve volunteering crime victims explaining their ordeal in awareness and learning sessions. It may not always do much good, but anything is better than marginalising, criminalising or even hospitalising solitary detainment. Such solitary detainment carries strong undertones of: 'It's the rest against the offender'. In civilised criminal law, no one needs to be alone. (A recent and well-publicised San Francisco penal experiment in confined community building seems to have been highly successful so far.)

5. *Justice for victims without offenders*

If offenders cannot or may not be rightfully forced to pay for the full costs of crime and criminal procedure, the state is to supplement public funds covering all costs of crime. But this is not all of it. In more than a few cases of crime, only victims are available. Of course, even in a completely civilised criminal legal order more than a few offenders will go free. No public administration can be totally effective against getting away with crime, certainly not as long as it acts within reasonable limits to investigative powers protecting citizens' rights and interests.

As far as minor offences against public interests are concerned, this may be no problem at all. There ought to be a reasonable balance between the costs of crime and the costs of enforcement, both in terms of public administration expenses and of nuisance to citizens as subjects of vigilance and control. But what are the fates of individual victims of serious crime committed by offenders who escaped the strong arm of criminal justice?

This is not all of it. If suspects do get arrested, there may be all kinds of reasons why they still go free, even if they may be directly related to the crime committed. Thus offenders may be acquitted or more leniently sentenced for reasons of procedure (but see §§ 8 and 9 on limits to this in civilised criminal law) or they may be found to be not deserving of punishment because they were not (completely) responsible for what they did. Why are victims to be left alone, in such 'offenderless' cases?

In current criminal procedure, a few victims may relish doubtful satisfaction through arrested and sentenced offenders' suffering. Most others are condemned to charity, if available at all from public means (and hopefully to love and understanding from fellow human beings). These others are deprived of any real answer to their resentment, as there are no offenders to be forced to stand up for what they did wrong, just as all others will get no answer to their moral resentment as well.

If victims of crime instead of offenders are to be the primary *dramatis personae* of criminal law, then an obvious difference between current practice and civilised criminal law must be full compensation for victims of crime without arrested and/or sentenced offenders. Of course, in general it is no victims' responsibility that more than a few offenders escape (part of) their punishment. In such cases, the state is to pay. Extra state payment is due as symbolic replacement of the loss of symbolic satisfaction for victims and others through penal servitude by offenders themselves.

Such payment may even be regarded as a kind of compensatory punishment against the state. Crime victims may indeed reproach the state for not preventing crime and feel resentment about it in the first place. For more or less good reasons, the state exercises exclusive rights to enforce criminal law, thus taking away at least part of victims' powers and possibilities (or even natural rights, according to some) to resolve matters themselves. The same state may not sit still after not having done its due, simply stating that it is of course as impossible to prevent all crime as it is to arrest and get sentenced all offenders afterwards.

Supposedly non-responsible offenders pose special problems. Victims' perception of actorship, malice and guilt may differ from scientistic or even implicitly determinist conceptions of forensic psychology and psychiatry. In normal human understanding and communication, actorship is the norm, compulsion the exception to be further explained in other than obvious cases. As already explained in some detail in § 3, actorship is of paramount importance for human communication and community. There cannot be but fundamental differences between what people do toward each other on the one hand and what happens to them on the other. There can be no respect and self-respect without imputation of actorship. This is all the more important when serious harm is to be answered in some or other way. Crime victims have rights to penal servitude as compensation for what they perceived as done to them, as basically different from what happened to them.

In normal perception, actorship and responsibility go together in some or other way. The important distinction is not a distinction between responsible and non-responsible actorship, but between responsible actorship on the one hand and what happens to somebody and its consequences on the other. Such responsibility may then be further qualified in terms of intention, malice, guilt and negligence and related notions. Thus there is an obvious difference between hitting somebody in the face and inadvertently hitting somebody as a consequence of epilepsy. Rather less obvious, if not even more or less irrelevant in normal human communication are differences between responsible and non-responsible actorship. Offenders carefully preparing and skilfully executing their crimes clearly display actorship as distinct from what happens to them, at least to their victims and to others in terms of normal human understanding. (Note echoes here of Beccaria's [1764] belittling of criminal malice and guilt as determining factors for degrees of punishment, as such 'inner factors' are not visible to the public and thus are to be left out of account in determination of general prevention against the same public through punishment.)

Still, forensic psychiatry and/or other forensic sciences may offer plausible or even convincing explanations of such behaviour in terms of inner compulsion. Courts may exclude offenders' responsibility on such grounds. Non-responsible offenders may not be punished, then, though of course they may be locked up for purposes of special prevention and/or compulsory treatment. As noted by Szasz (1977) and others, forensic sciences have an understandable tendency to try to explain heinous and absurd cruelty in terms of pathology, as normal human motives seem to be incompatible with committing such crimes. Thus offenders seem to be relieved of full responsibility to the degree of cruelty of their crimes (see also Dershowitz, 1994).

Crime victims may not understand and accept this. They may well feel deprived of what they are entitled to one more time, as they do not receive their dues for what they experienced as harmful consequences of responsible actorship. Thus victims of serial rapists surely had to witness application of means-ends rationality in offenders' commitment of crimes against them, like perception and calculation of opportunities to strike, or even explicit communication with victims in terms of threats in order to subdue them. Normal persons may not explain this in terms of no more than inner compulsion in the first place. They witnessed actorship, to be imputed to offenders and not to inner compulsion independent from offenders themselves.

This is not all of it. Withholding responsibility from offenders implies that victims are guilty themselves. At least, this is what more than a few victims may think and feel, with fateful consequences. Responsibility has to reside somewhere, it seems, so it ends up with the victim. Thus victims are not just deprived of compensation through penal servitude, but are saddled with responsibility for their harm and suffering as well. A sad fate indeed, possibly leading to lifelong trauma.

How to resolve this conflict between 'victim' perspectives and 'forensic-scientistic' perspectives on actorship and responsibility? In a few extreme cases, victims may be convinced by forensic-scientistic explanations excluding responsibility. Victims may even be consoled by the thought that compulsory offenders did not really have bad intentions toward them. The standard solution would be the state stepping in for offenders again. The same state explained offenders' responsibility away, thus the state pays full compensation to victims, including extra compensation for loss of satisfaction through penal servitude.

But this is obviously unsatisfactory. Money cannot really compensate for victims' loss of penal servitude. The same victims experienced actorship and its consequences, not to be explained away from offenders. Related to this, the problem of transfer of guilt is not solved either. Why not turn things round? Normal conceptions of action and related responsibility are to determine penal servitude and other civilised sanctions, forensic explanations excluding responsible action are not so much to determine what is to be done for victims, but what is to be done to such offenders by the state, in compensation for sanctions imposed on them as if they were fully responsible.

Thus psychiatric diagnosis of the same serial rapists may come down to insuperable inner compulsion, explained in terms of psychopathology. Still, such rapists may be put to work, in order to more or less compensate for what they did wrong in the eyes and minds of their victims and of other citizens. The state takes care of them as a consequence of what happened to them as determined from forensic standpoints. In practice, more than a few offenders forensically diagnosed as compulsory will be locked up anyway, for reasons of special prevention and/or compulsory treatment. Positive effects of penal servitude may well be integrated into such treatment programs. This may seem mercilessly harsh. On the other hand, penal servitude is very much less harmful than mere imprisonment is. Even incorrigibly dangerous offenders indefinitely detained may lead better lives by doing something with their lives, even within walls.

Let it be noted that this is not meant to belittle forensic science and its practical importance, however contestable its results may be at times. Here it is argued only that insights from forensic psychology and psychiatry concerning absence of actorship, malice and guilt due to kinds of compulsion not readily visible to everybody are not decisive in determination of penal servitude serving victims' rights and interests. It is a matter of perspectives. Forensic sciences and its all-forgiving tendencies belong to the sphere of relationships between the all-understanding state caring for all citizens, especially citizens bereft of real autonomy in thought and action. But citizens may not be expected to display such all-enveloping understanding toward one another's misdeeds at all. They simply expect each other to be responsible for what they do, just as the state is expected to be responsible for all.

Difficult problems remain, of course. First, actorship of course does not completely determine degrees of malice, guilt and negligence. A rent-a-kill man cunningly picking his victims may not be compared to an unlucky lorry driver overlooking a right of way sign, inadvertently killing people by hitting a school bus. All kinds of problems may prop up between such extremes. Causation may be complex as well, as exemplified by lorry driver-like cases (see also Kaptein, 1999). Though the lorry driver may have committed a pure conduct crime in the first place, criminal consequences may well be determined in part by consequences of such crime. Overlooking right of way signs with no further consequences may be settled by simple payment of fine. Serious or even deadly consequences imply civilised sanctions, though of course the greater part of costs in such negligence cases is to be paid for by insurance companies and/or public funds. Killing for money on the other hand ought to be as costly as possible of course, at least in terms of penal servitude.

6. *Further advantages*

The advantages of civilised criminal law, not only in comparison to current criminal procedure and punishment, however highly developed, may be too obvious by now to require much further mention. Still, a few remarks may still more clarify things, and motivate much-needed reform.

Crime victims are no longer left alone in the very first place. Doubtful satisfaction through infliction of suffering, in as far as offenders were sentenced at all, supplemented by more or less public charity is replaced by recognition and realisation of crime victims' rights to legal restoration through penal servitude to be performed by offenders. Integration of forfeit, restitution and punishment in such penal servitude replaces irrationally unrelated and insufficient measures vainly intended to realise the same effects. Tortuous and often ineffective civil law suits for damages against more or less penniless and/or uninsured offenders will be things of the past, apart from special cases. Still, it ought to be kept in mind that no criminal procedure, however civilised, may ever alleviate all consequences of crime.

Offenders are better off as well. Instead of undergoing the pain of imprisonment, with all of its consequences in terms of marginalisation and criminalisation, they are to constructively contribute not only to restoration of victims' losses, but also to society and to themselves. Instead of the exclusion of imprisonment as the standard sanction against serious crime, inclusive community service in a wide sense is the norm. Penal servitude performed in relative freedom may well have all kinds of positive motivation and learning effects. Inclusive sanctions greatly facilitate reintegration as well. In a sense, there is no need for reintegration at all, as there has been no exclusion in the first place.

Penal servitude is rather less negatively shameful than imprisonment is, with its attendant marking of offenders as outcasts. Also, offenders having paid for what they did wrong may be more easily accepted as full members of society than offenders who suffered imprisonment without having done anything to really pay their debts to their victims.

Capital punishment is excluded in principle. Dead offenders do not seem to be able to perform any penal servitude any more. (Apart from the baffling fact that proponents of capital punishment purport to know what it is like to be dead, in order to determine the nature and possible justification of consequences of putting offenders to death, and apart from so many other overwhelming arguments against such killing 'in the name of the law'.)

Civilised criminal law is equalising in a positive sense. Though so-called retribution through infliction of suffering may be equalising as well, in some sense, it produces highly negative results. Still more human suffering is what it all ends up with. Penal servitude on the other hand makes up for what was done wrong, thus adding to the good of society, in restoring original positions as they were before crime destroyed them. In fact, civilised criminal law is nothing but redistribution of labour for overriding reasons of retribution in its original sense.

Related to this, civilised criminal law is rather less expensive than current practice, in monetary and much more importantly in human and social terms. Apart from offenders' accountability for the costs of criminal procedure, there is rather less senseless suffering by offenders and their relatives to begin with. There will be less criminalisation as a consequence of long-term imprisonment, still apart from the huge monetary costs of current penal institutions. Less public means will be needed to pay for the costs of victim assistance and recovery programs as well. Greatly adding to this of course is the basic fact that crime victims are much better off as well.

Civilised criminal law may lead to depenalisation of conduct not wrongly harmful to individuals and/or society. Drug-related offences may be done away with for this reason alone, as self-inflicted harm ought not to be covered by criminal law. The full force of civilised criminal law ought to be limited to serious harm done to others and/or to general interests, in clear violation of individual and collective rightful interests and rights.

Civilised criminal law may elicit rather less public resistance than other reform proposals on behalf of victims, like informal restorative justice often regarded as insufficiently punitive. Indeed, retribution as restitution not only satisfies a generally rather punitive public opinion, but also such retribution is an answer to fellow citizens' moral resentment as a consequence of criminal harm done to other people. In this sense, punitive attitudes are not so much outright irrational as reasonable reflections of public rights to retribution of crime. Adding to this, taxpayers' resentment against spending money on offenders, accompanied at times by pleas for 'cheap' capital punishment, may be abated by the basic idea that the costs of crime are to be paid for by offenders themselves in the first place.

Special and general preventive and repressive effects are not lost in civilised criminal law either. Apart from confinement of dangerous offenders, special preventive effect may also be one more positive result of penal servitude, for example through confrontation with consequences of crime. This may range from litter-louts sweeping the streets to drunken drivers cleaning hospital rooms. Also, reintegration through penal servitude performed in relative freedom may have important effects of special prevention, curbing crime again. On the other hand, general preventive effects of unattractive prospects of penal servitude may not be strong enough in all cases of serious crime, though it remains doubtful of course whether sufficient preventive effect may be expected from any punitive measures against offenders (including capital punishment).

7. *Possible problems*

Of course, even civilised criminal law is not without its drawbacks, though more than a few obvious criticisms against it may be no more than basic misunderstandings. Here again, it ought to be kept in mind that no possible answer to crime in the real world may be effective in every respect.

If compensation and reparation for victims is the core of civilised criminal law, then victims' harm is to determine what counts as a criminal offence. Or: if no possible harm, then no offence, if possible harm, then all kinds of conduct causing such harm ought to be criminalised, it seems. The no harm no offence issue may be readily conceded, though of course offences may not be directly related to individual harm and suffering (think of offences against public order: see § 4). Though possible harm is a necessary condition for criminalising conduct, it is not a sufficient condition for it. Self-inflicted harm, harm as a consequence of fair competition and other kinds of 'rightful harm' are to be excluded (see again Feinberg, 1984-1988).

But what to think of betrayal and other kinds of malicious conduct in personal life, with possibly lifelong traumatic consequences, inflicted by parents to children, by superiors to their subordinates and by so many other people to more or less defenceless victims? Gouldner clearly expressed the problem (1971, pp. 306 ff.):

> One man may alienate the affection and love of another's wife, but neither the wife nor the seducer is clapped into jail. A man may undermine the authority of another, violate his obligations as a friend, lie, and cheat, and misrepresent, all to his own advantage and all in flagrant violation of the other's role 'rights'. For the most part, all that the injured party can do is call upon his friends to rally round, ask that onlookers observe the violation of the elementary decencies, and seek the unorganised protection of his immediate community. (In other words, the victim is in serious trouble.) In the normal course of role relationships, one man can destroy the life work of another and, in the process, violate the most sacred role obligations, yet he may at most be subject only to frowns, criticism, or loss of reputation. But heaven

> help him should he deliberately walk off with the other man's hat. The police apparatus would be mobilized, weapons inspected, warrants issued, jail keys turned.

From a victim point of view, such betrayal and related misbehaviour is incomparably much more harmfully criminal than petty theft may ever be. However many well-known reasons there may be to treat all kinds of theft as crimes and to leave personal betrayal and like misbehaviour out of account, boundaries remain unclear, of course not just concerning theft and betrayal. Problems of evidence and proof (theft may be readily established in court, betrayal in personal life may escape any conclusive determination) are of course not to be decisive here. Civilised criminal law seems saddled with its ambition to compensate all kinds of wrongful suffering caused by all kinds of offenders. More or less arbitrary codification is the only answer here. (Such codification is the only answer to the problem of differentiating criminal offences from torts as well. Of course, vague boundaries between criminal law and tort law is not just a civilised criminal law problem.)

Codification of offences carries codification of sanctions with it, in terms of payment to victims and/or to the state. Against this, it may be specifically objected that payment to victims reduces criminal codes to crime price lists, which would be totally unacceptable to crime victims and to society (see on this objection Watson *& al.*, 1989, Zedner, 1994 and Wright, 1996). Since Roman law times, in which the rich reportedly beat up the poor in the streets for the fun of it, and next had servants following in their wake pay victims for harm done, it is taken for granted that punitive criminal law must be different from compensatory civil law. Criminal law ought to have at least *pouvoir symbolique de condamnation* (Van de Kerchove, 1987).

Still apart from the question whether tort law itself may really be regarded as concerning tort price lists only, punitive penal servitude is of course the essence of civilised criminal law. The real price of serious crime goes rather further than just payment of money. Here it may be remarked again that offenders are to pay for all costs of crime for victims, including all immaterial costs. Adding to this, offenders' accountability for the costs of criminal procedure and for other general costs of crime may make the price of crime, if this still is an appropriate expression at all, too high for any sensible calculation. On the other hand, such calculation may of course play a role in any kind of criminal law, however harshly punitive. Also, more than a few serious offenders against other peoples' life and limb do not really calculate at all (just like more than a few law-abiding citizens are not motivated to their peaceful behaviour by fear for punishment in the first place: see already § 2).

Anyway, retribution as full restitution afterwards comes first. This leads to a rather more serious problem: may there be any fitting restitution for immeasurable harm caused by crimes like murder, rape and bodily assault with lasting consequences? The only real answer may be frustratingly simple: there is none. Nothing in the world can really undo consequences of such crime. Some victims may do better after some time, but generally such scars never disappear, not even through offenders' penal servitude for life and its rewards for victims.

Sometimes, lifetime penal servitude performed in confinement may be the only answer, if only to give victims peace of mind in the knowledge that offenders will never reappear in real life (see § 4).

Less serious crimes lead to the same kind of question. Material harm caused by theft may be calculable and thus lead to a certain amount of penal servitude, the rewards of which are to equal material costs of harm. But then theft and like crimes lead to immaterial harm too. Common assault is another example. Material harm may be negligible, mental and emotional harm may be traumatic. Still, offenders are to pay for everything, again including the costs of criminal procedure. Codification may prescribe standard supplements added to material costs of crime. Thus theft may lead to less immaterial harm than common assault and may therefore be less costly for offenders in immaterial terms. Also, crime victims may be more interested in the symbolism of full payment than in any semblance of exact actuarial determination of all kinds of harm done. Anyway, a certain arbitrariness in the imposition of reasonable limits of penal servitude may be inevitable here, both in codification and in adjudication. This holds good for crimes without specific victims anyway, like carrying firearms.

Basically the same answer may be given to queries concerning rather different victim reactions to seemingly identical offences. Some victims may be most vindictive, a few other victims may be rather indifferent toward any possible offenders. Victims may actively oppose legal action against 'their' offenders. Some victims of common assault may simply walk away from it, other victims may suffer fatal revival of childhood traumas related to like harm. A few of these victims may even end up in mental institutions. Thus material and immaterial cost of seemingly small offences may be quite high in some cases. Again, codification and adjudication are to set limits. Remaining costs may be paid for by public funds and/or insurance money.

Codification and adjudication are to be based upon 'the counterfactual victim', in terms of generalisations in as far as available, and not on 'the actual and always rather different victim' in the first place. Symbolic aspects of penal servitude are no less important than amounts of material means directly or indirectly transferred from offenders to victims. Offenders may not be held responsible for possibly far-reaching differences between individual victims. Justice implies that offenders pay on the basis of generalisations (unless offenders knew better, of course). On the other hand, all kinds of individual differences are far from unimportant for all kinds of care for crime victims apart from criminal procedure.

In the line of this, it may even be asked why victims would be interested in any offenders' reaction at all. Relatives and friends need reconciliation and everything necessarily preceding it, if they are to go on together. Strangers however may think and feel nothing about each other at all, not even after harm was inflicted. Thus victims may think and feel about offenders in terms of sad and worthless aberrations of the living world (or in even worse terms). Such 'doing away with offenders' by reducing them to less welcome phenomena of nature may do good to some victims. On the other hand, again, who else apart from offenders themselves are to pay for the consequences of crime?

It may even be thought that recognition of victims' suffering and compensating for it deepens such suffering, or even creates the subjective semblance of it in the first place. Though this may be true in some cases, such supposedly autopoietic effects of civilised criminal law cannot stand in the way of compensation for obviously wrongful harm. Of course, things are expected to work out the other way round: recognition and reparation of wrongful harm is to restore victims' self-respect and well-being.

Such problems of fitting retribution and different victim reactions are related to issues of immoderate victim claims, on the basis of allegedly more or less infinite suffering, to be alleviated at all cost. Much criticised as such immoderation and its background pathologies of modern man and society may be, the issue as such does not really touch upon civilised criminal law. Harm and suffering of whatever moderate or immoderate kind not caused by clearly identifiable actors do not count at all. The basic difference between what is done to somebody (to be accounted for, by criminal procedure or otherwise) and what simply or not so simply happens to somebody is apposite here too. Civilised criminal law is related to actorship and associated resentment only. In this basic sense, it does not fit in with general trends of victimisation as a consequence of whatever influences outside victims' own powers, 'loss of tragic consciousness' and so on. Thus civilised criminal law is no victimisation in underestimation of victims' autonomy, as it does not at all deny that victims' responsibility for dealing with harm comes first. Wrongful harm committed by or at least related to offenders is the one important exception here. Such harm only is dealt with by civilised criminal law.

But what about offenders' autonomy? Actorship and responsibility are at the core of civilised criminal law. Offenders and nobody else are to pay for what they did, because they did it and because nobody and nothing else did it. This very starting point may amount to gross overestimation of individual autonomy or even free will. It is all too obvious that more than a few offenders against life and limb are products of all kinds of unlucky, unhappy or even tragic circumstances, from possibly genetic factors to upbringing and education, outright poverty, marginalisation and worse, still apart from mental and emotional disorders without any clear causes at all. Is not civilised criminal law both an outright denial of a wealth of criminological evidence and intensification of social injustice by burdening the socially disadvantaged one more time? Thus regarded, civilised criminal law seems just one more simplistically anti-social right wing political conception.

Against this, it may be answered again that the state is to play the role of the anonymously all-understanding, all-caring and all-forgiving institution, whereas individual citizens, strangers to each other as they normally are, cannot but take the normal semblance of individual responsibility as the basic starting point for reciprocity. There can be no civil society without individual responsibility (see §§ 3 and 5). Thus the state ought to play both roles: all-caring for everybody, but still extorting retribution from offenders on behalf of victims. Also, emphasis on actorship and its consequences in matters of crime does not imply any so-called right wing politics in general. In fact, civilised criminal law is compatible with a wide range of political conceptions.

Related to this it ought to go without saying by now that civilised criminal law is essentially public law. The state represents and acts on citizens' resentment against offenders, on behalf of victims. Well-known objections against restorative justice as incompatible with the necessarily public nature of criminal law, based on the supposedly personal, private or even emotional nature of victim satisfaction need not be further discussed by now (see also §§ 4 and 8 on the public nature of civilised criminal law).

Anyway, civilised criminal law may well survive such and other problems of principle. What remains is real civilisation of criminal law and its no doubt numerous foreseeable and unforeseeable practical problems. Such realisation may well lead to rethinking matters of principle again, as unexpected consequences may come to light.

8. *Procedural justice for all*

How to realise civilised criminal law in specific cases? If possible, victims may take the law into their own hands. Informal restorative justice may lead to acceptable results in some cases (see § 4). Still, administration of criminal justice according to the rules is the core of civilised procedure, though formalisation of conflict carries its own costs. In this respect, important principles of current criminal procedure may remain in force. (Here again, emphasis is upon handling crime, not upon public order and preventive aspects of criminal procedure.) Thus codification of offences and sanctions goes along with independent courts in order to determine just and fair application of the law in specific cases. Though consequences for offenders may be less harsh than under current procedure, meting out punishment by public administration authorities ought to be limited to public order offences not inflicting individual harm, with full recourse to independent courts.

Public prosecution offices and their monopolies in formally addressing crime have pride of place too. Just as citizens are to be safeguarded against each others' free interpretation and implementation of criminal justice or even club-law, crime victims are not to be left alone in their quest for justice. One more important reason for this is the rather limited investigative power of individual victims, both in technical and in legal terms. Public prosecution is there to proceed against criminal violations of general interests as well. Administrative discretion in prosecution is to be limited to such general interests issues. Crime victim rights leave no room for weighing of interests concerned. Still, public prosecution offices may decline to proceed against petty crime, just as they may give due consideration to possibilities of false claims (though this is a problem in current criminal and civil procedure as well).

Given prospects of justice and fairness in court, public prosecution authorities may try to reach settlements out of court to the satisfaction of all concerned. Offenders may co-operate in the knowledge that court decisions may be less favourable to them than the outcomes of three party negotiations may be, directly or indirectly involving victims, offenders and public prosecution officers. In such ways, informal restorative justice may return to the scene, this time backed by the possibility of formal proceedings.

Indeed, both public prosecution and public trial are to express the essentially public nature of civilised criminal law. In a sense, the moral resentment of fellow citizens is translated into public procedure as expression of solidarity with victims. Solemnly rule-governed aspects of trial sessions may serve to emphasise this, though of course many a silly formalisation may be done away with.

Also, ceremonially authoritative determination of criminal liability may do crime victims much good. Official identification of offenders removes burdens of guilt from victims: offenders did it (apart from rare cases of victims' shared criminal liability), victims are not left alone with possibly traumatic doubts concerning their own responsibility for what was done to them (see also § 5 on the importance of 'removing' guilt from victims). This may be experienced by crime victims as even more important then any further measures against offenders, though reparation through penal servitude may be more welcome to victims than punishment as infliction of pain.

Civilisation of criminal procedure toward a three party system may lead to more basic changes, compared to current principle and practice. First, victims' roles preceding and during trial need careful reconsideration. Though not all victims may profit from active participation in any processes involving offenders, all possibilities to such participation ought to be available. Before all, crime victims are to be allowed to speak out in court, whether their testimonies are necessary or not. Dangers of influencing court members to the disadvantage of offenders do not seem to be decisive against this.

Second, one more consequence of compensation for all crime victims is criminal trial without any defendant, as more than a few offenders do not get arrested at all. The state has to pay for everything, then (see § 5). Such trials may lead to difficult issues of evidence and proof, and to misuse of compensation possibilities by fake victims again. On the other hand, in clear cases public prosecution authorities may offer full compensation out of court.

Third, consequences of errors of procedure or even outright offences against criminal suspects and defendants are to be reconsidered. The standard sanction against such authorities' misconduct in current legal procedure is partial or complete protection against punishment by the very same state who offended against suspects and defendants concerned. In many current legal orders, this ranges from milder punishment to barring the public prosecution. Of course such barring, ending criminal procedure, is the only thing to do in cases of irreparable tinkering with evidence or worse. But what to do with crime victims in such cases? They had nothing to do with any police or public prosecution misconduct. Are they to be barred from full compensation by offenders in their turn?

In the 'two party' system of old, direct compensation of offenders' wrongs with wrongs committed by the state against them may seem both rational and effective. State misconduct simply acts against the state itself in the end, by withholding (full) punishment. In a 'three party' system, crime victims may be compensated by the state as well, for their loss of satisfaction through offenders' penal servitude and payment. Still, more than a few victims and others may think of this as a nasty (hat)trick, as if guilty offenders going free were not guilty after all (or they would not have gone free). Instead of state compensation for victims, offender compensation by public means and sanctions against misbehaving officials may be more apposite in cases of criminal misadministration. Penal servitude for victims is no longer wrongly limited, then, just as suspects and defendants may be more adequately protected than under current sanctioning of rules of procedure (see also Kaptein, 2001).

Lastly, boundaries between criminal and civil procedure may be partly done away with. Thus there may be non-criminal harm as a consequence of crime, like serious bodily harm as a consequence of minor traffic offences (however difficult it may be to distinguish between criminal harm and tort). In order to simplify matters of procedure and proof, one and the same court may both decide criminal issues and damages to be paid for by insurance companies in most cases.

Anyway, clarity on the meaning and purpose of material criminal law may much clarify principles of criminal procedure. Discussion of this has long suffered from one-sided attention to suspects' and defendants' rights and interests, in the light (or darkness) of lack of any clear sense of punishment as infliction of pain. Basically important as such rights and interests are, a fair balancing against crime victims rights and interests is to determine criminal procedure as well. Though no Bentham-style instrumentalising of procedure is intended here, it is still the results that count.

Such results are to be realised in the shortest possible span of time. Though this probably goes without much further saying, criminal justice cannot be done by leaving harm done to the passage of time, with still more harmful consequences for victims and all others concerned. Reversal of harmful courses of history ought not to be hindered by more or less senseless procedures standing in the way of timely justice.

9. *Civilised rules of evidence and proof*

In current criminal procedure under the rule of law, most suspects simply confess. Such confessions may next be tested, among other things in terms of offenders' knowledge of facts and circumstances only available to them if they really committed the offence concerned. In this sense, there may be no great problems of evidence and proof in most cases. Adding to this in civilised criminal law is the relative lack of importance of possibly intractable problems of forensic establishment of malice and guilt. Proof of actorship comes first, complexities of criminal motives and/or psychopathological causes need not always be deeply inquired into in order to determine fitting penal servitude (see § 5).

Still, doubtful and difficult cases remain. Such cases are not amenable to informal settlement anyway, as one obvious presupposition for such settlement is certainty on facts concerning the offence committed for all concerned. Transformation through mediation of all kinds of facts related to the case, leading to better mutual understanding, may be most important in dealing with crime too. But the facts of the offence itself ought to be established beforehand. In some cases, offenders may be encouraged to co-operatively confess in the light of possibly more formal proceedings and its consequences against them.

Current procedures of evidence and proof are designed to protect the innocent in the first place, at least on paper. First, and related to the presumption of innocence, the burden of proof is taken to be on the public prosecution. Criminal defendants are not expected to offer evidence of innocence (though of course they are free to do so). Second, this proof is to be conclusive, if there is to be any criminal conviction. Punishment against the innocent is rightly regarded as rather more unjust than freedom from punishment for offenders.

Another asymmetry behind such principles may be less discussed. In current criminal law, punishment is conceived of as serving general interests only. From this it may be inferred that sufficient levels of punishment may sufficiently serve such general interests. From such a point of view, punishment against every offender is not necessarily the goal, in as far as possible at all.

As far as offences against general interests are concerned, nothing is to be brought in against such principles. Of course, presumptions of innocence are expressions of deeper principles of decent society. Citizens, including public administration officials, are to treat each other as if they are in good faith, as long as there is no convincing counter-evidence. If some offenders get away with their crimes by this, so be it. But then individual crime victims may not agree with this at all. They may feel that no justice is done to them, on the basis of principles of evidence and proof designed to protect criminal defendants in the first place.

May this lead to 'civilisation' of procedures of evidence and proof in civil law directions? Though of course one important background assumption of civil law evidence and proof is the same kind of presumption of good faith in the absence of counter-evidence, division of burdens of proof may be rather different. Thus the burden of proof is on the party stating the facts, then, just as it may even be assumed that facts are taken for granted as long as no convincing evidence is brought against them.

May some criminal defendants thus be burdened with some or other proof of their innocence in some cases, that is, if they contend to be innocent? (European criminal law adjudication already suggests this in 1996, though possibly not for the right reasons.) Difficult issues and dangerous suggestions no doubt, but still it is apparent that current divisions of proof do not do justice to all crime victims.

Another kind of civilisation may be no less contestable. In more than a few systems of civil procedure, parties are expected to inform the court on everything possibly important for dealing with the case at hand. Parties found to hide facts may be treated rather harshly, for example by barring them from further procedure. In civilised criminal law, a suitable sanction against all too taciturn criminal defendants may be (still) more penal servitude.

Such a rule of procedure is not at odds with the presumption of innocence. Whatever defendants' obligations or even duties to tell the truth as far they know it, they are still to be treated as if they are innocent until the courts decide otherwise. One consequence of this is that criminal defendants may no longer lie in court, a prerogative long established in several current criminal legal orders. Also, criminal lawyers' confidentiality and partisanship may be suitably qualified (see on this Kaptein, 2003). On the other hand, such rules are *nuda praescripta* in more than a few cases, however harshly sanctioned on paper.

Related to this (and already discussed in § 8, concerning errors of procedure) is the issue of improperly obtained evidence. Such evidence is to be used in full, as long as its factual content is not disputable. Harm done to suspects and criminal defendants by improper collection of evidence is to be compensated again, just as officials concerned ought to be properly sanctioned for it.

Next, criminal procedure and trial in the absence of any suspects and defendants may create special problems of evidence and proof, as there are no possible offenders to speak out (see §§ 5 and 8). On the other hand, and notwithstanding real possibilities of misuse, standards of proof need not be very strict then, as the state only is to pay for the consequences in such cases.

Victims may stay away from public court sessions in their turn. That is, if there are criminal defendants on trial. Contrary to current standard rules of testimony, possibilities of victim testimonies outside court ought to be considered, if offenders' presence is felt to be too menacing.

Many other issues remain to be addressed of course, like lifting bans on *ne bis in idem* as possible consequences of newly found evidence. Also, no civilisation of criminal procedure will ever ward off dangers of sentencing the innocent. No real consolation may be found in the fact that, in cases of wrongful conviction, penal servitude may be more or less undone by full compensation, whereas consequences of punishment as serious infliction of pain may be wellnigh irreversible.

10. *Agenda*

Doris Lessing (1986, p. 15) wrote about prisons we choose to live inside, a metaphor or even reality all too apposite as far as painful current criminal procedure and punishment are concerned:

> I spend a good deal of time wondering how we will seem to the people who come after us. This is not an idle interest, but a deliberate attempt to strengthen the power of that 'other eye', which we can use to judge ourselves. Anyone who reads history

> at all knows that the passionate and powerful convictions of one century usually seem absurd, extraordinary, to the next.

The other eye would like to see civilisation of criminal law. Is a paradigm shift needed in order to end endless suffering through punishment as suffering? If this is to be understood in its original, 'Kuhnian' sense, the answer must be in the negative. Paradigm shifts cannot be instigated at will, they happen. (Also, paradigm shifts as discussed by Kuhn and others, are matters of natural science in the first place and thus do not seem to relate to normative issues of criminal law and punishment.) No paradigm shifts are needed to clarify relationships of offence, resentment, reparation and reconciliation as the basis for civilised criminal law. Internal essentialism explains such relationships as irreplaceably there in human life, however much this may have been neglected, not only in criminal law theory and practice and attendant radical misinterpretation of retribution as infliction of pain (see § 3 on the idea of internal essentialism). Also, civilised criminal law is not categorically different from current criminal law. Essential elements of codification and procedure remain in force.

It would seem more apposite to develop theory and practice together, in order to test principles of civilised criminal law in their practical applications and probably unexpected consequences, just as there can be no justice and fairness in criminal practice without recourse to such principles again. Reflective equilibrium of principles and practice is the goal, guiding thought and action on behalf of crime victims, offenders and in fact everybody in the real world, however slow motion and marginal such progress may be (see on the idea of reflective equilibrium briefly but convincingly Rawls, 1999).

Complete codification of practicable principles would seem outlandish in any near future. On the other hand, public and political resistance against more than a few restorative justice projects, due to their perceived lack of public and punitive nature, may indeed be met with by the core idea of civilised criminal law. Offenders do not get away with their crimes, as penal servitude is the price to be paid. In such a way, uneasy and marginal roles of crime victim assistance within systems oriented toward the completely different goal of punishment as infliction of pain may be done away with in favour of integration of punishment and realisation of crime victims' rights and interests.

Still, doubts on preventive and repressive effect of such penal servitude, rightly perceived as milder than current punishment in most cases, may hinder realisation of civilised criminal law. Deeply rooted are primitive ideas implying that only prospects of suffering as a consequence of crime can make people behave properly and that such 'social engineering' by brute force is the prime method of keeping citizens within bounds. Or, one should say, other citizens, as most spokespersons for such persuasions probably do not relate such primitive but still politically and legally authorised club-law to themselves.

Doing away with such dangerously deeply rooted misunderstanding may be not much less important than civilisation of criminal law in itself. Which is not to deny that prevention of crime comes first. But it ought to dawn to all concerned that criminal law and punishment cannot play more than subordinate roles in prevention and repression of crime. Other means come first, means sadly neglected in even the most developed modern societies, however much difference of opinion there may be on causes of crime. Social justice is a tragic case in point. Decriminalisation may also have great preventive effects: think again of the senselessly legal war on drugs and its ravages. Cracking down on real or imaginary crimes already committed and not doing much about prevention of crime in the first place is betrayal of citizens. Every serious crime against life, limb and personal possession is nothing less than one more defeat of the state in realisation of its very first duties toward individual citizens and general interests.

So try to prevent serious crime in the very first place. Care for inevitable crime victims, with all means available, however imperfect. Do not forget that no merely legal means may ever adequately care for crime victims. Try not to commit any harmful offences to anybody, whether such offences are criminally codified or not. But do know that nobody can be without sin, in the sense of never committing any offence. Answer to resentment, then, try to repair consequences of wrongdoing, in order to restore communication, respect and self-respect. This is the cement of society. But remember Elizabeth Hardwick (1994):

> There is no equity in life or in judicial decisions. In any case, you can't go to heaven on other people's sins.

And be driven by resentment against punishment as infliction of pain, in furthering the cause of civilised criminal law.

References

T. Baldwin, 'Punishment, Communication and Resentment' in M. Matravers ed., *Punishment and Political Theory* (Hart Publishing, Oxford & Portland, Oregon, 1999)

R.E. Barnett, *The structure of liberty: justice and the rule of law* (Clarendon Press, Oxford / New York, 1998)

R.E. Barnett & J. Hagel ed., *Assessing the Criminal: Restitution, Retribution, and the Legal Process* (Ballinger Publishing Company, Cambridge, Mass., 1997)

C. Beccaria, *Dei Delitti e delle Pene* (1764 and many later editions)

J. Braithwaite, *Restorative Justice and Responsive Regulation* (Oxford University Press, Oxford, 2002)

J. Braithwaite & P. Pettit, *Not Just Deserts: A Republican Theory of Criminal Justice* (Clarendon Press, Oxford, 1990)

M.E.I. Brienen & E.H. Hoegen, *Victims of Crime in 22 European Criminal Justice Systems: The Implementation of Recommendation (85) 11 of the Council of Europe on the Position of the Victim in the Framework of Criminal Law and Procedure* (Wolf Legal Productions, Nijmegen, 2000)

J. Butler, *Sermons* (1726), also in W.E. Gladstone ed., *The Works of Joseph Butler, Vol. II* (Clarendon Press, Oxford, 1896)

M. Cavadino & J. Dignan, 'Reparation, Retribution and Rights' in A. von Hirsch & A. Ashworth ed., *Principled Sentencing: Readings on Theory and Policy* (Hart Publishing, Oxford, 1998)

J.L. Coleman, *Risks and Wrongs* (Cambridge University Press, Cambridge, 1992)

A.M. Dershowitz, *The Abuse Excuse: And Other Cop-Outs, Sob Stories, and Evasions of Responsibility* (Little Brown & Company, New York, 1994)

R.A. Duff, *Trials and Punishments* (Cambridge University Press, Cambridge, 1986)

The European Court of Human Rights, 'John Murray v. the United Kingdom' judgment of 8 February 1996 (*Reports of Judgments and Decisions* 1996-I)

J. Feinberg, *The Moral Limits of the Criminal Law* (four vols., Oxford University Press, Oxford, 1984-1988)

A.W. Gouldner, *The Coming Crisis of Western Sociology* (Heinemann, London, 1971)

E. Hardwick, 'The Menendez Case' *The New York Review of Books* (17-2-1994)

H.L.A. Hart & A.M. Honoré, *Causation in the Law* (Clarendon Press of Oxford University Press, Oxford, [1959,] 1985)

H.J.R. Kaptein, 'Causation, Criminal' in C.B. Gray ed., *The Philosophy of Law: An Encyclopedia* (Garland Publishing, New York / London, 1999)

H.J.R. Kaptein, 'Improperly Obtained Evidence and the End(s) of Punishment' in C.M. Breur, M.M. Kommer, J.F. Nijboer & J.M. Reijntjes ed., *New Trends in Criminal Investigation and Evidence, Vol. 2* (Intersentia, Antwerpen / Groningen / Oxford, 2001), pp. 375-384

H.J.R. Kaptein, 'Just criminal lawyers? Professional ethics and problems of punitive justice: restorative perspectives' *Archiv für Rechts- und Sozialphilosophie* (Beiheft Nr. 88, 2003), pp. 141-149

J.W. de Keijser, *Punishment and Purpose: From Moral Theory to Punishment in Action* (Thela Thesis, Amsterdam, 2000)

M. van de Kerchove, *Le droit sans peines: aspects de la dépenalisation en Belgique et aux Etats Unis* (Facultés Universitaires Saint-Louis, Brussels, 1987)

D. Lessing, *Prisons We Choose to Live Inside* (CBC Enterprises, Toronto & Jonathan Cape, London, 1986)

J.L. Mackie, 'Retributivism: A Test Case for Ethical Objectivity' in J. Feinberg & J. Coleman ed., *Philosophy of Law* (Wadsworth/Thompson Learning, Belmont, CA, 1999)

J. Mason ed., *The Family of Man* (Maco, New York, 1955)

S. Morimura, 'Libertarian Theories of Punishment' *Archiv für Rechts- und Sozialphilosophie* (Beiheft Nr. 85, 2002), pp. 131-140

M. Nussbaum, 'Human Functioning and Social Justice' *Political Theory* (20/2, 1992)

R. Posner, *The Problematics of Moral and Legal Theory* (Belknap Press, Cambridge, Mass., 1999)

P. Probst, 'Ressentiment' in J. Ritter & K. Gründer ed., *Historisches Wörterbuch der Philosophie* (Schwabe & Co., Basel, 1971/1992)

J. Rawls, *A Theory of Justice* (Belknap Press, Cambridge, Mass., [1971,] 1999)

S. Schafer, *Compensation and Restitution to Victims of Crime* (Patterson Smith, Montclair, NJ, [1960,] 1970)

P.F. Strawson, 'Freedom and Resentment' *Proceedings of the British Academy* (1962), also in Strawson, *Freedom and Resentment, And Other Essays* (Methuen, London, 1973)

P.F. Strawson, *Scepticism and Naturalism: Some Varieties* (*The Woodbridge Lectures, 1983*) (Columbia University Press, 1985)

T.S. Szasz, 'Psychiatric Diversion in the Criminal Justice System: A Critique' in R.E. Barnett & J. Hagel ed., *Assessing the Criminal: Restitution, Retribution and the Legal Process* (Ballinger Publishing Company, Cambridge, Mass., 1977)

R.J. Wallace, *Responsibility and the Moral Sentiments* (Harvard University Press, Cambridge, Mass. & London, 1994)

D. Watson *& al.*, 'Reparation for retributivists' in M. Wright & B. Galaway ed., *Mediation and Criminal Justice: Victims, Offenders and Community* (Sage Publications, London, Newbury Park & New Delhi, 1989)

M. Wright, *Justice for Victims and Offenders: A Restorative Response to Crime* (Open University Press, Milton Keynes & Philadelphia, 1996)

L. Zedner, 'Reparation and Retribution: Are They Reconcilable?' *The Modern Law Review* (57, 1994)

H. Zehr, *The Little Book of Restorative Justice* (Good Books, Intercourse, PA, 2002)

6. Victims on View: Are Victims Served by the Principle of Open Justice?

Marijke Malsch*

Case 1

On August 21, 1998, 11-year old Hans and two friends of the same age were riding their bicycles along the cycle path on Station Street. They accelerated to get through the traffic lights before they turned red. Hans was the only one able to cross the road in time. A small truck, driving in the same direction as the boys, turned right without giving right of way to Hans. The truck hit the little boy, who fell and landed under the truck's wheels. He died immediately.

Ronald, the driver of the truck, was accused of negligently causing Hans' death. Although the statements of the accused and witnesses contradicted on a number of points, the prosecutor had decided to bring the case before the court because he was of the opinion that Ronald had acted negligently by not looking carefully in his mirror before turning right. Ronald stated that he had looked into the mirror prior to turning right, but had not noticed the victim. At the court session, held about one year after the accident happened, some twenty members of the victim's family entered the courtroom. A number of the defendant's relatives also attended. The courtroom was completely silent. When the defendant entered, he was pale as a ghost.

Before the actual trial started, the president of the court gave the relatives of the deceased boy an opportunity to say a few words about their experience of the accident and Hans' consequent death, and how they had led their lives since. The boy's father gave a short characterisation of Hans, how he had done at school and what his hobbies were. Then he described the moment that the family had been notified at home of what had happened. In the year since his son's death, he and his wife and other children had regularly attended a certain church. The accused was also a member of this church. Ronald had contacted the family, and had visited them a number of times since the fatal accident. The father explained that Hans' family highly appreciated this contact.

After these words, the president started the trial. She gave each non-professional process participant plenty of time to tell his or her story. Even after a year, the defendant still found it difficult to talk about what had hap-

* Netherlands Institute for the Study of Crime and Law Enforcement (NSCR) and Leiden University, The Netherlands.

pened. He evidently felt extremely guilty about the little boy's death. After the trial concluded, the defendant left the courtroom together with his own family and the victim's family.

Case 2

Hamid is standing trial for a number of robberies from females. These offences were all conducted in a similar way. The woman would be riding a bicycle when a car would bar her way. Three youths would be sitting in this car. One of them would get out and threaten the woman with a knife, before taking her bag and other belongings. He would then get back in the car, which would drive off quickly, leaving the terrified woman behind. Three women had fallen victim to these crimes before the youths were arrested.

One of these women was present at the trial, with a friend. She had submitted a claim for compensation of damage before the court session. Her claim consisted of a material part and a non-material part. Under the present law, victims submitting such a claim are not obliged to attend the court session, but this woman wished to see how the court would deal with the case. The police had interrogated her as a witness several times, and the police reports were included in the dossier. In principle, under current Dutch law, the judge does not need to hear witnesses again at the public hearing of a case.

During the process, a number of ambiguities became apparent. The police had not done their work with due care, and the court wanted further detail as to exactly what had happened to the women while they were being robbed. The president of the court cautiously enquired who the two women in the courtroom were. The victim answered that she was the victim of the crime being processed by the court. She looked extremely startled by the president's direct questioning and immediately added that she would not speak about the crime in front of the defendant, who had turned around and looked her in the face. The judges left the courtroom for a while to deliberate what to do next. When they returned, the victim had left with her friend and did not come back.

Introduction

The rights of the victims of crime have come to achieve far greater recognition in many countries in the course of the last decades. Detailed descriptions of the increased attention paid to victims of crime and accompanying new legislation are given elsewhere in this book. This chapter focuses on a limited number of still highly important aspects of the victim's experience in the criminal process.

Most research in the field of victimology has been concerned with new rights accorded to victims, new policies related to these rights, and implementation problems. Little attention has been paid to the 'older' principles of justice and how they work out in legal practice with respect to victims and their position in the criminal process. One of these central principles of justice, which emerged as a reaction to legal practices during the Inquisition in Europe, is the principle of open justice. At the time of the Inquisition in the 16th Century, criminal processes were held in secret. The suspect was often unaware of the crime he was accused of, and the proof as well as the actual trials were kept secret. Only the execution of the penalty – in many cases hanging or decapitation – was carried out in public. In the centuries following the Inquisition, trials gradually came to be constructed in such a way that openness for the public was secured. Anyone who was interested could attend a trial, and the media were allowed to report on legal procedures and court decisions. This enabled the 'general public' to keep a democratic check on the decisions of judges. Establishing judges' accountability for their treatment of cases and their decisions was more and more deemed to be necessary (Hoekstra & Malsch, 2002).

The principle of open justice has a number of consequences for victims of crime, both in their role as witness and in their role as claimant of compensation of damages suffered. This chapter focuses on these consequences. The central question of this chapter is, therefore: what is the scope of the principle of open justice, and does open justice serve victims? First, the principle of open justice will be explored. This principle cannot be investigated independently of the legal system in which it operates. In other words, the principle has a different character and scope in the Dutch system as compared with, for example, an Anglo-American system. This chapter, therefore, also describes certain relevant characteristics of the Dutch legal system. A number of aspects of open justice are elaborated on in a later section of the chapter. The provision of information, the accessibility of trials, the visibility of justice and the justification of court decisions are all of great relevance to victims of crime. This chapter discusses each of these aspects and how they influence the victim's position in the trial.

A new law was recently proposed in The Netherlands, enabling victims to give oral statements at the actual court session, describing the crime and how it impacted on their private life. The proposed law would promote victims' input into the sentencing process and, in certain respects, would increase the openness of the criminal trial. This chapter discusses the advantages and drawbacks of this new law, and draws some final conclusions.

The principle of open justice

The principle of open justice[1] is one of the fundamental pillars of the Dutch criminal justice system. In all democratic Western countries, a well-established principle is that courts should generally be open to anyone who wishes to attend. This is extremely important in the Dutch system, which is mainly inquisitorial and from which the lay-element has almost totally disappeared. The Dutch system does not make use of juries and lay judges do not, with a few exceptions, sit in criminal cases. In contrast, most adversarial systems, as well as some inquisitorial, provide a direct public influence on the adjudication of cases in the form of lay juries. Moreover, many countries have far more

1. *Openbaarheidsbeginsel* in Dutch.

cases in the form of lay juries. Moreover, many countries have far more extensive media coverage of trials than The Netherlands, providing the general public with greater insight into events in the courts. The Dutch system, resting almost entirely on professional process participants, offers far fewer opportunities for public control than other countries. This makes the principle of open justice extremely important (Hoekstra & Malsch, 2002).

The principle of open justice, as defined in Dutch law, refers to the accessibility of the criminal process to both process participants and the general public. Process participants need access to all documents and reports produced in a case to check the propriety and legal correctness of all actions taken by the police and other investigative officers. This aspect of open justice is generally referred to as the 'internal openness' of the trial, or the right of access to documents. In addition, the general public needs access to the public hearing of cases, in order to exert democratic control on the adjudication of cases. Criminal processes are not held in secret, as happened during the Inquisition, but in open court. This aspect of the principle of open justice is generally referred to as the 'external openness' of the trial, or the right to attend court sessions (Hoekstra & Malsch, 2002). This chapter concentrates on the external aspect of open justice.

The principle of open justice, when realised in legal practice, can be expected to have a number of side effects that may help realise particular goals of punishment. Knowing what types of punishment are to be imposed for which crimes may have a preventive effect on potential perpetrators. This is known in The Netherlands as the *general preventive effect* of punishment. The prospect of public identification and the risk of being convicted and sent to prison may act as a disincentive to commit crimes, at least so utilitarian penologists claim (Walker, 1991). Openness of the courts may enhance this preventive effect of punishment by enabling the media and the public to become familiar with the adjudication of cases.

A similar effect, though limited to the individual offender, may result from standing trial and being convicted in open court. This is also a proclaimed effect of punishment, in The Netherlands generally known as the *special preventive effect* of punishment. Although this effect is largely attributed to the serving of a prison term, the shaming effects of standing trial and being convicted in front of the 'public' and the media may also reinforce it. This may prevent an individual offender from recidivism (Braithwaite, 1989). The principle of open justice might also be expected to cause this effect to be more significant. Another side effect of the principle of open justice is public denunciation of criminal conduct (Roche, 1999). These effects and functions, in combination with the primary aim of making the judiciary more democratically accountable, make open justice an extremely important principle (Hoekstra & Malsch, 2002).

Although the principle of open justice is primarily directed at the general public and at the accused (in terms of the internal openness of cases), victims testifying in open court are also directly affected. Testifying in open court, before the accused, the judges, prosecutor, counsel and the public in the gallery, can be a traumatising experience for victims. The second case described at the beginning of this chapter illustrates victims' reluctance to appear in open court and to be questioned in front of the defendant. The trauma is substantially increased if the accused denies having committed the alleged act.

Traumatisation or secondary victimisation is not the only conceivable effect of testifying in open court. On occasion, as for instance in the first case described at the beginning of this chapter, victims may positively evaluate being able to relate to the judge in court how they experienced the crime and how it affected their well-being. The experience may help them deal with the crime on a personal level, and resume their 'normal' life afterwards. Certain restorative effects may result from such an appearance in court, especially if the accused and the victim have established some kind of rapport.

Victims' satisfaction may be increased by the offender being convicted, a punishment being imposed, possibly by compensation being paid or even by re-conciliation with the offender. Public recognition of the crime and the damage it caused from all process participants, denunciation of the crime or the offender as well as being able to talk about what happened are extremely important to victims. Some victims may even feel a need to confront the offender with their experiences of the crime. But not all victims wish to explain in open court what their feelings were during and after the crime. Many victims just want to be left alone, and hence refuse to appear in court. It is not easy to predict in advance, however, which victim will give a positive evaluation of appearing in open court, and which victim will give a negative evaluation.

Open justice in practice: characteristics of the Dutch criminal justice system

The present Dutch Code of Criminal Procedure, drafted in 1926, originally designed the Dutch criminal process as a mainly 'oral' process: all evidence should, in principle, be presented, explained, and evaluated at the trial session. In the same year that this new code came into force, the Dutch Court of Cassation (*Hoge Raad der Nederlanden*) ruled that lower courts would, nevertheless, be allowed to use reports that relate statements made by witnesses (or experts) out of court.[2] Moreover, statements in which a person (witness, expert, or police officer) relates what he or she heard a third party say, were considered as constituting acceptable evidence. Both types of statements are known as *de auditu* (hearsay) statements. As a consequence of this ruling by the Court of Cassation, the Dutch criminal process became substantially less 'oral' and relied increasingly on reports of interrogations of witnesses, defendants, and experts written down by the police and other investigation authorities. The dossier became the backbone of the case. It moved from the police to the prosecution, from the prosecution to the investigating judge, and then on to the trial judges, clerks and defense counsel. Each official added reports and other documents to the case-file. These reports were considered an adequate reflec-

2. HR 20 December 1926, *NJ* 1927, 85.

tion of all investigative actions performed in the case (Nijboer & Sennef, 1999).

On hearing the case in court, the presiding judge summarises these reports of interrogations of witnesses, defendants, and experts, and reads aloud a summary of extensive reports on the defendant's personality drawn up by various mental health experts. The Dutch trial is dominated by paperwork. The legal systems of most other countries, both of an adversarial and an inquisitorial nature, award far more importance to the presentation and examination of evidence at the actual trial session than the Dutch system, and the trying of each case takes more time. In those other countries, witnesses and experts are more often summoned to appear at the public hearing of the case than in The Netherlands.

Dutch cases, on the other hand, reach an actual trial more often than criminal cases in some other countries. A substantial proportion of cases in the US system is plea-bargained. Such a common practice does not exist to an equal extent in The Netherlands (Hoekstra & Malsch, 2002), though certain highly 'consensual' methods for deciding cases are employed in the stage preceding the hearing of the case. In these cases, there is no judge to decide on the defendant's guilt and impose penalties. The public prosecutor, or even a police official, offers the defendant the option of paying a certain amount of money, for which in exchange the prosecution is stopped (Kaptein, 2001).[3] This procedure also has ramifications for the openness of the legal system, since neither plea-bargained cases, nor those cases in which the prosecution or the police stops prosecution when the defendant pays a certain sum of money, are open to the public.[4] These cases are not systematically publicised either, so a review by the general public is not possible. The number and seriousness of Dutch cases decided without a judge is growing over the years, reducing the openness of the criminal law system as a whole.

Victims who wish to claim compensation of damage can do so within a criminal process, not only *at* the public hearing of a case, but also *before* the trial. Cases mediated by the police or the prosecution can also involve payments of compensation (Malsch & Carrière, 1999). Guidelines governing the manner in which the police and the prosecution ought to treat victims have been developed in The Netherlands. These guidelines stipulate that the police and prosecution should try to reach a pre-court arrangement between the accused and the victim on the compensation of damage by the accused. If this mediation (*bemiddeling*) results in compensation, the case is either dismissed or the prosecutor requests a lower penalty at the court session. Most mediating procedures do not cover compensation for non-material damage; in most cases only easily assessable material losses are taken into account. The mediation procedure takes place largely through the exchange of letters and by telephone;

3. *Transactie* in Dutch.

4. No exact figures can be found for the number of cases tried in open court as compared to cases not reaching a trial. The annual report of the Dutch Prosecutions Service suggests that over half of criminal cases do not reach a trial in open court.

the so-called mediator is a kind of intermediary. Direct confrontation between the accused and the victims hardly ever takes place. Mediators do not consider organising face-to-face meetings to be one of their tasks. Those victims who wish to avoid direct contact with the accused, therefore, may prefer to be involved in such pre-trial arrangements through the police or the prosecution, rather than submit a claim at the public hearing of the case. This type of procedure however does not serve the principle of open justice, since the general public has no direct view of the outcome and procedure of these cases.

The emphasis of the investigation in each Dutch case has been placed largely in the stages preceding the court session. Victims are, therefore, usually heard before the open trial, during interrogations by the police or the investigating judge. The accused is not present at the questioning. The defendant's counsel may be present when the investigating judge interrogates the victim, but the defendant himself is not. At the court session, however, any of these persons may be present unless, as rarely happens, the judge decides that they should be absent.

Victims are generally reluctant to be heard in open court in front of the defendant, his counsel and the public seated in the gallery. The Dutch emphasis on the pre-trial stages can, from that point of view, be considered as advantageous to many victims acting as witnesses. Countries that adhere more strongly to the principle of immediacy[5] than The Netherlands do not offer this advantage to victims of crime. In most cases abroad, victims who serve as witnesses are summoned to appear at trial. Likewise, in The Netherlands, victims who wish to submit a claim for compensation of damage can do that prior to the court session. This enables them to avoid a public confrontation with the accused. In conclusion, the interests of many victims, acting either as witnesses or as claimants of compensation, seem to be served by the Dutch criminal law system, in which most investigation in a case occurs before the public trial.

Aspects of openness

Dutch law does not explicitly define open justice. The phrasing of the principle of open justice in the law seems to apply only to the accessibility of court sessions: the law says that court sessions are, with a few exceptions, open to the general public. Court decisions are *always* pronounced in open court; no exceptions apply there. Since openness of the courts is such a fundamental pillar of the criminal law process, the legal system and the officials working within it can be expected to do more to realise this goal than merely open the doors to the general public. Law enforcement officials should take a more active role in realising open justice than is currently the case.

The focus of the (external) principle of open justice is primarily on the general public. Certain aspects of the principle are, however, of special relevance

5. The term 'immediacy' refers to all evidence being presented in its original form before the judge.

to victims of crime: the information provided regarding developments in a case, the accessibility of trials, the visibility of justice, and the justification of court decisions. The next section deals with these aspects of openness and how they influence the victim's position in the trial (Malsch, 2001).

The provision of information

Any system that, as a matter of principle, is open to the general public, can be expected to take the initiative in providing information about procedures employed and cases heard. The criminal law system, therefore, can be expected to give information about cases tried as well as their outcomes. Dutch courts increasingly make use of the Internet and dedicated officials to disseminate information about cases and procedures. Although the law does not specify an obligation to inform the general public about developments in cases *before* the actual trial, victims have a right to such information. Guidelines drafted over the last twenty years oblige the police and the prosecution to inform victims of crime about case developments, to ask victims whether they want compensation of the damage caused by the crime, and to treat victims with respect (Wemmers, 1994, 1996; Malsch & Carrière, 1999). Unfortunately, a recently conducted study shows that these guidelines have not substantially improved the provision of information to victims of crime in the Dutch criminal law system (Kool & Moerings, 2001).

The media play an important role in informing the general public about the trial. Although the principle of open justice does not, in fact, apply to the work of the media, their function in providing information about the operation of the criminal justice system deserves some attention. The media report on crimes, actions taken by law enforcement officials, cases tried and decisions taken by courts. The court allows them limited access to trials. In doing their work, the media may invade the privacy not only of defendants but also of victims. By disclosing information about the private lives, relationships, habits, names, addresses, drug or alcohol use of victims, the media may label victims to the same extent as defendants. In comparison with the media in other countries, the Dutch media are fairly reserved about detailing the private lives of process participants. Nevertheless, they may reveal details about persons who wish to remain anonymous. In this respect, openness may not always be in the interest of victims participating in a criminal process.

Visibility and audibility

Visibility, audibility and comprehensibility of the criminal process are further highly important aspects of open justice (Van de Pol, 1986). The trial of cases in open court must be visible, audible and comprehensible for all present, including the media. An observation study, conducted in Dutch courts, showed that public trials are not always sufficiently visible and audible, due to a number of factors (Malsch & Hoekstra, 1999). In courts with public galleries separate from the courtroom, even process participants have poor visibility and audibility.

Poor visibility and audibility may affect victims to an even greater extent than other attendees of a trial. Most victims are admitted into the courtroom; courts generally decide that they should not have to sit in the separate public gallery among members of the defendant's family. But even in the courtroom they may have difficulty hearing and seeing everything. This may heighten the victims' sense of not being involved in the process. The use of complicated legal language by professional process participants may further increase this sense.

Accessibility

A third aspect of open justice to be discussed in relation to the position of victims is the accessibility of trials. Trials should be open to anyone who wishes to attend, but especially to the victims of the crimes being tried in court and to victims' relatives. No physical obstacles should prevent victims reaching and entering the court building. Information should be easily obtainable about how to get to court, in which room the trial will take place and at what time. This aspect of open justice requires law enforcement personnel to have a responsive and alert attitude. Court personnel should be friendly and offer help when needed.

In addition, public galleries and courtrooms should be tidy and pleasant for those attending a court session to sit in. The observation study reported above, however, showed that most galleries that are separated from the courtroom are dirty and unpleasant to visit (Malsch & Hoekstra, 1999). These aspects may appear of low relevance, but they help determine the degree of accessibility of court buildings and sessions, and therefore the openness of court trials.

Most victims come to the court building to fulfil a task: they have been asked to testify before the court. Because this may be a frustrating or even traumatising task for them, they should be treated with the utmost respect. Having a separate waiting room for victims is an important way of alleviating the victim's task. Unfortunately, such rooms are often lacking or not in use in the older court buildings (Van der Leij, 2002). It may happen that a victim of a crime, waiting outside the room for the trial to start, finds himself or herself sitting beside the defendant!

Justification of court decisions in comprehensible language

The final aspect of open justice to be discussed here is the justification of court decisions. Decisions that are adequately justified can be considered to be more 'open', or 'public', than decisions that are not or poorly justified. The use of simple and adequate language in court decisions can help people understand why certain decisions on proof and punishment were taken. If unnecessarily difficult and complicated language is employed, sentences may be substantially less accessible than when simple language is used. Research has shown that justification of court decisions is generally poor (Nijboer & Sennef, 1999). Insufficient reasons for a decision are often given and standard phrasings are generally used, which do not disclose the real reasons why a certain decision was made.

In general, legal language is difficult and complicated, both when spoken and when written. At the actual court session, the language employed is more colloquial than the language used in written court decisions. Nevertheless, participants in a session, including the victim, sometimes do not understand what the professional process participants are talking about. Unexplained ambiguities at trial substantially reduce comprehensibility and, as a consequence, the 'openness' of the trial. Professional process participants should encourage the non-professional process participants to ask questions if they do not understand something. Investigating judges, who hear victims (and other non-professional process participants) in closed sessions, offer them such opportunities to resolve issues more often than judges at public hearings do (Van der Leij, 2002). The reason for this difference is that procedures employed during the hearing by the investigating judge are substantially less formal than during the public hearing at the court session.

In conclusion: to serve the principle of open justice, more elaborate and adequate justifications should be given. In addition, more colloquial language should be employed during the public hearing of cases and in written decisions. Although Dutch law does not explicitly require that court decisions be written and pronounced in understandable, colloquial language, it follows from the principle of open justice that these decisions should be comprehensible for people without legal education. This puts some restrictions on the use of over-complicated juridical and technical language, and requires an open and responsive attitude from professional process participants.

Victim impact statements: openness about consequences of crime

The Dutch criminal law system, under the influence of the European Court of Human Rights (ECHR), has become more inclined towards presenting all evidence at the public hearing of cases (Swart, 1999; Malsch & Nijboer, 1999). During the course of the last ten years, the principle of immediacy has been more widely acknowledged in Dutch court procedures. An increase in immediacy indirectly serves to realise the principle of open justice: the more the evidence of a crime is presented in its original form at the court session, the more the general public and non-professional process participants are able to understand what is happening in court and the more they can review court decisions.

A comparable influence of foreign legal regulations can be discerned in the draft for a new law enabling victim impact statements in The Netherlands. Other countries, both in Europe and in other parts of the world, already have such legislation, and The Netherlands seems set to follow the examples of these foreign legal systems (Brienen & Hoegen, 2000). The newly proposed law[6] gives victims of crime, or their surviving relatives, the right to ask the prosecutor to call them to the court session in the case against the defendant, in order to make a statement about the consequences of the crime. To date, vic-

6. TK 2000-2001, 27 632, nr. 1-5.

tims have only occasionally been offered an opportunity to speak at the public trial about the consequences of the crime they had experienced, at the president's discretion. The new law proposes that the victim should have a right to do so. The draft only allows statements about the consequences of the crime for the victim; he or she may not speak about the defendant or about whatever penalty they consider to be adequate. The court can use these statements during sentencing. The statements have a fourfold goal: they may contribute to the victim's recovery after the crime (a therapeutic goal); they may inform the sentencing court (an informational goal); and they may promote both individual and general preventive effects.

When introduced, this new law will enhance the immediacy and comprehensibility of public trials. The amount of information provided at the actual court session will increase because victims will make a statement about what has happened to them since the crime took place. The general public and the media, in addition to process participants, will be better informed on the consequences of crime for victims. The victim's information will be provided in a direct, oral manner. In this sense, the new law will deviate from the norm in the Dutch criminal law system, which emphasises reporting in a written form.

Although the new law can be applauded for its contribution to the openness of cases and immediacy, some serious criticisms have been voiced concerning the basis for the proposal and the arguments employed in its accompanying Memorandum (for an overview, see De Keijser & Malsch, 2002). One important objection made against the introduction of victim impact statements in the Dutch criminal law system is of a fundamental nature. In using these statements, punishments might be determined by only slightly relevant or even *ir*relevant circumstances or coincidental consequences of the crime, instead of the degree of the defendant's culpability. Articulate victims may have a disproportionate influence on the judge's decision compared to victims who talk less eloquently. In addition, the crime's consequences may be coincidental, and not related to the intent and degree of guilt of the defendant. Relatively minor crimes, such as a simple burglary, could lead to disastrous effects if the homeowner who tried to stop the burglar were to slip, fall and break his neck. It is, in this example, highly questionable whether the defendant can be held accountable for these consequences. His degree of culpability is unrelated to these extreme and unexpected consequences. Victim impact statements will introduce into the trial of the case aspects that, in principle, should not be immediately relevant to the court's sentence.

Research in other countries, where victim impact statements have been introduced and evaluated at an earlier point in time, has found that these statements have no or only a minor influence on the penalties imposed (Erez & Roeger, 1995; Erez & Tontodonato, 1992; Davis & Smith, 1994; Erez, Roeger & Morgan, 1997; Brienen & Hoegen, 2000). The explanation for this finding is that judges are used to deciding cases without receiving direct information from victims about the consequences of the crime they have experienced. They probably feel no need to use this type of information. It may also be the case that judges already have access to most of this information in other parts of the file, and that the new information provided by victims is considered to be redundant.

Victim impact statements appear not to lead to overall satisfaction of victims. Some research findings report increased feelings of satisfaction, but others show that many victims cannot even remember having made such a statement (Erez & Roeger, 1995; Erez & Tontodonato, 1992; Davis & Smith, 1994; Erez, Roeger & Morgan, 1997; Brienen & Hoegen, 2000). There is always a risk of unfulfilled expectations if victims make an impact statement and then expect the trial to have a certain outcome.

Other objections against the introduction of victim impact statements in The Netherlands revolve around the question as to whether such statements may be used instrumentally for achieving certain goals of criminal law, such as, for example, prevention of new crimes. These goals have nothing to do with the victim's case, and it is doubtful whether 'using' a victim to achieve these goals is justified. The principle of open justice plays an important role in the presumption that such an effect would exist: defendants, people in the public gallery, and those who read journals and watch television – all those who hear the consequences of crimes as described by the victims may refrain from offending or from relapsing into criminality. It is not clear whether hearing such information in an open trial has such a consequence. It would be highly interesting to study these presumed effects of the public hearing of cases.

Conclusions

The two cases described at the beginning of this chapter show that different victims of crime can perceive open justice quite differently. Not all victims take a positive view of being able to talk at a public trial in front of the defendant, the process participants, the media, and the people in the public gallery. Some victims may, however, find relief in telling the court about the consequences of the crime on their personal life, and hearing the court's decision on guilt and punishment. In some exceptional cases, such as the first one described in this chapter, where the victim's family and the defendant had been in positive contact since the alleged crime took place, speaking at a public trial may help both sides of the conflict deal with the crime and its consequences. Certain restorative effects may follow in these cases.

In this chapter it is contended that the principle of open justice should be understood in a broader sense than merely the openness of the courtroom doors. The operation of the principle in legal practice should also encompass such aspects as the provision of information by legal professionals to process participants and the general public, the visibility, audibility and comprehensibility of the trial, the accessibility of court buildings, and an adequate and comprehensible justification of court decisions. These aspects are of relevance to every person who attends a public trial, but especially so for the victim, since he or she risks being injured psychologically by a lack of due care in processing cases and any disrespectful treatment by law enforcement professionals.

References

J. Braithwaite, *Crime, Shame and Reintegration* (Cambridge University Press, Cambridge, 1989)

M.E.I. Brienen & E.H. Hoegen, *Victims of Crime in 22 Criminal Justice Systems: The Implementation of Recommendation (85) 11 of the Council of Europe on the Position of the Victim in the Framework of Criminal Law and Procedure* (Wolf Legal Productions, Nijmegen, 2000)

Y. Buruma, *De aandacht van de strafrechter* (Gouda Quint, Arnhem, 1996)

R. Davis, 'Impact Statements: Not Having Much Effect' *NOVA Newsletter* (9, 1992), pp. 1-7

R.D. Davis & B. Smith, 'The Effect of Victim Impact Statements on Sentencing Decisions: A Test in an Urban Setting' *Justice Quarterly* (3, 1994), pp. 453-469

J.W. De Keijser, *Punishment and Purpose: From Moral Theory to Punishment in Action* (Thela Thesis, Amsterdam, 2000)

J.W. De Keijser, & M. Malsch, 'Is spreken zilver en zwijgen goud? Spreekrecht en het ontstemde slachtoffer' *Delikt & Delinkwent* (1, 2002), pp. 5-20

E. Erez & P. Tontodonato, 'Victim Participation in Sentencing and Satisfaction with Justice' *Justice Quarterly*, (9, 1992), pp. 393-427

E. Erez, 'Victim Participation in Sentencing: And the Debate Goes On...' *International Review of Victimology* (3, 1994), pp. 17-32

E. Erez & L. Roeger, 'The Effect of Victim Impact Statements on Sentencing Patterns and Outcomes: the Australian experience' *Journal of Criminal Justice* (23, 1995), pp. 363-375

E. Erez, L. Roeger & F. Morgan, 'Victim Harm, Impact Statements and Victim Satisfaction with Justice: An Australian Experience' *International Review of Victimology* (5, 1997) pp. 37-60

R. Hoekstra & M. Malsch, 'The Principle of Open Justice in The Netherlands' in P.J. van Koppen & S. Penrod ed., *Adversarial Versus Inquisitorial Justice* (Kluwer Academic / Plenum, New York, 2003)

H.J.R. Kaptein, 'Materieelrechtelijke (de)legitimatie van strafvorderlijke openbaarheid en publiciteit' in C.J. de Poot & M. Malsch ed., *Bivakmuts, politiepet en toga: wisselwerking tussen criminaliteit en rechtshandhaving* (Boom Juridische uitgevers, Den Haag, 2001), pp. 121-148

M. Malsch & R. Carrière, 'Victims' Wishes for Compensation: The Immaterial Aspect' *Journal of Criminal Justice* (3, 1999), pp. 239-249

M. Malsch & R. Hoekstra, 'De publieke tribune: controlemiddel voor de rechtspraak of opvangruimte voor daklozen?' *Delikt & Delinkwent* (29, 1999), pp. 737-755

M. Malsch & J.F. Nijboer ed., *Complex cases: perspectives on The Netherlands criminal justice system* (Thela Thesis, Amsterdam, 1999)

M. Malsch, 'Openbaarheid en herstel' *Tijdschrift voor herstelrecht* (3, 2001), pp. 33-43

J.F Nijboer & A. Sennef, 'Justification' in M. Malsch & J.F. Nijboer ed., *Complex Cases: Perspectives on The Netherlands Criminal Justice System* (Thela Thesis, Amsterdam, 1999), pp. 11-27

D. Roche, *Restorative Justice: The Need For Public Accountability and the Role of Open Justice* (Paper presented at the Third International Meeting on Restorative Justice for Juveniles, Leuven, 1999)

C.A. Studebaker & S. Penrod, 'Pretrial Publicity: The Media, the Law and Common Sense' *Psychology, Public Policy, and Law* (2/3, 1997), pp. 428-460

B. Swart, 'The European Convention as an Invigorator of Domestic Law in The Netherlands' *Journal of Law and Society* (1, 1999), pp. 38-47

U. Van de Pol, *Openbaar terecht: Een onderzoek van het openbaarheidsbeginsel in de strafrechtspleging* (Dissertation, Vrije Universiteit, Amsterdam, 1986)

J.B.J. Van der Leij, *Bejegening op maat: de behandeling van getuigen in strafzaken* (Proefschrift Universiteit Leiden, Kluwer, Deventer, 2002)

N. Walker, *Why Punish?* (Oxford University Press, Oxford, 1991)

J.M. Wemmers, *Evaluatie Terwee: Slachtofferonderzoek wet en richtlijn Terwee: Eindrapport* (Ministerie van Justitie, Centrale Directie Wetenschapsbeleid en Ontwikkeling, The Hague, 1994)

J.M. Wemmers, *Victims in the criminal justice system* (WODC/Kugler Publications, Den Haag / Amsterdam / New York, 1996)

7. Victims and the International Criminal Tribunal for the Former Yugoslavia

Åsa Rydberg*

1. *Introduction*

In 1993, following reports of widespread and flagrant violations of international humanitarian law in the territory of the former Yugoslavia, the UN Security Council acted under the powerful Chapter VII of the UN Charter and set up the *ad hoc* International Criminal Tribunal for the former Yugoslavia ('Tribunal' or 'ICTY'). It acted with determination to put an end to these crimes and to bring to justice the persons responsible for them.[1] Since then, the Tribunal has become a reality and is now in full operation.[2]

In this article I will focus on matters which, in my view, are likely to be of particular importance to many victims of the conflicts in the former Yugoslavia. After a brief description of the mandate and organisation of the Tribunal, I will examine the applicable rules and practices with regard to the following four matters: the basis on which indictments are brought against the accused; the role of victims – testifying as a witness; compensation and restitution of stolen property; and sentencing. This will be followed by a discussion on the limited victim participation in the ICTY proceedings and I will conclude with some remarks on the need for public outreach to the victims in the region. The article will not cover the work of the *ad hoc* International Criminal Tribunal for

* International Criminal Tribunal for the former Yugoslavia. The views expressed in this article are those of the author and do not necessarily represent those of the ICTY or the United Nations.

1. UN Security Council Resolution 827 (1993) of 25 May 1993. For general information about the establishment of the Tribunal, see for example V. Morris & M.P. Scharf, *An Insider's Guide to The International Criminal Tribunal for the Former Yugoslavia* (Transnational Publishers, Irvington-on-Hudson N.Y., 1995), C. Bassiouni & P. Manikas, *The Law of the International Criminal Tribunal for the former Yugoslavia* (Transnational Publishers, Irvington-on-Hudson N.Y., 1996).

2. For an overview of the work of the Tribunal, the ongoing cases, statistics and other information, see the ICTY Internet homepage: <http://www.un.org/icty/>. Another useful source of information is the ICTY Annual Report, which covers the activities of each organ of the Tribunal and is submitted each year by the President of the Tribunal to the Security Council and the General Assembly. See for example the Eighth ICTY Annual Report, A/56/352 - S/2001/865, 17 September 2001, which is available, *inter alia*, on the ICTY Internet homepage.

Rwanda ('ICTR')[3] or the future International Criminal Court ('ICC').[4] However, it should be noted that many of the rules and practices of the ICTR are very similar to those of the ICTY.[5]

2. *Mandate and organisation of the ICTY*

As set out in the Security Council resolution, the Tribunal was established 'for the sole purpose of prosecuting persons responsible for serious violations of international humanitarian law committed in the territory of the former Yugoslavia between 1 January 1991 and a date to be determined by the Security Council upon the restoration of peace'.[6] The Security Council has not yet set an end date to this jurisdiction.

In the resolution, the Security Council adopted the Statute of the Tribunal ('Statute'), which sets out the competence and organisation of the Tribunal. It also deals with procedural matters, which have been further detailed in the Rules of Procedure and Evidence ('Rules').[7] The Statute provides that the Tribunal has jurisdiction over the following crimes: Grave breaches of the Geneva Conventions of 1949; Violations of the laws or customs of war; Genocide; and Crimes against humanity.[8] Individual persons can be prosecuted on the basis of individual criminal responsibility, which includes superior responsibility.[9]

The Tribunal, which is located in The Hague, The Netherlands, has three main organs. The Office of the Prosecutor is responsible for carrying out investigations, gathering evidence and indicting and prosecuting those suspected of crimes falling within the jurisdiction of the Tribunal.[10] In Chambers, the judges

3. The International Criminal Tribunal for Rwanda was established by Security Council Resolution 955 (1994).
4. The Rome Statute of the International Criminal Court was adopted by the United Nations Diplomatic Conference of Plenipotentiaries on the Establishment of an International Criminal Court on 17 July 1998, UN Doc. A/CONF.183/9 (1998). It came into force on 1 July 2002, although it is likely that it will take some years before it becomes a fully functioning court.
5. On the other hand, the ICC Statute and Rules of Procedure and Evidence provide for a much stronger position for victims.
6. UN Security Council Resolution 827 (1993) of 25 May 1993.
7. Article 15 of the Statute provides that the Judges of the International Tribunal should adopt the Rules of Procedure and Evidence. The Rules have been amended several times to take into account evolving needs and unforeseen circumstances of pre-trial, trial, and post-trial proceedings before an international criminal tribunal. The latest amendment of the Rules came into force on 5 August 2002, IT/32/Rev.24.
8. Articles 2-5 of the Statute.
9. Article 7(1) and (3) of the Statute.
10. Article 11 of the Statute. In 1998, the Statute was amended by the Security Council to provide for a third Trial Chamber. Security Council Resolution 1166 (1998) of 13 May 1998. In 2000, the Statute was amended again to establish a pool of *ad litem* judges, who can serve with permanent judges in some cases. Security Council Resolution 1329 (2000) of 30 November 2000.

carry out the judicial functions of the court. Chambers comprise three main Trial Chambers and an Appeals Chamber.[11] Three judges serve in each of the Trial Chambers and five judges serve in the Appeals Chamber.[12] Finally, the Registry is responsible for the administration and servicing of the Office of the Prosecutor and Chambers.[13]

3. *Indictments against the accused*

A victim of, for example, deportation – or indeed anybody who has lived through an armed conflict during which war crimes, crimes against humanity or genocide were committed – may want to see the wrongdoers brought to justice. However, it is not unusual that the views differ with regard to who should be brought to justice and for which reasons. This brings us to the following question: how, and on which grounds, are indictments against the accused brought at the Tribunal?

Indictments are brought solely by the Prosecutor, who acts independently and whose office is a separate organ of the Tribunal.[14] Individuals, States or organisations cannot bring cases before the Tribunal. In other words, a victim cannot decide 'to bring the perpetrator to the court in The Hague.' However, the Statute provides, *inter alia,* that the 'Prosecutor shall initiate investigations ex-officio or on the basis of information obtained by any source [...]'[15] and a victim can therefore provide relevant information to the Office of the Prosecutor regarding allegations of crimes falling within the jurisdiction of the ICTY.[16] On the other hand, it is worth stressing that the Statute provides that the Prosecutor shall not seek or receive instructions from any Government or any other source.[17]

Thus it is entirely within the Prosecutor's discretion to initiate investigations. However, as noted by the Appeals Chamber, this broad discretion is

11. Articles 11 and 12 of the Statute.
12. Article 12 of the Statute.
13. Article 17 of the Statute.
14. Article 16 of the Statute.
15. Article 18(1) provides: 'The Prosecutor shall initiate investigations ex-officio or on the basis of information obtained from any source, particularly from Governments, United Nations organs, intergovernmental and non-governmental organisations. The Prosecutor shall assess the information received or obtained and decide whether there is sufficient basis to proceed'.
16. See further for example Å. Rydberg & K.D. Askin, 'International Criminal Tribunals: Refugees and Internally Displaced Persons Who May Be Witnesses Before The Tribunals' in J. M. Fitzpatrick ed., *Human Rights Protection for Refugees, Asylum-Seekers, and Internally Displaced Persons: A Guide to International Mechanisms and Procedures* (Transnational Publishers, Ardsley N.Y., 2002), pp. 499-503.
17. Article 16(2) of the Statute.

limited by the Statute and the Rules of the Tribunal and more generally by the principles of human rights.[18]

Upon determination that a case exists, the Prosecutor shall prepare an indictment containing the facts and the crimes with which the accused is charged and transmit the indictment to a Judge for review and confirmation. The reviewing Judge shall confirm the indictment, in whole or in part, if satisfied that a *prima facie* case exists against the suspect. If not so satisfied, the indictment will be dismissed.[19] As explained in a reasoned review decision, the purpose of this exercise is 'to determine whether there is a fit case to justify the commencement of proceedings against the accused on the indictment and to ensure that there is material to support the allegations in it, thus preventing the commencement of proceedings for which there is no support '[20]

So whom does the Prosecutor indict? Because the Tribunal has a limited mandate, scope of jurisdiction and resources, as a general rule the Prosecutor will attempt to prosecute primarily, but not exclusively, the leaders and most serious offenders. This prosecutorial strategy became clearer in 1998, when charges against 14 lower level accused were withdrawn. Louise Arbour, then Chief Prosecutor, stated that this was due to the steady increase in accused who had either been arrested or who had voluntarily surrendered. She noted that she had to balance the available resources within the Tribunal and that the withdrawal of charges against these accused was consistent with her office's investigative and prosecutorial strategies.[21]

This policy has been further developed by the current Chief Prosecutor Carla Del Ponte. In an address to the Security Council (concerning both the ICTY and the ICTR) she stated:

> It goes almost without saying that my focus [...] is on the leaders. Any lower level cases that are going through the system can either be explained in terms of the history of the Tribunals' development, or they concern notorious individuals whose conduct stands out despite the fact that they had no formal position in any hierarchy.[22]

18. In Delalić *& al.*, one of the grounds of appeal which the Appeals Chamber dealt with was an allegation of selective prosecution by the Prosecutor: Prosecutor v. Delalić *& al.*, Case No. IT-96-21-A, Appeals Chamber, Judgement, 20 February 2001, paras. 596-619. See also Prosecutor v. Milošević, Case No. IT-99-37-PT, Decision on Preliminary Motions, 8 November 2001, paras. 12-15.
19. Articles 18(4) and 19 of the Statute and Rule 47 of the Rules.
20. Prosecutor v. Milošević, Case No. IT-01-51-I, Decision on Review of Indictment, Judge Richard May, 22 November 2001, para. 2.
21. 'Statement by the Prosecutor following the Withdrawal of the Charges against 14 Accused' *ICTY Press Release* (314, 8 May 1998).
22. 'Address by the Prosecutor of the International Criminal Tribunal for the former Yugoslavia, Carla Del Ponte, to the UN Security Council' *ICTY Press Release* (642, 27 November 2001).

Two aspects of this policy were explained in more detail. First, it was stated that the Office of the Prosecutor has not investigated all crimes, but has concentrated on the areas in which the worst massacres occurred. Although it has been established that the ethnic cleansing in Bosnia was the result of a highly organised enterprise by many individuals, the Prosecutor said that she does not expect to prosecute all those at such command levels. Second, at the same time the Prosecutor stressed that one should not fall into the trap of polarising accused into 'big fish' and 'small fish', and noted that a number of the accused under investigation played a nasty role somewhere in between these two extremes as key organisers and motivators at the district or local level. The Prosecutor stated that for the victims and survivors,

> ... it was these people who brought their world to an end, not the remote governmental architects of the overall policy of genocide. Unless these local leaders are brought to justice [...] the ordinary population will not come to terms with the past, and the process of reconciliation and building a stable peace will suffer accordingly.'

She concluded that this 'is why these cases justify my attention and that is why the choice of cases to pursue is not at all simple.'[23]

In this connection it should be stressed that the Statute of the Tribunal provides for concurrent jurisdiction with national courts. Thus, while the Statute grants the Tribunal primacy over national courts and the Tribunal can formally request national courts to defer competence to it, cases not prosecuted by the Tribunal can be prosecuted before national courts.[24] However, the current trend is rather the reverse: Judge Claude Jorda, President of the Tribunal, recently submitted a report to the Security Council, which proposes that in order to achieve its current objective of completing all first instance trials by 2008, the Tribunal should refer certain cases to national courts. The report recommends that the ICTY should concentrate its work on the prosecution and trial of the perpetrators of crimes most prejudicial to international public order, *i.e.* the highest-ranking civilian, military and paramilitary leaders. It is suggested that now, when peace has returned to the region, the time is right for referral of cases involving intermediary and lower-level accused to the competent national jurisdictions. In the case of Bosnia and Herzegovina, the report further recommends the creation of a specific Chamber within the State Court for the cases involving the intermediary-level accused (with international judges serving alongside national judges).[25] The Security Council has endorsed the proposed broad strategy of referring cases to national courts and seemed positive to the

23. *Id.*
24. Article 9 of the Statute.
25. Report on the Judicial Status of the International Criminal Tribunal for the former Yugoslavia and the Prospects for Referring Cases to National Courts, 10 June 2002, S/2002/678; 'Address of Judge Claude Jorda, President of the International Criminal Tribunal for the former Yugoslavia, to the United Nations Security Council', 23 July 2002, *ICTY Press Release* (690, 26 July 2002).

idea of creating a specific Chamber within the State Court of Bosnia and Herzegovina.[26]

In conclusion, indictments can only be brought by the Prosecutor, who has developed a strategy according to which there is a principal focus on the leaders and others responsible for planning and orchestrating the crimes. Thus many crimes which fall within the Tribunal's jurisdiction will not be prosecuted and tried by it. Instead, it is expected that many intermediary and lower-level perpetrators will be tried before national courts.

4. *The role of victims: Testifying as witnesses before the ICTY*

A victim may wish to take part in the proceedings against an alleged perpetrator. He or she may want to present his or her views on a particular aspect of the proceedings or perhaps tell the world precisely what happened during an attack of a village or how the detainees were treated in a concentration camp. What are the possibilities to do so, and what happens if he or she is called to testify as a witness before the Tribunal?

In fact, there is no specific role or special place for victims in the proceedings before the ICTY other than as witnesses. There is no *partie civile* or similar role for victims or people acting on their behalf. As witnesses, victims play an important role at the Tribunal. Unlike the Prosecutors at the Nuremberg International Military Tribunal who had access to the Nazi's carefully kept documentation of the atrocities committed during World War II, the Prosecutor of the Tribunal must generally rely on the testimony of eye-witnesses to the war crimes committed in the former Yugoslavia.[27]

Witnesses can be called either by the Prosecutor, the Defence or occasionally, by the Trial Chamber.[28] During the investigation of alleged crimes and during the preparation for trial, the Office of the Prosecutor is usually in contact with a vast number of people who provide information or give statements relating to the alleged crimes. However, depending on the prosecutor's strategy, testimony of previous witnesses and logistical arrangements, only a few of the persons providing evidence will eventually appear as prosecution witnesses before the Tribunal.[29] Consequently, a victim who is not called to testify as a witness does not have any right or possibility to appear before a Trial Chamber to tell his or her story. Moreover, it should be pointed out that even if a victim

26. Statement by the President of the Security Council, 23 July 2002, S/PRST/2002/21.
27. As noted by Bassiouni, among others, the alleged perpetrators of the former Yugoslavia did not leave a similar paper trail or documentary record. See C. Bassiouni, 'Former Yugoslavia: Investigating Violations of International Humanitarian Law and Establishing an International Criminal Tribunal' *Fordham International Law Journal* (18, 1995), pp. 1191-1206.
28. Pursuant to Rule 98 of the Rules, a Trial Chamber can call witnesses at its own initiative.
29. See further Å. Rydberg & K.D. Askin, *op. cit.*, p. 502.

is called as a witness, this may not necessarily mean that he or she may give testimony about all the things that, according to him or her, are of relevance or importance in relation to an incident. The testimony will normally be limited to the topics or questions that the party calling the witness is raising in court.

Although a high number of the witnesses before the Tribunal are victim witnesses, there are also other witnesses, such as people who served as peace-keepers or monitors during the conflict, forensic experts, and demographers. So far, over 2000 witnesses have testified before the Tribunal.[30]

At an early stage of its existence, the Tribunal recognised that in giving testimony before it, some witnesses will have to re-live their experiences in a country far away from their own and without the support from relatives and friends which they would normally receive if testifying in an ordinary court of law in their own country, in time of peace. Moreover, it was also recognised that some witnesses may have legitimate concerns about reprisals.[31] The Victims and Witnesses Section of the Tribunal ('VWS') was established in order to alleviate these anxieties as far as possible and to create an environment for witnesses where they can give their testimony with dignity and in safety.[32] Thus the VWS is tasked with the support and protection of victims and witnesses, as provided in the Rules.[33] The VWS deals with all witnesses, regardless of whether they will appear for the Defence or the Prosecution. It is placed within the Registry of the ICTY. This is a neutral place, which enables it to take into consideration the interests of the witness – rather than the interests of the accused or the Prosecutor – regardless of the role the witness will play in the trial.[34]

The VWS is responsible for the administrative and logistical arrangements in connection with the witnesses' travel to The Hague. Thus VWS gained experience in solving practical problems with visas and identification papers. It has developed policies for a witness to be accompanied by a support person when travelling to The Hague to testify; childcare; compensation for lost wages and daily allowances, etc. Further, it will provide emotional support and arrange for specialist medical and psychological assistance if needed.[35]

With regard to witness protection, it should be noted that as a general rule, the ICTY hearings are held in public with full disclosure of the identity of the

30. According to the VWS, by the end of February 2002, approximately 2080 witnesses have testified before the ICTY.

31. Second ICTY Annual Report, UN Doc. A/50/365 (1995), para 109.

32. *Id.* para 110.

33. Rule 34 of the Rules.

34. See further Å. Rydberg, 'The Protection of the Interests of Witnesses: The ICTY in Comparison to the Future ICC' *Leiden Journal of International Law* (12, 1999).

35. In developing the policies, the VWS has applied the relevant United Nations standards, such as the 1985 General Assembly Declaration of Basic Principles of Justice for Victims of Crime and Abuse of Power, GA. Res. 40/34 (1985), Second ICTY Annual Report, UN Doc. A/50/365, para 116. *See further e.g.* Å. Rydberg, 'The Protection of the Interests of Witnesses: The ICTY in Comparison to the Future ICC' *op. cit.*, pp. 462-465, and Å. Rydberg & K.D. Askin, *op. cit.*, pp. 503-507.

witness.[36] A Trial Chamber may in exceptional circumstances and in the interests of justice, authorise the receipt of testimony via video-conference link for witnesses who are unable to travel to The Hague to testify.[37] In accordance with the Rules, a Chamber may order various measures for the privacy or protection of the witness, provided that the measures are not inconsistent with the rights of the accused. As always with witness protection, a balance has to be found between the need for witness protection on the one hand and the procedural rights of the accused on the other.[38] Some of the measures that are frequently applied in court have also been developed in practice. A Judge or Chamber can order that the name and identifying information be removed from the Chamber's records. In such a case, the witness will be assigned a pseudonym, like 'Witness R', which will be used for all purposes at the Tribunal. Moreover, a Judge or Chamber can order non-disclosure to the public of any records identifying the victim. The Chamber can also order image altering and voice distortion devices that will leave the witness's appearance or voice unrecognisable on the court television and in the public gallery of the courtroom.

Which protective measures, if any, are granted will depend on a variety of factors, including preference of the witness and assessment of the danger or threat of harm, physically and mentally. Ultimately, however, the Trial Chamber has the final responsibility for determining which protective measures are most appropriate. When doing so, the Chamber can consult with the VWS on what protective measures would be appropriate in a particular situation.[39]

Needless to say, these are protective measures for the courtroom, which have been designed to minimise the need for protection after the testimony. However, in some cases there may be a need for post-trial protection. If so, arrangements will be made with the local police authorities in the country of residence of the witness. In the event that this would not suffice, there is a witness relocation program designed for witnesses who, as a result of their appearance before the Tribunal, cannot return to their homes, due to serious concerns for their safety. For these rare cases, the Tribunal has concluded a number of agreements with States that are willing to accept such witnesses and their close family members.[40]

36. Articles 20(4) and 22 of the Statute and Rules 75, 78 and 79 of the Rules.

37. Rule 71 *bis* of the Rules.

38. Rule 75 of the Rules. See for example F. Mumba, 'Ensuring a Fair Trial whilst Protecting Victims and Witnesses – Balancing of Interests?' in R. May *& al.* ed., *Essays on ICTY Procedure and Evidence In Honour of Gabrielle Kirk McDonald* (Kluwer Law International, The Hague, 2001), p. 359.

39. It is also noteworthy that Rule 75 allows for the VWS to independently request the Trial Chamber that certain protective or privacy measures for victims and witnesses be implemented.

40. As the agreements concern the safety and security of witnesses, the terms and details of these agreements are confidential. See 'United Kingdom becomes first state to agree to provide enhanced assistance to witness protection efforts of International Tribunal' *ICTY Press Release* (258, 7 November 1997), see also C. Châtelot & C. Tréan, 'Témoins sous

In short, victims can only participate in the proceedings before the Tribunal as witnesses. Their live testimony is crucial to ICTY, and as witnesses they can request protective measures and support.

5. *Can victims seek compensation and restitution at the ICTY?*

The next issue to be discussed concerns compensation and reparation. Naturally, many victims of the conflicts may want to seek compensation for their injuries or losses. In other cases, a victim may simply want his or her former house or possessions back.[41]

The Statute is silent on the matter of victim compensation and the founding resolution of the Tribunal provides that 'the work of the International Tribunal should be carried out without prejudice to the right of the victims to seek, through the appropriate means, compensation for damage incurred as a result of violations of international humanitarian law.'[42] Thus, the Security Council was clearly conscious of the issue of victim compensation, but appears to have implied that the Tribunal should not deal with the matter.

Although there are no provisions on direct victim compensation, the Rules of the Tribunal address the matter in that they provide that when a convicted person has caused injury to a victim, claims for compensation may be brought before national courts or other competent bodies. For the purposes of such a claim, a judgement of the Tribunal shall be final and binding as to the criminal responsibility of the convicted person.[43] This rule appears to be of limited practical use, as no such compensation claims have yet been based on an ICTY Judgement.

In September 2000, following an initiative by the Chief Prosecutor, victim compensation was discussed by the ICTY Judges during the 22nd Plenary Session of the Tribunal. As stated in a press release, they concluded that the victims of crimes within the jurisdiction of the Tribunal have a legal right to seek compensation for their injuries. The Judges made a recommendation to the Security Council and to the Secretary-General 'that methods of compensating victims of crimes in the former Yugoslavia, be seriously considered by the appropriate organs of the United Nations'.[44] In other words, it was acknowledged that the victims of crimes within the ICTY jurisdiction have the right to compensation, but concluded that the Tribunal is not the appropriate organ to

---

haute protection' *Le Monde* (19 February 2002); Å. Rydberg, 'The Protection of the Interests of Witnesses: The ICTY in Comparison to the Future ICC' *op. cit.*, pp. 463-465.

41. See generally S. Malmström, 'Restitution of Property and Compensation to Victims' in R. May *& al.* ed., *Essays on ICTY Procedure and Evidence In Honour of Gabrielle Kirk McDonald* (Kluwer Law International, The Hague, 2001), p. 373.

42. UN Security Council Resolution 827 (1993) of 25 May 1993.

43. Rule 106 of the Rules.

44. 'The Judges of the ICTY Acknowledge the Right of Victims of Crimes Committed in the former Yugoslavia to Seek Compensation: UN Invited to Consider Methods of Compensation Victims' *ICTY Press Release* (528, 14 September 2000).

deal with such matters. A few months later the Chief Prosecutor raised the matter again, in an address to the Security Council. She stated that her office had had considerable success in tracing and freezing large amounts of money of the accused, and that in the event of a conviction, this money could be used to compensate 'the citizens who deserve it.' Consequently, the Prosecutor asked the Security Council to give 'serious and urgent consideration to any change that would remove this lacuna in our process.'[45] However, thus far, the Security Council has neither designated an appropriate organ that could handle compensation claims (as requested by the Judges), nor changed the ICTY Statute to allow for victim compensation (as requested by the Prosecutor).

Concerning restitution of stolen property, the Statute and the Rules actually provide that a Trial Chamber of the Tribunal may make special findings in this regard. If a Trial Chamber finds an accused guilty of a crime and concludes from the evidence that unlawful taking of property by the accused was associated with it, the Chamber shall make a specific finding to this effect in the judgement. Following such a finding, a Trial Chamber may, *proprio motu* or at the request of the Prosecutor, after a special hearing, order restitution of the property (or the proceeds thereof) to the rightful owner.[46] Thus, under the Rules a victim does not have standing to directly request a Trial Chamber to order restitution of his or her property.

To date, no findings relating to restitution have been made by the Trial Chambers of the Tribunal. However, these rules may be applied in the future, as the Prosecutor has requested restitution of property in an on-going case.[47]

In conclusion, victims cannot request compensation before the Tribunal. There are rules which allow a Trial Chamber to make specific findings concerning restitution of property. However, victims do not have standing to make a direct request to a Trial Chamber to order such restitution.

6. *Sentencing*

Sentencing is a matter which is usually of great importance to many victims. Opinions often differ with respect to what kind of sentence should be imposed on a convicted person and on what is generally appropriate in the circumstances. Given that, it might be useful to briefly examine the applicable rules and practices in relation to sentencing at the Tribunal.

45. The Prosecutor also stated that in her view, the voices of survivors and relatives of those who were killed are not sufficiently heard, and suggested that victims be given a more prominent role in the processes before the International Tribunal. 'Address to the Security Council by Carla Del Ponte, Prosecutor of the International Criminal Tribunal for the former Yugoslavia and Rwanda' *ICTY Press Release* (542, 24 November 2000).

46. Article 24(3) of the Statute and Rules 98 *ter* (B) and 105 of the Rules.

47. Prosecutor v. Naletilić & Martinović, Case No. IT-98-34-PT, Prosecutor's Pre-Trial Brief, 11 October 2000, paras 4.186 - 4.199.

Following a trial against an accused, the Trial Chamber shall pronounce a public and reasoned judgement and, if the accused has been found guilty of any of the counts charged in the indictment, it shall impose a sentence.[48] The Statute provides that any penalty imposed should be limited to imprisonment.[49] In other words, life imprisonment is an allowed penalty, whereas the death penalty is not.[50] To date, the Chambers of the Tribunal have imposed sentences ranging from three to 46 years.[51]

The practice of the Tribunal reflects two main objectives of sentence: the need to punish an individual for the crimes committed and the need to deter other individuals from committing similar crimes.[52]

The Statute and the Rules offer little guidance when it comes to sentencing of a convicted person. When determining a sentence, a Trial Chamber must take into account the general practice regarding prison sentences in the courts of the former Yugoslavia, the gravity of the offence as well as the individual circumstances of the convicted person.[53] Further, any aggravating and mitigating circumstances must also be considered.[54] In the practice of the Tribunal, the gravity of the offence is the most important factor to be taken into account in imposing a sentence.[55]

As noted recently by a Trial Chamber, assessing seriousness of crimes is not a mere matter of comparing and ranking crimes in the abstract: a Trial Chamber must assess the gravity of the crimes in the light of their individual circumstances and consequences, which 'presupposes taking into account quantitatively the number of victims and qualitatively the suffering inflicted on the

48. Article 23 of the Statute. See generally on sentencing among others J.C. Nemitz, 'Sentencing in the Jurisprudence of the International Criminal Tribunals for the Former Yugoslavia and Rwanda' in H. Fischer *& al.* ed. *International and National Prosecution of Crimes Under International Law: Current Developments* (Spitz, Berlin, 2001), S. Beresford 'Unshackling the Paper Tiger: The Sentencing Practices of the Ad Hoc International Criminal Tribunals for the former Yugoslavia and Rwanda' *International Criminal Law Review* (1, 2001, 33), A. Marston Danner, 'Constructing a Hierarchy of Crimes in International Criminal Law Sentencing' *Virginia Law Review* (87, 2001), W.A. Schabas 'Sentencing by International Tribunals: A Human Rights Approach' *Duke Journal of Comparative and International Law* (7, 1997).

49. Article 24 of the Statute.

50. It should also be noted that fines cannot be imposed as a penalty to serious violations of international humanitarian law.

51. For an overview of the sentences imposed thus far, see the ICTY Internet home page: <http://www.un.org/icty/> under 'Judgements'.

52. Prosecutor v. Krstić, Case No. IT-98-33-T, Judgement, 2 August 2001, para. 693. See also, for example, Prosecutor v. Kunarac *et al.*, Case Nos. IT-96-23-T & IT-96-23/1-T, Judgement, 22 February 2001, paras. 836-844; Prosecutor v. Aleksovski, Case No. 95-14/1-A, Judgement, 24 March 2000, para. 185.

53. Article 24 of the Statute.

54. Rule 101 of the Rules.

55. Prosecutor v. Delalić *& al.*, Case No. IT-96-21-T, Judgement, 16 November 1998, para. 1225.

victims.'[56] Some judgements include a separate section on the impact of the crimes on the victims.[57]

The Appeals Chamber has stated that the 'Trial Chambers exercise a considerable amount of discretion (although it is not unlimited) in determining an appropriate sentence. This is largely because of the overriding obligation to individualise a penalty to fit the individual circumstances of the accused and the gravity of the crime.'[58] The Appeals Chamber will not intervene in the Trial Chamber's discretion with regard to sentence unless it has made a 'discernible error'.[59] Given this position, it hardly surprising that the Appeals Chamber has refrained from establishing any sentencing guidelines.[60]

With regard to sentencing upon a guilty plea, it should be noted that in recent practice Trial Chambers have considered a timely guilty plea and substantial co-operation with the Prosecutor to be important mitigating factors. Expressions of remorse, including a wish to contribute to the reconciliation in Bosnia and Herzegovina, by the accused have also been taken into consideration, albeit to a lesser degree.[61] In fact, even accused who have entered guilty pleas at a late stage of the proceedings have been given some credit for doing so 'because a guilty plea contributes directly to one of the fundamental objectives of the International Tribunal: namely, its truth-finding function.'[62]

Sentences are served in prisons in States, which have agreed to enforce sentences of the Tribunal. The imprisonment shall be in accordance with the applicable laws of the enforcing State.[63] However, in the event that the convicted person becomes eligible for early release, commutation of sentence or pardon pursuant to the applicable domestic laws of the enforcing State, the matter will

56. Prosecutor v. Krstić, Case No. IT-98-33-T, 2 August 2001, paras. 700-703.
57. See for example the Krstić judgement, which contains a section on 'The Impact of the Crimes on the Bosnian Muslim Community of Srebrenica' Prosecutor v. Radislav Krstić, Case No. IT-98-33-T, Judgement, 2 August 2001, paras. 90-94.
58. Prosecutor v. Delalić *et al.*, Case No. IT-96-21-A, Judgement, 20 February 2001, para. 717.
59. In Aleksovski the Appeals Chamber found that there had been a discernible error in the Trial Chamber's exercise of discretion in imposing sentence, Prosecutor v. Aleksovski, Case No. 95-14/1-A, Judgement, 24 March 2000, paras. 182-190; Prosecutor v. Tadić, Case Nos. IT-94-1-A & IT-94-1-A*bis*, Judgement in Sentencing Appeals, 26 January 2000, para. 22.
60. See further S. Beresford 'Unshackling the paper tiger – the sentencing practices of the ad hoc international criminal tribunals for the former Yugoslavia and Rwanda' *op. cit.*, pp. 82-86.
61. Prosecutor v. Todorović, Case No. IT-95-9/1-S, Sentencing Judgement, 31 July 2001, paras. 74-92, 108-115; Prosecutor v. Sikirica *& al.*, Case No. IT-95-8-S, Sentencing Judgement, 13 November 2001, paras. 148-152, 192-199, 227-230.
62. Prosecutor v. Sikirica *& al.*, Case No. IT-95-8-S, Sentencing Judgement, 13 November 2001, paras. 148-152.
63. Article 27 of the Statute, Rule 103-104 of the Rules. The United Nations has concluded agreements on the enforcement of ICTY sentences with the following States: Austria, Finland, France, Italy, Norway, Spain, and Sweden.

be referred to the President of the Tribunal, who will decide if such a measure should be granted or not.[64]

Thus, in imposing a sentence on a convicted person, a Trial Chamber has a relatively broad discretion in determining an appropriate sentence. While assessing the gravity of the crime, a Trial Chamber will take into account the number of victims as well as their suffering. Accused who have plead guilty and who have co-operated with the Prosecutor have received reduced sentences in recent practice.

7. *Reasons for the limited participation of victims in the ICTY proceedings*

Having examined the above matters, it can be concluded that the Tribunal does not allow for much direct input or participation of victims as victims in its proceedings. In my view, this can be explained by the fact that the Tribunal is not a court that was created primarily for the benefit of the individual direct victims of the conflicts in the former Yugoslavia. Had that been the intention, the Security Council would have made provision for a type of court that could handle a large number of cases and the Statute would have provided for the possibility for victims, among other things to be heard as a *partie civile* in the various stages of the proceedings; to request compensation for the losses and injuries; or perhaps to independently submit victim impact statements in connection with sentencing.

The Security Council established the Tribunal for 'the sole purpose of prosecuting persons responsible for serious violations of international humanitarian law', in order to halt and effectively redress such violations and with the aim of contributing to the restoration and maintenance of peace.[65] Thus, rather than focusing on the individual victims, the Tribunal was established with a broader, more general goal: namely the restoration of peace. As stated by the President of the Tribunal the court's mission is

> ... to promote reconciliation through the prosecution, trial and punishment of those who have perpetrated war crimes, crimes against humanity and genocide. By ensuring that people are held individually responsible for crimes they committed, the International Tribunal must prevent entire groups – be they national, ethnic or reli-

64. Article 28 of the Statute, Rules 123-125 of the Rules, Practice Direction on the Procedure for the Determination of Applications for Pardon, Commutation of Sentence and Early Release of Persons Convicted by the International Tribunal, IT/146. See also D. Tolbert, 'The International Tribunal for the former Yugoslavia and the Enforcement of Sentences' *Leiden Journal of International Law* (11, 655, 1998), and D. Tolbert & Å. Rydberg, 'Enforcement of Sentences' in R. May *& al.* ed., *Essays on ICTY Procedure and Evidence In Honour of Gabrielle Kirk McDonald* (Kluwer Law International, The Hague, 2001), p. 533.

65. UN Security Council Resolution 827 (1993) of 25 May 1993.

gious – from being stigmatised and must ensure that others do not resort to acts of revenge in their search for justice.[66]

8. *Reaching out to all the victims?*

If, however, the ultimate objective of the Tribunal is to apply the legal process in helping to create conditions for reconciliation leading to peace, it is critical for the success of the court that the victims and perpetrators of the crimes, as well as the general populations of the States in which the crimes occurred are made aware of it and its activities.[67] Unfortunately, this was not the case during the first years of the Tribunal's existence: an Expert Report noted that there appeared to be a large-scale lack of knowledge about the Tribunal throughout the former Yugoslavia. Furthermore, to the extent that its existence was known, misconceptions of its work were common.[68]

In order to address this situation an Outreach Programme was established in 1999. This programme, which operates primarily in the languages of the former Yugoslavia, aims to strengthen contacts between the Tribunal and communities in the region and to provide education and information about the objectives and activities of the court. It 'operates on the understanding that the Tribunal works as an agency of justice and reconciliation in South East Europe, working in partnership with and for the benefit of citizens in the region to strengthen the rule of law'.[69] More concretely, the Outreach Programme has, *inter alia*, established field offices in various places of the former Yugoslavia, arranged for on-line audio broadcasts of the proceedings on the ICTY internet site in the relevant languages, and organised numerous symposia about various aspects of the work of the Tribunal.[70]

If the Tribunal is to have a positive impact on the peace and reconciliation process in the former Yugoslavia, it is crucial that it manages to build a posi-

66. 'The ICTY and the Truth and Reconciliation Commission in Bosnia and Herzegovina' speech by President Claude Jorda in Sarajevo (Bosnia and Herzegovina), on 12 May 2001, *ICTY Press Release* (591, 17 May 2001).
67. L.C. Vohrah & J. Cina, 'The Outreach Programme' in R. May *& al.* ed., *Essays on ICTY Procedure and Evidence In Honour of Gabrielle Kirk McDonald* (Kluwer Law International, The Hague, 2001), p. 550.
68. See Report of the Expert Group to Conduct a Review of the Effective Operation and Functioning of the International Criminal Tribunal for the Former Yugoslavia and the International Criminal Tribunal for Rwanda, A/54/634, 22 November 1999, at para. 97. See also S. Coliver, 'The Contribution of the International Criminal Tribunal for the former Yugoslavia to Reconciliation in Bosnia and Herzegovina' in D. Shelton ed., *International Crimes, Peace, and Human Rights: The Role of the International Criminal Court* (Transnational Publishers, Ardsley N.Y., 2000), pp. 20-23.
69. See 'Support from the United Kingdom Foreign and Commonwealth Office to the ICTY Outreach Programme' *ICTY Press Release* (579, 23 March 2001).
70. The Outreach Programme has offices in Sarajevo (Bosnia and Herzegovina), Zagreb (Croatia), Pristina, (Kosovo, Federal Republic of Yugoslavia ['FRY']) and Belgrade (FRY).

tive and direct relationship with those affected by the crimes it was created to prosecute.[71] In my view, the Tribunal is certainly moving in the right direction: it is fully operational with several on-going trials; there is an increasing number of arrests, including arrests of high-level indictees; and, a much needed public outreach to the region has been undertaken. These and other developments have led to a growing impact of the Tribunal and will hopefully contribute the processes of reconciliation in the region.[72] At the same time I believe that expectations of what the Tribunal can achieve must be realistic. Peace-building and reconciliation are slow processes which take place at various levels and by different means in a society. The work of the Tribunal can only contribute to one part of these processes. However, if the Tribunal is successful in fulfilling its mandate by contributing to peace and reconciliation, it would play an important role for all the victims in the former Yugoslavia. In that sense, it will reach out to all the victims.

71. L.C. Vohrah & J. Cina, 'The Outreach Programme' *op. cit.*, p. 548.
72. S. Coliver, 'The Contribution of the International Criminal Tribunal for the former Yugoslavia to Reconciliation in Bosnia and Herzegovina', *op. cit.*, pp. 24-28.

8. The Rights and Needs of Victims in the Criminal Justice Process

Martin Wright*

The social context of justice

Let us begin by thinking about the whole picture: not only restorative justice, but the purpose of the criminal law, which I assume to be to create a just and stable society. I will not say much about the problems of conventional justice, which we all know, or the theory of restorative justice; I will concentrate on how it could work in practice, and I hope that the theory will be reflected by the practice.

Returning to the ideal of the just and stable society, I believe that this would be based as much as possible on consent and as little as possible on coercion. I would summarise this as a society which. aims to *persuade* people to stay within acceptable boundaries without the use of repression. This would be done partly by rewarding people, not only in a material way but through the approval of others, and also by *enabling* them to survive without behaving in unacceptable ways. Only then would we consider what to do when people went outside those boundaries; and the principle of maximum consent, minimum coercion, would apply here also.

I will begin by looking at some of the words we use, and by considering how restorative justice can be used within the context of conventional criminal justice. Then we can consider a more radical vision of how a society could respond when one person harms another. Do we need to use the criminal law at all? If so, how would it work restoratively, with especial reference to the victim's point of view? This includes the process itself, the administrative structure, and the way in which it is integrated into the system. I will refer to some frequently asked questions about restorative justice; and finally, returning to society as a whole, we will consider how a restorative approach could transform it.

Terms

First, some of the words. 'Crime' is defined in English as behaviour which is against the law and can be punished; in other languages this way of looking at things is built into the words themselves: the Dutch *strafrecht*, German *Straf-*

* University of Sussex, Brighton, United Kingdom.

recht, French *droit penal*, for example. But this policy has been described as *het repressief model,* and punishment is not necessarily the response to law-breaking, as we shall see. The Norwegian criminologist Nils Christie (1982) has reminded us that punishment is the infliction of pain, and the word 'deterrent' has the same root as 'terror' (and the same is true in Dutch: *afschrikkend* and *schrik*); do we really want to live in a society ruled by repression and fear?

The simple assumption that offenders should be punished is extremely problematic: it is based on the assumptions that punishment is (a) effective and (b) ethical, both of which are, to say the least, questionable (Wright, 1999). It may be more helpful to think of the action as not necessarily punishable, but 'criminal', from the Latin *crimen,* fault or accusation; it is also an action which causes 'harm'. Even if we remove the link to punishment, it is probably useful to have a law which lists the main ways in which people harm each other, as a declaration by society that they are not acceptable. To question the usefulness of punishment does not mean that there is no response to crime, but we can use a more neutral word such as a 'sanction' or 'measure' (*maatregel*).

'Restorative justice' takes a problem-solving approach: an individual (or the community) has been harmed, what is the best way of resolving the event in the best interests of those who are affected by it? It is based on the premise that this question should be resolved, if possible, by the victim and others affected by the harm, and by the person who caused it. 'Mediation' and 'conferencing' are different methods of arranging for this resolution to take place, and will be described below; so will the concept of 'reparation'. 'Mediator' and 'facilitator' will be used interchangeably.

Restorative justice in the criminal justice system

What should we do when one person harms another? The criminal justice process has not treated victims well. They are kept waiting, without adequate information, and the procedure is not explained to them. Sometimes they must endure distressing questioning by lawyers. Although efforts are being made to improve this situation, for example through the Vaillant guidelines on the treatment of victims in 1987, the Terwee guidelines of 1993 on referral to victim assistance (*Aanwijzing Slachtofferzorg*), and the *Victims charter* of 1990 and 1996 in Britain, the process is still centred on the offender. Restorative justice takes the victim as its starting point. Its basic principle is to offer help to the person who has been harmed; dealing with the offender comes later. This is how we respond after an accident: first we help the casualties, then we look for the causes, and only then do we ask who was to blame (Wright, 1977).

How does restorative justice work, from the victim's point of view? Every case is different, but I will describe one which shows some of the possibilities. This one took place within the framework of the existing law: the offender was convicted and sentenced before restorative justice was used.

Tom, aged 18, with no driving licence, was driving a stolen car and knocked down a six-year old girl, Sally. She was in intensive care and for a short time her life was in danger, but she recovered; however, she suffered from nightmares and a phobia about being in the bath, because it made her think of being underneath the car.

Tom, who came from a difficult background, was sentenced to four months in a young offenders institution, and a mediation worker visited him there. He was willing to apologise, though not enthusiastic. The worker then visited Sally and her parents, who at first were distressed and did not want to listen, but became interested, and although the mother did not want to meet Tom, the father and Sally agreed to do so. There had been a suggestion that he might offer her a teddy bear as a present, and the parents agreed that this would be appropriate.

Tom was terrified before the meeting, but made his apology (in very few words) and offered the teddy bear. Sally left her father, walked across to take it, and gave Tom a hug. He was very moved by this, and so were the mediators. The father asked to speak to him alone; the mediators said that they must be present. He described his feelings when he was called from his work to the hospital, and how he was so angry that he might have killed Tom if he had met him then. But he recognised that Tom had been brave in coming to the meeting, and said that it had helped him to get over his anger. Sally had no more nightmares, and was able to bathe without being afraid.

Tom felt pleased at having taken part. But he was later arrested for stealing another car.

This story illustrates several points relating to victim/offender mediation. It is important to prepare people to take part so that they know what mediation would be like, and do not have unrealistic expectations; and they need time to make up their minds. Most workers feel that it is best to contact the offender first, so that the victim does not have the stress of making a decision when there is a possibility that the offender will refuse to take part, or that a meeting will be considered inappropriate. If this is done, it can help the victims to let go of their anger, which is helpful to them as well as to the offender.

Also, its success can be measured by its effect on the victim, not only by whether it prevents the offender from re-offending. In this case, it is worth noting that the young offenders institution also did not prevent re-offending; such institutions can be terrible places, and it is even possible that if the mediation had taken place *instead of* the custodial sentence, he might not have committed a further offence. There are also questions to be asked about whether, after the mediation, Tom received the help he needed to cope with the problems in his own life. In theory mediation results in a kind of contract between the victim and the offender, but in reality the community is also a party to it, so that if all does not go well, we should ask whether individuals and agencies, relatives, employers and social services, have given all necessary support. Perhaps they, as well as the offender, have not kept their contract.

Some of what I shall describe is already happening; it will be concerned with practical details, but I shall try to give it a conceptual framework, and in some cases a different emphasis; for example, I will suggest that the process of mediation can be more important to victims than receiving some money as compensation. As you know, these forms of conflict resolution are already being introduced in The Netherlands. As I understand it, the only one which is used everywhere is settlement of claims by the public prosecution department (*schaderegeling door de parketten*), but in some places there is also community mediation (*buurtbemiddeling* in six municipalities[1] and *Justitie in de Buurt*[2]), settlement of disputes in the public prosecution department (*conflictregeling door de parketten*[3]), and reparative mediation (*herstelbemiddeling*[4]) to assist after sentence in coming to terms with the pain on the part of the victim and the guilt on the part of the perpetrator in serious criminal cases, including some where death ensued (Ministerie van Justitie, 2000). In Austria, Belgium, France, Germany, Poland, the United Kingdom and other European countries there is a variety of initiatives, and a European Forum for Victim/Offender Mediation and Restorative Justice has been formed to promote an exchange of ideas, experience and good practice. All these are encouraging signs, but there is an important warning: restorative justice must be done well if it is to benefit victims, offenders and the community, and win public and political support. Well-planned projects with adequate resources and evaluation will show how the idea can work, as a basis for extending it through the country; otherwise it will not be given a fair trial and the opportunity will be lost.

A radical vision

Harm: a civilised response

Do we need a criminal law at all? Radbruch said that we should only try to create a better criminal law until we can find something *better than* criminal law. The Dutch criminal lawyer Louk Hulsman has pointed out that often the same action can be treated as criminal or as a civil wrong (a 'tort' in the English legal language which we imported from France 900 years ago). Like his Norwegian colleague Nils Christie (1982), he sees punishment as a barbaric way for a state to treat its citizens; according to him the three greatest historical causes of human suffering have been famine and pestilence, war, and criminal justice. Most crimes are also civil wrongs, and in some countries the criminal process is accompanied by a civil one. This can also be enforced, but in a different way, by civil injunctions and officers of the court. So why,

1. Rotterdam, Zwolle, Gouda and district, Almere, Amsterdam and Amersfoort.
2. Amsterdam (several), Arnhem, Enschede, Groningen, Haarlem, Maastricht and Rotterdam (several).
3. Almelo.
4. The Hague.

Hulsman asks, cannot the whole process be 'civilised', in both senses of the word?

This is already happening where *victims and offenders know each other.* The ideal, of course, is to use mediation at an early stage to *prevent* conflict from getting worse, but if that has not been done, some disputes between neighbours or workmates lead to an act of violence which can be classified as a crime. Possibly some private accusation offences (*klachtdelicten)* such as insults would fall into this category. It may be more helpful to resolve the dispute than to treat it as a crime. Consider this case:

Mr Roberts was annoyed at the way his neighbour Mr Johnson parked his car. Mr Johnson answered him rudely, and complained about the noise Mr Roberts' children made. The relationship got worse, and Mr Roberts attacked Mr Johnson. Quite serious crimes can have such trivial origins. Mr Johnson could accuse Mr Roberts of assault. But who is the victim and who is the offender? If Mr Roberts pleaded self-defence or provocation, and the court dismissed the case because it considered that both were in the wrong, the court's time would have been wasted and the two people's relationship would not get better. More important, if Mr Roberts was found guilty, so that Mr Johnson's action resulted in Mr Roberts receiving a criminal conviction, the intervention of the criminal justice system would have made the relationship worse than before. In fact Mr Johnson did go to the police; they suggested that it would make more sense not to treat the incident as a crime at all, and that he should go instead to the community mediation service. A mediation was arranged, with trained volunteer mediators, and they were both able to tell each other details of their lives which the other person had not known (and which would not have been regarded as relevant in a court of law); this helped them to agree how they will behave towards each other in the future.

This is also an example of another feature of restorative justice: to involve ordinary members of the community as much as possible, as facilitators.

Crime: a restorative response

Supposing however that the incident is classified as a crime, how can it be dealt with in a restorative way? We can consider three main situations: where someone has become a victim but the offender is not known; where victim and offender are known and are willing to take part in a restorative process; and where, for various reasons, mediation is not possible.

Crimes committed by a stranger who is not detected These are some of the commonest reported crimes. This is where assistance to victims fits in to the restorative process, and it is already well developed in The Netherlands, the United Kingdom and elsewhere. In countries where victim assistance is provided by volunteers, this is another example of participation by the community, and helps to implement the principle: As much State as necessary, but as little State as possible. Some victims, if they cannot meet 'their' offender, welcome the chance to meet groups of other offenders and victims who have been involved in the same type of crime.

If victims need more than a friendly listener, for example a counsellor or therapist, volunteers are trained to refer them to professional services, provided by the community through its formal structures, local and national government. For physical injuries, either they should be cared for by the national health service, in countries which have one, or they should receive the money to pay for medical attention; in the United Kingdom many victims also receive compensation for their pain and suffering. The maximum award, for the most serious brain damage, is £250,000, with the possibility of additional compensation for loss of earnings or special expenses. In New Zealand compensation by the state for victims of crime is 'civilised': it is included with the system for accident compensation, of which it is only a very small fraction, compared with the other injuries and traumas which people may suffer, and this is another point made by Louk Hulsman.

Victim assistance and state compensation are restorative, because they help to repair the consequences of the crime; but they are not fully restorative, because they do not involve the offender.

Crimes committed by a stranger, where a suspect is found As before, the victim's needs, and injuries if any, should be attended to first. Since the offender is known, it is only right that he or she should be held responsible – but how? This is one of the ideas at the centre of restorative justice. It aims to address some of the major weaknesses of conventional criminal justice, for example that the victim is allowed no proper role in the process; that offenders, although nominally at the centre of the process, also have no active part in it because they have lawyers to speak for them; and that because the system is mainly based on punishment, offenders naturally wish to avoid it, and their lawyers try to deny, minimise or even justify the harm which the offender did to the victim. Prosecutors also take part in this, in Anglo-Saxon countries at least: in the process known as plea-bargaining, they drop a more serious charge if the offender will admit a less serious one. This saves the court's time. For example, the offender may have committed a robbery, which is theft with violence; but if the offender admits the theft, the prosecutor may forget the violence. But the victim does not forget it.

What does restorative justice offer instead? It offers the victim and the offender the opportunity to speak for themselves under the guidance of a mediator (or 'facilitator'), and, if they wish, to speak to each other in less formal surroundings than a court room. (If either of them does not want to meet the other, they can communicate indirectly.) This is more than a negotiation about compensation. Although they did not know each other before, the crime has created a kind of conflict between them, and this process enables them to resolve it. The victim can tell the offender how much the crime has affected him or her; often the offender had not thought about this, or had 'neutralised' it by telling himself that the victim could afford the loss, or was covered by insurance.

For this reason the method is most suitable for cases where the crime has had a serious effect on the victim; but there has been a tendency to use it only for minor cases. What do victims want from the process? First of all, they often find the process itself helpful. They want to understand why this person harmed them, whether there was a reason why they were chosen as the target, and whether they are likely to be victimised again. Research has suggested that telling the offender about the effects, and asking questions which only the offender can answer, is more important for many victims than obtaining money as compensation (Umbreit and Roberts, 1996, Tables E-1 to E-4: of the victims who participated in mediation, the percentages who stressed the importance of telling the offender the impact of the crime (90 per cent), of receiving answers (80 per cent) and of receiving an apology (73 per cent) were greater than the percentage who attached importance to restitution (65 per cent)).

At the beginning victims are sometimes still angry and want compensation from the offender, for example the full value of the things that were stolen; but after getting to know the offender and his background, the money often seems less important. They do however want the offender to do something to show that he or she is sorry; one woman wanted the young man who had robbed her to do some work for people less fortunate than himself. It was arranged that he should work on a project teaching disabled children to ride. Another common reaction is to want the offender to do something to make it less likely that he will offend again; for example to attend school, undertake training, go to live with relatives, tackle abuse of alcohol or drugs. These are things which have previously been labelled as 'rehabilitation', and it sometimes seemed that more was being done for the offender than for the victim; but in restorative justice the offender is doing it, not having it done to him, and he is doing it for the sake of the victim as well as himself. So in this context all these activities can be counted as 'reparation'.

What does this offer to the offender? Many offenders are sorry for what they have done, and welcome the chance to say so, and to offer some explanation of their behaviour. Some show no remorse immediately, but change their attitude after they have met their victim.

This is how restorative justice *can* work; but it cannot be fully applied in all circumstances.

Where mediation cannot take place, or is unsuccessful If the victim or the offender does not want to take part in victim/offender mediation, the case will have to go to court. It is important that the victim should not feel burdened, or even threatened, by having the responsibility of making this decision. It should therefore be possible for conferencing to proceed without the victim, and for victim/offender mediation to be replaced by a 'victim awareness' session or a 'positive experience' (*positieve ervaring*) as in the *Herstelbemiddeling* project in The Hague. If the offender is willing but the mediation or conference cannot proceed because there is no identifiable victim or for some other reason, it would not be fair if he or she would receive a more severe punishment. In this case the offender should have the possibility of showing that he was sorry by 'giving something back' in the form of service to the community.

There will also be some cases where the facilitator does not consider that both parties would benefit or where mediation was unsuccessful; and there is a minority of accused persons who deny the act with which they are charged. Such cases will also have to be dealt with by a court. It would be expected, however, that any sanctions imposed by courts would be restorative ones, such as compensation (if the victim wishes to receive it), or community service, or reparation in the sense described above.

Models, structures, and integration into the system

There are three policy decisions which a country will have to make when it introduces restorative justice: what model(s) of mediation or conferencing to use; who will provide the service; and what will be its relationship with the criminal justice system.

Models The details of the victim/offender mediation process vary; I will emphasise the victim's point of view, because some projects which use the term 'restorative justice' have treated it more as a way of dealing with offenders, thinking of reparation mainly in terms of an amount of money or a number of hours' work. It is important also to look at the process, step by step, to make sure that it is 'victim-friendly'.

Some people talk of different models of mediation; I suggest that it may be more helpful to think of them as points on a spectrum. At first the victim and offender are visited. If they decide to go ahead, they may exchange messages or letters, and nothing more. (This stage is referred to either as visiting, or as indirect victim/ offender mediation.) Or they may then agree to meet one-to-one, perhaps with parents or other supporters present (direct mediation). This can be taken a stage further by inviting the offender's extended family and other significant people, and the victim can bring their family or other supporters as well (conference). (Notice how the words 'mediation' and 'conference' emphasise the process, rather than the outcome.)

There are also different styles for running conferences. In a 'community conference', the discussion is mainly about the way in which the victim and the offender resolve the situation, and everyone is present all the time; but where there are problems within the young person's family, which do not concern the victim, a 'family group conference' may be more suitable, in which at one stage of the process the offender and his or her family have 'private time' with no one else present; then everyone comes together again and the offender and family explain their 'action plan'. This can be discussed further if the victim does not agree.

Structures The way a victim/offender mediation service looks after the needs of victims, and the way in which it is perceived, depend not only on its processes, which we have just been looking at, but on its administrative structure. The model which encourages the greatest community involvement is a non-governmental organisation, whose management includes representatives of the statutory agencies (police, prosecutors, probation service, and others), supported by legislation to ensure that it is recognised as an essential part of the system. If one of these agencies alone runs the service, it is likely not to be perceived as independent – and is vulnerable to changes of policy, as the service in West Yorkshire, England, has found: a new chief probation officer has greatly reduced mediation work in order to transfer resources to other activities. But it can also be provided by a single state agency created for the purpose (such as the Youth Justice Conferencing Directorate in New South Wales), or a multi-agency group. Whichever is used, it is important that the management structure includes presence of a victim assistance organisation.

Another question is Who should be the mediators? Here again there is an opportunity for involvement of the community, as some projects in The Netherlands have found: with professional supervision and support, volunteers can be good mediators. In some places they are paid a small fee for each session, but they are still members of the general community. In other countries a new profession of mediator is growing up; this has advantages, but it limits the number of mediations that can be undertaken, because the state is never likely to employ as many as are needed. Members of existing agencies can be trained as mediators, although there is a risk that they may not be perceived as neutral. Whichever method is used, it is essential that they have specific training in mediation, paying especial attention to the importance of considering the needs of both victims and offenders. The training of social workers, police and probation officers is not the same as the training of mediators; although it has some similarities, in other ways it has a very different approach. Other staff need to be trained to organise reparation, by finding opportunities for community service (including arrangements for safety and insurance) and liaising with rehabilitative agencies.

Integration into the system It will be convenient to make a division of offences into four broad categories, least serious, less serious, more serious and most serious – and in a restorative system these distinctions would take account of the effect on the victim, not only of an arbitrary legal category. The actual borderlines between them will of course vary at different times and in different countries.

The *least serious* offences would be diverted out of the system either informally (by the police officer who says 'Go home and don't do it again') or formally (where an official caution or warning is given by the police, prosecutor or court), and no further action is taken. This warning would be given in a 'restorative' way, that is, by emphasising the harm caused to others rather than by threatening punishment if the offence is repeated.

Less serious offences would be those where the accused admits the act (though not necessarily guilt in the legal sense) and where there has been enough of an impact on the victim to make it worth asking if they would be willing to take part in mediation or a conference, but the intervention of a court is not necessary. There should be a minimum below which mediation is not normally used.

More serious offences require the supervision of the court to confirm that the accused has committed the act charged; but then the court can refer the case to a conference to decide on an 'action plan' for the offender. This is brought back to the court, which in most cases confirms it, but may add to it or reduce it. If it does make a change, however, the court should explain to the victim and the offender why it was felt necessary to alter their agreement.

The *most serious* offences will have to deal with by courts, and until restorative justice is better known and accepted, sentences will continue to be decided on a retributive basis; but the aim is that these sentences should also be based on reparation. In addition courts would impose *restriction* of liberty when necessary, such as suspension of a driving licence, restrictions on movement, or disqualification from following a certain occupation or profession, but *deprivation* of liberty (imprisonment) would be kept to the minimum required for the protection of the public; it would be protective custody and not punitive custody, and prisoners should also have the opportunity to make reparation in the sense outlined above.

Distinctions of this kind are already made in 'out-of-court offence settlement' (*aussergerichtlicher Tatausgleich, ATA*) in juvenile law in Austria, where only offences punishable with more than five years' imprisonment are in the 'more or most serious' categories, and in New Zealand, where only homicide and some very grave rapes and assaults are heard in the High Court, and pre-sentence FGCs are used even then (McElrea, 1996; Akester, 2000).

Some frequently asked questions

Of course there are problems and questions that need answering. Legitimate points have been raised about safeguarding human rights, especially of offenders. Some of these, however, come from lawyers who take the conventional theory of criminal law as a basis, and try to fit restorative justice into it. I have nothing against lawyers – some of my best friends are lawyers! – but I would suggest, with the greatest respect, that it would be better to ask the question in a different way, namely, to accept that restorative justice starts from a different philosophical base, and ask how it can be implemented in a way which respects the needs, and the human rights, of the victim, the offender, and other members of the community who are affected. These are questions which the advocates of restorative justice need to ask: There are serious issues about, for example, whether the process enables the accused to obtain advice from a lawyer. Many of them have been taken into account in the Youth Justice Conferencing Scheme in New South Wales, Australia (Trimboli, 2000). Where lawyers are involved, they should be familiar with the principles of restorative justice. These objections are not a reason for dismissing restorative justice; the movement is addressing them, and will welcome help from lawyers and other practitioners in finding restorative solutions.

Lawyers also ask whether restorative justice can deal with 'victimless' crimes and attempts, regulatory offences, and so on. These have not yet been fully addressed, but can be approached in a similar 'restorative' way. As an Australian social theorist David Moore says:

> When we ask not 'Who did it and what is to be done to them?' but 'What happened, how have people been affected, and what do we need to do now?' we get a very different sort of justice. We get a justice process that involves the acknowledgement of conflict, then the transformation of conflict into co-operation (Moore, 2000, p. 330).

For misleading descriptions of goods offered for sale, for example, instead of a fine, the offender might be required to discuss the effects of inaccurate labels and to contribute to the cost of enforcing the regulations: offenders might have to pay the same as if they had been fined, but the message given to them would be different.

A common question is, Will restorative justice deter crime, or is it a 'soft option'? There are several answers to this. One is that meeting a victim can be a stressful experience, as it was for Tom, the young man described above; another is that deterrence is not very effective, as he also showed. In a restorative system the reduction of crime would be based, logically, on crime reduction strategies. Even if it is less punitive than the alternative, why should it not be? If offenders receive a reduced sentence for confessing the crime, or for co-operating with the police, why not also for taking part in a process which requires them to do something constructive, instead of passively enduring punishment, and which in addition offers advantages to the victim?

The Truth and Reconciliation Commission in South Africa has shown us forcefully that severity of punishment has to be weighed against the probability of discovering the truth. In that country far more wrongdoing was uncovered in a far shorter time by offering an amnesty in exchange for full disclosure than could ever have been achieved by attempting to detect, prosecute and punish the offenders – although those who did not confess could still be prosecuted. Archbishop Desmond Tutu, who chaired the Commission, maintains that this process 'encourages accountability rather than the opposite. It supports the new culture of human rights and acknowledgement of responsibility...'. Retributive justice, he says, is not the only form of justice. In restorative justice, the central concern is reintegration, the redressing of imbalances, the restoration of broken relationships, in the spirit of what is called in some South African languages *ubuntu,* the quality of being 'generous, hospitable, friendly, caring and compassionate' (Tutu, 1999): Although South Africa still has serious problems, with intolerable levels of unemployment and crime, it is generally believed that any other policy would have produced far worse results, and the South African Law Commission has proposed a new Child Justice Bill based on restorative principles (SALC, 2000).[5]

5. Other questions relating to voluntary participation, standards, rights, and other matters, are considered by Czarnecka-Dzialuk and Wójcik (1999, pp. 125-132).

Towards transformation of society?

It was suggested at the beginning that restorative justice could offer an alternative to criminal justice. It can be used even more widely, beginning in schools: children are being encouraged to use mediation to resolve playground disputes and disputes between the child and the school. This can reduce the amount of bullying and the number of children excluded from school for bad behaviour.

Neighbourhood mediation can deal with conflicts between neighbours, some of which would otherwise take up time in the civil courts or lead to a violent act and a criminal court. We see mediation (alternative dispute resolution) being used in disputes in the workplace, business disputes, environmental disputes, disputes concerning the care of elderly people, in reaching agreement on the conditions for separation and divorce, and many more besides.

As regards criminal offences, several countries are using mediation or conferencing in the juvenile justice system, and some of them are extending it to adults. There is every reason to hope that this in turn could reduce the prison population. For those who do still have to be sent to prison for the protection of the public, there are several possibilities. Offenders can make indirect reparation by work for people less fortunate than themselves, for example by repairing wheelchairs for use in Africa or transcribing books into Braille for blind readers. Mediation can be used to resolve disputes between prisoners, or between prisoners and staff – and this does not only resolve disputes, it shows them *how* to do so.

No one need fear that the proposal is a step towards abolishing courts. They will have two roles. Firstly, since the mediation process requires the consent of the victim and the offender, and cannot be used in all cases, they will be needed to hear the cases where for any reason mediation or conferencing does not take place or does not succeed; and secondly, they will oversee the justice process, as they do in New Zealand, to make sure that it is genuinely restorative and respects the rights of all concerned.

These principles can be applied in other parts of society, and above all in schools, where the foundations can be laid for a society based on respect for all individuals and constructive ways of resolving conflicts. Restorative, problem-solving methods, unlike those based on punishment, bring us closer to the ideal of a stable society, in which people would respect each other's individuality and acknowledge their responsibilities to each other within the community.

References

K. Akester, *Restoring Youth Justice: New Directions in Domestic and International Law and Practice* (Justice, London, 2000)

N. Christie, *Limits to Pain* (Martin Robertson, Oxford, 1982)

B. Czarnecka-Dzialuk & W. Dobrochna ed., *Juvenile Offender-Victim Mediation* (Oficyna Naukowa, Warsaw, 1999)

F.W.M. McElrea, 'The New Zealand Youth Court: A Model For Use With Adults' in B. Galaway & J. Hudson ed., *Restorative Justice: International Perspectives* (Kugler, Amsterdam, 1996)

D.B. Moore, 'Community Conferencing: A Supply Side Contribution to Prison Abolition' in W. Gordon West & R. Morris ed., *The Case For Penal Abolition* (Canadian Scholars' Press, Toronto, 2000)

South African Law Commission, *Report On Juvenile Justice* (Project 106, 2000) <www.law.wits.ac.za/salc/report/project106.html>

L. Trimboli, *An Evaluation of the NSW Youth Justice Conferencing Scheme* (NSW Bureau of Crime Statistics and Research, Sydney, 2000) <www.lawlink.nsw.gov.au/bocsar>

D. Tutu, *No Future Without Forgiveness* (Rider, London, 2000)

M. Umbreit & A.W. Roberts, *Mediation of Criminal Conflict in England: An Assessment of Services in Coventry and Leeds* (Centre for Restorative Justice and Mediation, School of Social Work, University of Minnesota, 386 McNeal Hall, 1985 Buford Avenue, St Paul MN 55108, USA, 1966)

M. Wright, 'Nobody Came: Criminal Justice and the Needs of Victims' *Howard Journal* (16,/1, 1977), pp. 22-31

M. Wright, *Restoring Respect for Justice: A Symposium* (Waterside Press, Winchester, 1999)

Index

Note: numbers in brackets preceded by *n* are note numbers.